# Developing Mathematical Talent

a Guide for Challenging and Educating Gifted Students

# Developing Mathematical Talent

a Guide for Challenging and Educating Gifted Students

by
Susan
Assouline
&
Ann
Lupkowski-Shoplik

PRUFROCK PRESS, INC.

Prufrock Press, Inc.
P.O. Box 8813
Waco, Texas 76714-8813
(800) 998-2208
Fax (800) 240-0333
http://www.prufrock.com

To Jose, Jason, and Sonja—always an inspiration
In memory of Jacqueline N. Blank—still an inspiration

S.G.A.

To Mike, Helena, and Anthony, with all my love.

A. L. S.

# Table of Contents

# List of Tables

# List of Figures

# Foreword

IN THE EARLY 1970s AT JOHNS HOPKINS
University, I started annual talent searches and
special, supplemental, accelerated, academic
courses for seventh graders who reasoned exceptionally well mathematically. This kept me and
a small staff, especially Lynn Fox, Daniel
Keating, and William George, busy experiment-
ing during that decade. We tried many identification    and    instructional    procedures    to
determine which were most effective. These
early efforts resulted in    our first book,
*Mathematical Talent*, published by the Johns
Hopkins University Press in 1974.

In 1979, I "gave the shop away" by founding
what is now the Center for Talented Youth and
relinquishing control. This quickly led to similar regional programs at Duke University,
Northwestern University, and the University of
Denver. In the 1980s, I basked in the reflected
glory of their great success, but was perhaps a bit
at a loss to fill the work vacuum created by my
no longer running the Study of Mathematically
Precocious Youth (SMPY).

Then along came a brilliantly foresighted foundation executive, Raymond Handlan, who pointed out that I should be training postdoctoral students in our philosophy and methods. I gladly accepted his offer to fund three postdoctoral fellowships. How the field of giftedness has benefited from those! Two of the most outstanding learners and performers were Ann Lupkowski, who spent 3 years with us, and Susan Assouline, who spent 2. They are the coauthors of this remarkably helpful book. Until their coming, SMPY and its later offshoots were working chiefly with seventh and eighth graders, even though we realized that many mathematically highly able boys and girls need educational facilitation far earlier than that. We have become accustomed to finding even kindergartners who are far advanced beyond 1 + 1 = 2. One was doing number-theory research shortly after his fifth birthday! (We verified that.)

Ann and Susan developed a collaboration that has lasted over the years across considerable distance, Pittsburgh versus Iowa City. Their first contribution was a major innovation, the profoundly helpful but simply titled *Jane and Johnny Love Math: Recognizing and Encouraging Mathematical Talent in Elementary Students*. This current book grew out of that predecessor as their hands-on experience with many mathematically talented youth helped them revise and update their ideas and recommendations. The result should be widely useful to teachers, parents, educational administrators, methods-of-teaching courses, and even mathematically talented students themselves.

What happened to the other postdocs whom Mr. Handlan's foundation supported financially? After a fantastically successful research career at Iowa State University, Camilla Benbow is now dean of Peabody College of Vanderbilt University. Linda Brody heads the Study of Exceptional Talent (mathematical and/or verbal) in the Center for Talented Youth (CTY) of Johns Hopkins University. Elaine Kolitch is a math education professor at a state university in New York state. Each postdoc helps enrich the others.

The moral has become clear to us: Start as early as possible in helping intellectually talented boys and girls. Capitalize

on their already-developed and fast-developing predisposi-
tions. Be sure they get a well-rounded, full education, but
without holding them back in the areas where they have the
greatest potential. If one of these areas is quantitative reasoning, this volume is essential. Probably no one else in the world
is as well equipped as Drs. Assouline and Lupkowski-Shoplik
to guide the needed supplementation of the mathematics curriculum for the early school years.

Julian C. Stanley
Center for Talented Youth
Johns Hopkins University

# Introduction

*Where are we going?*
*Are we there yet?*

*—Any child at the*
*start of a trip.*

WE ALL TOO OFTEN HEAR about students who are "bored to tears" in math classes, their boredom stemming from frustration with the underchallenging mathematics curricula in our schools. This frustration is similar to the frustration and sense of helplessness children express when they are unaware of the destination of a trip. Mathematically talented students entering school expect to start on an exciting educational journey that will take them to their destination of talent development. However, their journey seems to go nowhere because neither the destination nor the road are readily apparent. Although educators are sincere in their commitment as teachers, their training typically has not included information about teaching mathematically talented children. Educators, as well as parents, are unsure of the educational destination of gifted students and, for that reason, they are not sure of the path to that destination. The result is a sense of helplessness and a need for guidance.

We think the educational destination for mathematically talented students should be a learning environment that encourages and develops their unique talents. Of course, this is the desirable pedagogical goal for all students, but mathematically talented students require a different path to reach it. Mathematically talented students will have more time, energy, and need for further exploration than the typical student. It is possible that their paths will lead to destinations not dreamed of by parents or teachers. The drivers for this journey are educators, but parents are partners, and they will often be the map readers for the trip.

Educators willing to embark on this exciting journey are dedicated. However, dedication—admittedly a huge aspect in arriving at the destination—typically will not match the navigational skills needed. From our work with mathematically talented students over the past 20 years, we have realized that the current educational landscape discourages mathematically talented students, as well as their educators and parents. We concluded that a guide was needed, and we wrote this book as a resource for parents and educators to establish educational programs that are appropriately challenging for mathematically talented students. In keeping with the map/journey metaphor, this book is intended to inform and increase the navigational skills for the journey, including recognizing students' abilities, identifying appropriately challenging curricula and programs, and matching them to the abilities of students in order to facilitate and encourage the development of mathematical talent.

Recognizing that both parents and educators will be reading this book underscores our philosophy about the development of mathematically talented students: Talent development is multifaceted and requires that parents and educators understand that their roles in developing students' mathematical talent are complementary. Although the chapters of this book are intended to guide both parents and educators, there are 2 chapters that have a specific emphasis: Chapter 2, "Advocacy," is aimed at parents, and Chapter 8, "Teaching Mathematically Talented Students," is aimed at educators. Nonetheless, we are confident that educators will benefit by reading the chapter on advocacy, and parents will benefit by reading the chapter on professional development.

We also considered it important that the scope of the book represent the broader educational landscape. Consequently, throughout the book we briefly visit some important educational topics, including the general issues around curriculum standards, educational reform, and ability grouping, as well as more specific issues such as social/emotional development or working with students who are twice-exceptional (i.e., gifted and learning disabled). We provide references so that the reader who has additional interest in the topic can easily obtain more information.

As a special feature, we have drawn upon our clinical and practical experiences with mathematically talented students and interwoven them with a solid research base to produce chapters that tell compelling stories about mathematically talented students. The cases and examples presented throughout will resonate with the experiences of parents and educators. These examples are an outcome of our involvement with students, their families, and educators through the Connie Belin & Jacqueline N. Blank International Center for Gifted Education and Talent Development (B-BC) at the University of Iowa and the Carnegie Mellon Institute for Talented Elementary Students (C-MITES) at Carnegie Mellon University. These two centers provide opportunities for identification and programming for academically talented students, as well as resources and professional development opportunities for teachers.

Although our focus in this book is on the mathematically talented student, we incorporate a comprehensive view of the student as a "whole child." While most of our comments specifically target the student's development of mathematical aptitude, when relevant, we discuss the impact of our recommendations on the entire child.

Because the topics in each of the chapters are so integrated, we were challenged by the choice of what topic to put first. We decided to begin by addressing the myths associated with mathematically talented students. These myths include inaccurate assumptions and attitudes that impede identification and programming for talented students; thus, Chapter 1, "Myths About Mathematically Talented Students," a prelude to the subsequent chapters, presents and refutes 12 myths. Chapter 1 concludes with the introduction to the overarching myth, *the* myth that motivated us to write the book: *It is best to leave well enough alone and not deviate from the regular programming.* All the parents who have contacted us have expressed doubts about their perceived need to advocate for a change in their child's educational program. They are concerned that educators and other parents will view them as "pushy" parents. We always respond with a question: "If you don't advocate for your child, who will?"

Because parents typically are first to recognize the student's talent, we decided that the chapter to immediately follow should guide parents in their efforts to advocate for their student in the regular school setting. For both Chapters 1 and 2, we distilled the available research and integrated that research with our experiences as an introduction to objective information useful in a variety of educational settings.

Chapter 2, "Advocacy," views advocating for an appropriate program to challenge a gifted student as a process defined by a series of interactions between parents and educators. The parent-educator interactions are the focal point of Chapter 2, and the journey metaphor is applied extensively. The journey can be tedious because, for most people, the effort and activities needed to advocate are not familiar and require sustained attention. This chapter includes the presentation and discussion of a detailed case in which a parent advocated for curriculum and program change for her mathematically gifted student from kindergarten through middle school. Typically, parents will initiate the request. Very often, parents are also responsible for gathering objective information to be used in the decision-making process. They must then skillfully work with educators to implement a program based upon the information. Simple, but not easy.

Chapter 2 is the *raison d'être* for the book. The subsequent chapters are intended to facilitate the interactions between parents and educators by giving very specific, detailed information about assessment, curricula, programming, and resources.

Assessment and testing are the first steps to advocacy, and we devote three chapters (Chapters 3–5) to the topic. Both Chapters 3 and 4, "Educational Assessment" and "The Diagnostic Testing➤Prescriptive Instruction Model," respectively go into great depth regarding the process for conducting assessments of mathematically talented students and using that process to design individualized instruction for one student or a small group of students. In addition to detailing the process for an assessment, Chapter 3 also provides a review of tests that are useful in working with mathematically talented students. An exhaustive review of tests was impossible; however, the review that is presented is thorough and comprehensive.

Chapter 3 presents a report of an assessment conducted for a mathematically talented student. The purpose of the report is to demonstrate how a range of tests serves various purposes when generating recommendations for programming. One purpose of testing may be placement. However, in our view, placement is secondary to diagnosis and programming. That is why the next chapter, Chapter 4, describes a system for precisely determining where mathematically talented students should begin instruction so that they are challenged by new material and not stifled by material they already know. The system for diagnosing where to begin instruction is based upon diagnostic testing followed by a specific prescription for instruction based upon the results of the diagnostic testing. This approach is applicable to both individual students and small groups of students.

Parents and educators will find the contents of Chapter 4 very useful because a detailed, step-by-step explanation and several examples are provided. When the information in Chapter 4 is combined with the information in Chapters 3 and 5, parents and educators have the formula for implementing challenging math curricula and programming for individual students, small groups of students, or larger groups.

Chapter 5, "Talent Searches for Elementary Students," is the third of the three chapters detailing the goals, purposes, and benefits of academic testing. Talent searches are an important part of the history of gifted education, and are the primary method of discovery of mathematically talented students. Although talent searches were founded with the seventh- or eighth- grade student in mind, we have been involved in the application of the talent search model with elementary students since the late 1980s. This chapter presents the results of a decade of research regarding the benefits of young students' participation in the above-level testing provided by the talent searches. These benefits include educational diagnosis; educational programming and opportunities based upon talent search results; and opportunities for scholarships, awards, and honors.

Throughout Chapter 5, we offer a variety of examples in which talent search results are used to guide program placement and planning. This chapter uses charts and diagrams to emphasize that above-level testing is a powerful tool for distinguishing among bright students and identifying whether a curricular approach should be more accelerative or enriched. The results from the talent search emphasize to parents and educators the degree of academic aptitude among students. The talent search provides comparison information so that teachers and parents can recognize among a group of bright students who needs an enriched curriculum and who needs a more accelerated curriculum.

Since their inception, talent searches have spurred new opportunities for students and have motivated teachers to regard their students as individuals with unique needs for academic challenge. In its own way, the talent search is responsible for the multitude of students who participate in summer and academic-year programs that introduce them to advanced academic content. While reading about the talent search model, the reader is initiated into the discussion regarding program and curricular options, the major topics for the two chapters that follow.

Chapter 6, "Programming," contains information about programs currently available for mathematically talented students, ranging from enrichment in the regular classroom, to ability grouping, to individualized instruction and radical acceleration. No one option is the "right" choice for all mathematically talented students. In this chapter, and throughout the book, we emphasize that the goal is to find the "optimal match," in which the level and pace of the program are correctly matched to the abilities and achievements of the student. One of the options we discuss and advocate is acceleration, in which a student moves ahead in mathematics by taking a more advanced math class or by skipping a grade. Contrary to popular opinion, the long-term impact of acceleration is usually positive; research over the past 50 years has provided empirical support for acceleration as an appropriate and necessary program option for gifted youth. We have also described a number of exemplary programs to illustrate how different schools have provided appropriate educational opportunities for their mathematically talented students.

Chapter 7 provides an extensive review of curricula and materials. We argue that mathematically talented students should study a core curriculum presented in a systematic manner, not a random assortment of enrichment topics. Enrichment and acceleration should be used together to challenge mathematically talented youth. The curriculum offered in most schools is not challenging enough for mathematically talented youth, and the information provided in Chapter 7 provides guidance on how to supplement and differentiate that curriculum for individual students. We present a collection of resources and materials that teachers can use to differentiate the mathematics curriculum. Teachers can go beyond the material that is presented in the typical textbook by using manipulatives, math games, computer programs, and math contests.

Chapter 8, "Teaching Mathematically Talented Students," discusses the issues confronting the teachers who are expected to work with mathematically talented students. In the same way that Chapter 2, "Advocacy," had a specific target audience—parents—we wrote Chapter 8 for teachers. We had several goals in mind for this chapter, but we had no intention of providing a recipe or prescription for teaching mathematically talented students, nor did we intend to enhance the teacher's specific skill for teaching mathematics.

Rather, the purpose of Chapter 8 is to address both philosophical and pedagogical issues facing today's educators. In this chapter, we present our philosophy about the role of teachers in the lives of mathematically gifted students. We explore the teacher's evolving role as the student's grade and maturity level increase. We discuss the issue of quality of instruction versus quantity of instruction and explore this same issue with respect to teacher preparation. Although we do not provide a prescription to resolve these issues, we believe that, by highlighting them, we add an important voice to the discussion.

Chapter 9, "Case Studies," is the application of information presented in Chapters 1–8. Parents and educators alike seem to appreciate the lessons offered by the stories of the five cases presented, and we are grateful to the students and their families for their willingness to share them. In Zach's case, we address the common question, "Since there are lots of bright students in this school, why should we do anything different for Zach?" We think the case of Elizabeth is interesting for a couple of reasons. Elizabeth's progress had been monitored since she was a sixth grader, when we first met her and her parents. At that time, her parents "did not want her to be different from her classmates." Now, Elizabeth is a young adult and has chosen a field—physics—that has typically attracted very few females. Realization of her academic talent meant that Elizabeth was destined to be different.

An important rationale for presenting these case studies is to emphasize that students are resilient to some of the unfortunate programming and missed opportunities that have been part of the educational journey. We hope that parents and educators will see (a) the critical role of advocacy in providing appropriate programming and (b) that, even if students remain underchallenged for a (hopefully brief) period of their life, their abilities are not lost, although their enthusiasm may be jeopardized.

*Developing Mathematical Talent* concludes with a chapter of resources, several appendices of forms, and a glossary that should be helpful to parents and educators who are developing programs for mathematically talented students.

* * *

We could not have written this book without each other. Our collaboration started in 1988 when Julian C. Stanley, founder of the Study of Mathematically Precocious Youth at Johns Hopkins University, brought us together as postdoctoral fellows. Dr. Stanley and his associate, Dr. Linda Brody, worked extensively with mathematically talented youth in seventh grade through college. As our mentors, their work inspired us to branch into the study of younger mathematically talented students.

Dr. Stanley had an important goal for his associates and postdoctoral fellows: furthering the program of research that would foster the identification and talent development of mathematically gifted students. Dr. Linda Brody is now director of the Study of Exceptional Talent (SET), at Johns Hopkins University. SET evolved from Stanley's SMPY, which has moved to Peabody College at Vanderbilt University and is codirected by Dr. Camilla Benbow, Dr. Stanley's first postdoctoral fellow and current dean of Peabody College, and Dr. David Lubinski, a professor of psychology. The postdoctoral positions were funded by the Atlantic Philanthropies, and we are especially grateful for the personal interest and support that Keith Kennedy from the Atlantic Philanthropies gave us.

Our first collaboration resulted in the 1992 publication of *Jane and Johnny Love Math: Recognizing and Encouraging Mathematical Talent in Elementary Students*. *Jane and Johnny Love Math* emphasized the existence of mathematically talented students and delineated methods of addressing their needs. It was based upon our experiences with hundreds of talented elementary students. Our goal was to describe educational options that allow students to move systematically through the elementary mathematics curriculum while matching the curriculum to their abilities and achievements. That book has served its purpose well. However, there have been significant developments in the field of gifted education since its publication, and it was time for a new book about mathematically talented students for their parents and educators. Thus, *Developing Mathematical Talent: A Guide for Challenging and Educating Gifted Students* was written.

We have learned a lot since *Jane and Johnny* was first published, and we are looking to the future for lessons to be learned from *Developing Mathematical Talent*. We hope this book will enhance you professionally and personally.

# Acknowledgements

OUR CURRENT AND FORMER COLLEAGUES PLAYED an important role in the creation of this book. The Belin-Blank Center's director, Nicholas Colangelo, provided valuable advice and resources that helped bridge the miles between Iowa City and Pittsburgh. We are also grateful for support and assistance from the other center administrators, including Laurie Croft, Brian Sponcil, Ed McElvain, Damien Ihrig, Clar Baldus, Jan Warren, and Jerilyn Fisher. The extremely competent clerical staff, including Frances Blum, Pamela Bullers, Bridget Pauley, Rachelle Hansen, Lori Hudson, and Marie Villareal, were very helpful. Many graduate assistants from the Belin-Blank Center also assisted in researching and verifying the resources included in the book.

The Carnegie Mellon Institute for Talented Elementary Students (C-MITES) staff members Brianna Blaser, Raymond Budd, Connie Herold, Barbara Dunn, Pam Piskurich, Mary Ann Swiatek, Kathleen Trehy, and Lynne Young read earlier drafts of this book and offered their support throughout the writing process. We are also grateful to C-MITES teacher Francy McTighe, who provided many insights during long discussions about what works best for mathematically talented students. Marty Hildebrandt and Anne Burgunder suggested some of the resources that are listed in this book.

Christy Kendrick provided helpful editorial comments, and we appreciate Jim Kendrick's exemplary efforts in editing and layout for the document.

We are appreciative of Dr. Julian Stanley for the support he continues to show us in our professional careers. He brought us together as postdoctoral fellows at the Study of Mathematically Precocious Youth at Johns Hopkins University, and our long conversations with him continue to influence our work today. Julian has been both a mentor and a friend.

# 1 Myths About Mathematically Talented Students

*Myth: 1. Traditional story dealing with supernatural beings, ancestors, or heroes that informs or shapes the world view of a people, as by explaining aspects of the natural world or delineating the customs or ideals of society. 2. A story, a theme, an object, or a character regarded as embodying an aspect of a culture. 3. A fiction or half-truth, esp. one that forms part of an ideology.*
—*The American Heritage College Dictionary, 3rd. ed. (1993, p. 903)*

IN THIS CHAPTER, we present myths commonly associated with mathematically talented students. Some of the myths concern the students' cognitive and social/emotional development, whereas others are concerned with programming or curricular issues.

For example, two often-stated developmental myths are "He's too young to start algebra" and "Students who skip a grade will have social problems when they are teenagers." A commonly heard programmatic myth is "But, if you push her ahead now, she won't have any math left to study in high school." Perhaps you have heard statements like these with regard to your own child or other

1

mathematically talented students you have known. Although well-meaning individuals typically make these statements, there is rarely objective evidence to back up these claims. In fact, the myths about mathematically talented students are either fiction or, at best, half-truths; nevertheless, they have acquired mythical power and are often used by teachers, administrators, and other parents as roadblocks to developing appropriate interventions for mathematically talented students. The myths are summarized in Figure 1.1.

In this chapter, we will present and dispel each myth. The specific purpose of this chapter is to introduce parents and educators to objective information needed in their efforts to develop programming for mathematically talented students. Each of the topics will be more thoroughly addressed in subsequent chapters.

## The Myths

### Myth 1: Only students identified for a gifted program are mathematically talented.

This myth is pervasive due to the general nature of programming for gifted students. Many gifted programs are pull-out programs (i.e., students are pulled out of their regular classroom for gifted programming once or twice a week). The identification criteria for pull-out programs tend to emphasize the all-around gifted student. One typical identification criterion for a pull-out program is an IQ of 130 or higher as measured on an IQ test. In lieu of, or in addition to, the IQ criterion, a pull-out program may use a criterion such as a high percentile ranking on the composite score of a nationally standardized achievement test. A student who earns a score at or above the 97th percentile must therefore score in the high ranges on most sections of the test in order to qualify. However, this type of cut-off criterion effectively eliminates students who have a special talent in just one area and average, or even above-average, abilities in other areas. Thus, the mathematically talented student may not meet the criteria for his or her school's gifted program.

Myth 1:    Only students identified for a gifted program are mathematically talented.

Myth 2:    Results from standardized, grade-level testing are sufficient for identifying mathematically talented students.

Myth 3:    Gifted students respond equally well to the same curriculum.

Myth 4:    Students whose pace of instruction is accelerated cannot cover each section of the text and will have gaps in their mathematics background.

Myth 5:    Students who are mathematically talented demonstrate mastery of a topic by earning 100% on tests—including pretests.

Myth 6:    Mathematically talented students are computation whizzes.

Myth 7:    Mathematically talented students cannot be identified until high school.

Myth 8:    Early ripe, early rot.

Myth 9:    The best option for mathematically able elementary school students is enrichment.

Myth 10:   The best way to challenge mathematically talented students is to have them skip a grade and study the regular textbook in the regular classroom.

Myth 11:   If mathematically able students study mathematics at an accelerated pace, they will run out of math curriculum before they reach high school.

Myth 12:   Students—even those who are mathematically talented—shouldn't study algebra until eighth or ninth grade.

**Figure 1.1 Myths About Mathematically Talented Youngsters**

As an example of the situation described above, over 26% of mathematically talented students in one study did not participate in their school's gifted and talented program (Lupkowski-Shoplik & Assouline, 2001). Unfortunately, these students who are not in the gifted program are often prevented from receiving special services or participating in enrichment activities that would be appropriately challenging. For example, in one school, only students who are in the school's gifted program can participate in extracurricular math activities such as the Mathematical Olympiads for Elementary and Middle Schools (MOEMS). A third-grade student in that school (for whom we will use the pseudonym Jason) has mastered fractions, multiplication, and division and he grasps elementary algebraic concepts. However, Jason has a tested Verbal IQ of "only" 125, and the school requires an IQ of 130 in order to be identified as eligible for the gifted program. Therefore, Jason is not in the school's gifted program, and school policy prohibits him from participating in MOEMS. This is unfortunate because he clearly would benefit from participation in MOEMS, and the MOEMS team would probably also benefit from his participation. Also, and more importantly, although Jason is mathematically talented, because of the school's operational definition of giftedness, he does not receive specialized services in his talent area.

Providing special services to mathematically talented students only through the school's gifted program is a related version of the myth that only students who are identified for a gifted program can be mathematically talented. However, there is no guarantee that the mathematically talented student will actually receive, through the gifted program, advanced curricular opportunities that correspond to mathematical talent. This is because many gifted programs are driven not by students' identified strengths, but by the district's designated curriculum. In other words, many gifted programs do not provide specific programming for any of their identified students, despite the fact that the students may have been identified specifically for their mathematical ability. These issues are discussed more thoroughly in Chapter 6.

**Myth 2: Results from standardized, grade-level testing are sufficient for identifying mathematically talented students.**

Although grade-level testing information may be useful in finding mathematically talented students, it does not give information that is precise enough to generate a program. Using grade-level tests to assess exceptionally talented students is like using miles to measure something that should be measured in inches. For example, two students might earn identical scores on a grade-level test (such as a 99th percentile on the mathematics total section of a basic skills battery), but earn very different scores on an above-level test. An above-level test helps us to measure the students' abilities more accurately; therefore, it helps us to devise more appropriate programs for these students. The concept of above-level testing is the foundation upon which the talent search model was built (Chapters 3 and 5 provide more detailed information about above-level testing and talent searches). Additionally, much of the research used to dispel the myths presented in this chapter derives from the talent search data.

**Myth 3: Gifted students respond equally well to the same curriculum.**

Our research has shown that gifted students are a varied group with respect to their interests (Lupkowski-Shoplik & Assouline, 2001) and abilities (Colangelo, Assouline, & Lu 1994; Lupkowski-Shoplik & Swiatek, 1999). The curriculum for mathematically talented students should also reflect that diversity of talent (Sheffield, 1999a). That is why we don't recommend just one curriculum for all gifted students. (The diversity of ability within a highly able group of mathematically talented students is thoroughly discussed in Chapter 5.)

When thousands of gifted students were asked about their academic interests, the highest percentage of respondents (39%) indicated that mathematics interested them the most. Next was science (27%), and least was language arts (5%; Lupkowski-Shoplik & Assouline, 2001). Even if teachers did not take general intellectual ability or specific mathematical aptitude into consideration, the fact that gifted students are so varied in their interests suggests that one curriculum does not fit all.

For mathematically talented students, we advocate using resources that are readily available by adapting their school's math curriculum. This might mean using the curriculum from a higher grade level with younger students. Chapter 7 presents a wide range of ideas; used in combination with information provided in Chapter 6, these ideas can help school personnel devise the right level and pace of curriculum for talented students.

**Myth 4: Students whose pace of instruction is accelerated cannot cover each section of the text and will have gaps in their mathematics background.**

When mathematically talented students enter the regular classroom at the beginning of each school year, they bring with them knowledge of specific mathematical content, as well as a high aptitude for learning new mathematics. In fact, they already know much of the material that will be presented to them that year. How can they be challenged through an accelerated approach without risking that they will skip important concepts?

We advocate a simple, sensible model for developing a program plan for talented students. First, students should be pretested using the chapter tests provided by the textbook publisher. Students correctly answering 85% of the material should be permitted to move on to the next topic after they have covered specific topics related to any items they missed. This clarification of missed material might take as little as 15 minutes (Lupkowski, Assouline, & Stanley, 1990). After students demonstrate that they understand the concepts they missed, they can then move on to the next chapter or topic.

Although some teachers routinely offer pretests to their students, we hear too often about teachers who administer them to the whole class and then require all students to complete all the work in the chapter, regardless of the level of mastery they have demonstrated. Students who demonstrate mastery should be allowed to move on to something new.

Pretesting indicates readiness to move forward, but it also ensures that students do not miss any content. Then, students aren't stuck with the drudgery of studying each page of a math book. A more complete explanation of pretesting is described as part of Chapter 4.

This simple approach of pretesting is extremely helpful for students who are accelerating or skipping a year of mathematics. Students can take the pretests, final exams, or chapter exams from the course they are scheduled to skip. Then, if there are a few topics the students have not yet learned, they can study them. Students can easily fill in the gaps in their knowledge and be ready to move on to the next level as well prepared as any student who has studied the level for a year. They are not forced to trudge through the entire 180 days of curriculum in order to fill in a few gaps that may only take a few minutes or a few days to learn and understand.

## Myth 5: Students who are mathematically talented demonstrate mastery of a topic by earning 100% on tests—including pretests.

Implicit in this myth is the notion that talented students should not make errors. Because students in the primary grades often do not make errors on the assignments they are given, educators begin to adopt a mindset that mastery means getting 100% correct. The student version of this "mastery = 100%" mindset is known as *perfectionism*.

From the student and educator perspective, the "100% correct" definition of mastery is detrimental; however, if 100% correct on a test is not an appropriate indicator of mastery, what is? To answer this question, we turned to a variety of texts that are used in graduate classes in the field of gifted education. Much to our surprise, we didn't find a definition of mastery. In these texts, mastery was discussed, especially within the context of differentiation of curricula, but it was not defined. In our nonexhaustive search, we found two specific references to the notion of "instructional level." One of the references, *Instructional Strategies for Teaching the Gifted* (Parker, 1989), was specifically in regard to challenging the gifted reader. The second reference, *Being Gifted in School: An Introduction to Development, Guidance, and Teaching* (Coleman & Cross, 2001), also discussed a child's instructional level with respect to reading. Coleman and Cross stated,

> The rule of thumb is that the appropriate instructional level consists of 90% known information and 10% unknown information. Because data on this point in terms of giftedness are hard to locate, this seems to be a conservative criterion for beginning instruction with gifted children. An important mediating variable is student interest and commitment. Because there is no way to account for motivation until instruction begins, a 50:50 ratio might be reasonable in some content areas. (p. 407)

In our pursuit of a definition of mastery, we also reviewed texts used in graduate-level coursework on educational measurement and assessment. According to Nitko (1996),

> A frequently used passing score is 80% (or as near as you can come to this with the number of items you have for assessing a learning target). There is no educational justification for 80%, however. The important point is not the exact value of the passing score or passing percentage. Rather, it is the minimum level of knowledge a student needs to demonstrate with respect to each learning target to benefit from further instruction. This may vary from one learning target to the next. Use your own judgment, remembering that setting a standard too low or too high results in misclassifying students as masters or nonmasters. (p. 291)

These authors' comments parallel our thinking. Because on-grade-level mathematics tends to be so underchallenging, the mathematically gifted child typically answers almost all of the problems from a grade-level mathematics test correctly. As a result, that high standard is often carried over to advanced instructional settings. It isn't reasonable to assume that mastery is demonstrated only when students earn 100% on an achievement test. It is even less reasonable to assume that 100% should be earned on a pretest.

The purpose of pretesting should always be diagnostic in nature. A pretest should help the educator to identify where instruction should begin. If a student earns 100% on a pretest, the educator needs to move on rapidly to a new topic. Pretesting should continue until the student has missed enough problems to have further instruction, but is not frustrated by the difficulty level of the assessment. For problems missed on the pretest, it is helpful if the teacher asks the student to rework the problem, showing all his or her work. In this way, the teacher can determine if the student answered the question incorrectly because he or she did not understand the concept or because of a careless error.

## Myth 6: Mathematically talented students are computation whizzes.

Many of the mathematically talented students with whom we work have excellent conceptual skills, but their skills at computation are less developed. For example, Barb has an excellent understanding of how to multiply fractions, but she often makes mistakes when adding a column of figures. In this situation, teachers are often tempted to hold students back from learning advanced concepts until their "basic skills" catch up. This is unfair to the student and may actually be detrimental to his or her mathematical development. Research (Lupkowski-Shoplik, Sayler, & Assouline, 1994; Rotigel, 2000) has shown that many mathematically talented students have an excellent understanding of advanced mathematical concepts while simultaneously having relatively less-developed computation skills. This means that their computation skills may lag significantly behind their understanding of mathematics, resulting in a student who understands abstract mathematical ideas (such as a variable), yet frequently gets the wrong answer when multiplying fractions. As described in Lupkowski-Shoplik et al. (1994) and Rotigel (2000), students may show this weakness because:

1. they have demonstrated competence with a computational skill, but are not allowed to move on to another topic, so they make careless mistakes;
2. they may prefer to do computations in their heads to stimulate themselves intellectually because the material they usually study in school is not interesting or challenging;
3. some underlying cognitive construct may cause the difference;
4. direct instruction is generally required for students to learn computational skills, while students may develop a conceptual understanding on their own; or
5. teachers are impressed by these students' exceptional abilities and may assume that drill or practice on routine computation tasks is unnecessary.

Unfortunately, the typical elementary school curriculum doesn't allow these talented youngsters to demonstrate their reasoning skills. Nobody knows how good their conceptual skills are because so much time in the elementary curriculum is devoted to practicing rote tasks.

### Myth 7: Mathematically talented students cannot be identified until high school.

The general nature of the elementary mathematics curriculum might lead one to believe that it is only when students are at the secondary level that they are ready to be recognized as mathematically talented. However, it is necessary to identify mathematically talented students well before high school so that adjustments can be made in their educational programs.

Using above-level standardized tests, we have successfully identified students as young as third grade for challenging programs in mathematics at Carnegie Mellon University and the

University of Iowa. These students were identified through the Elementary Student Talent Search testing program described in Chapter 5. An above-level testing program has been effective in selecting students who will perform well in fast-paced, high-level summer classes for academically talented students (Swiatek & Lupkowski-Shoplik, 2000b). In many cases, the test results confirm what the parents have long suspected: that their child has a talent in mathematics.

Much anecdotal evidence is also available concerning mathematically talented children younger than age 8. Information provided by parents in these cases is especially helpful. Nancy Robinson and her colleagues (Waxman, Robinson, & Mukhopadhayay, 1996a) have systematically identified preschoolers and kindergartners for special programs in mathematics at the University of Washington. Students in the Waxman et al. study were first identified by their parents, and individual achievement tests confirmed the parent nominations. Chapter 9 illustrates this.

## Myth 8: Early ripe, early rot.

The issue of "burnout" seems to come up often, but our experience and the research evidence indicate that this is not the real problem. Rather, the real problem is the nondiscovery of students who are ready for a challenging curriculum. Mathematically talented students who are discovered at a young age and receive appropriate opportunities to develop their mathematical talent continue to excel in mathematics throughout their school careers and beyond. Waxman et al. (1996b) found that talented students maintained their advantage; children in their research group tested at the ages of 3–5 were tested at the end of first grade and again after second grade. As a group, they continued to score above their peers, and they made impressive gains over those years.

Julian Stanley, Camilla Benbow, and their colleagues have conducted a fascinating longitudinal study of exceptionally talented students whose academic talents were discovered at the age of 12 or 13 (Benbow & Lubinski, 1996; Benbow & Stanley,

1983). These students have been studied into graduate school and beyond. The results clearly show that, not only can students be identified at a young age, but also their abilities and achievements continue at high levels into adulthood. For example, in one cohort of high-achieving graduate students participating in the most selective graduate programs in the sciences, many of them had been identified early, enrolled in special programs in elementary school and junior high, participated in accelerative opportunities through high school, maintained stellar academic records, and gained admittance into the most select undergraduate colleges and universities. Most of them had taken advantage of research opportunities during their undergraduate years. "Clearly, we have here a pattern of excellence begetting excellence. . . . They took advantage of educational opportunities presented to them and this began early. It appeared to have a snowball effect on their achievement. With each stage their academic credentials stood out more and more" (Benbow, Lubinski, & Sanjani, 1999, p. 66). Exceptional talents that manifest themselves early do not disappear; when nurtured, they continue to develop.

### Myth 9: The best option for mathematically talented elementary school students is enrichment.

Although enrichment is appropriate and necessary for mathematically talented students, it is not the only option and it might not be the best option for any particular student. Acceleration should not be dismissed for talented students automatically because of their young age. Talented students who accelerate their mathematics education have more time for enriching activities that include studying mathematics in greater depth.

Enrichment can take a variety of forms, including activities unrelated to mathematics, problem-solving activities, or mathematically oriented enrichment activities (Lupkowski & Assouline, 1992). Unfortunately, it is a frequent practice in this country for gifted students to participate in pull-out programs where the topics they study are designed to be unrelated to the regular curriculum. For example, a mathematically talented student in a gifted program might be studying Shakespeare, growing plants for a science project, or participating in a community-service activity. While these are all valuable enrichment activities, they do not advance the student's understanding of mathematics.

Another form of enrichment related to mathematics is often called *problem solving*. Problem-solving activities may offer students the opportunity to think about challenging questions, and these activities can be very enjoyable and intellectually stimulating. However, even though these activities may have mathematics content, they are often totally unrelated to the regular mathematics curriculum the student is required to study. In that case, a student's regular mathematics curriculum cannot be said to have been adjusted to meet his or her needs.

For example, in one school district, a great deal of effort is put into identifying exceptionally mathematically talented students for a special mathematics program. The special program occurs only one day every six weeks. Students in this school district still participate in the regular mathematics curriculum and are expected to work at the same pace as the other students in their class even though they have been identified as exceptionally talented in mathematics. Even though they are studying advanced topics and working with difficult concepts, the students' regular mathematics is still unaffected. Again, this means that the curriculum has not really been adjusted for them.

Finally, a student might have the good fortune to be placed with a teacher who is capable of appropriately enriching the mathematics curriculum. That teacher would assign material that is at a greater depth than what is presented to students in the regular mathematics education program and would also bring in new topics that are not a part of the regular curriculum. The difficulty with this approach is that it depends heavily on having a teacher who is well prepared in mathematics and has the time and inclination to differentiate to a radical degree for the mathematically talented student. Also, there is the concern that the student will no longer have the same type of mathematically enriched curriculum once he or she goes to the next grade level.

For mathematics, good acceleration includes much enrichment, and good enrichment is accelerative (Julian C. Stanley, personal communication, May 1998). Mathematics builds upon itself so that, in reality, it is extremely difficult to "enrich" a student without actually accelerating his or her study of mathematics. All of these issues are discussed thoroughly in this book, especially in Chapters 4, 6, and 7.

*Myth 10: The best way to challenge mathematically talented students is to have them skip a grade and study the regular textbook in the regular classroom.*

Skipping a grade and studying mathematics in the regular classroom with older students may be an excellent option for some students. In this case, both short-term and long-term planning are critical. For example, will the student be able to take mathematics the following year with students in the older grade? How will the transportation issues be resolved in the future if the student must go to a different building for mathematics? What will happen to the student when he or she is a 12th grader? Will the student be able to take a mathematics course at a local college, or does the high school offer a course for accelerated students so that he or she may take mathematics during his or her senior year?

Even if the above questions are answered to the satisfaction of all parties (i.e., student, parent, and educators), studying mathematics with students who are a year older may not be the right option for some students, especially extremely talented students. The pace of instruction in the regular classroom will probably still be too slow even though the student is studying material usually reserved for older students. The level of instruction may not be challenging enough, and they may need mathematics instruction that is 2 or 3 or even more years advanced compared to their age. They would benefit from an individualized approach, such as that detailed in Chapter 4. Chapter 6 also details a variety of options that may be offered to mathematically talented students.

Myth 11: If mathematically able students study mathematics at an accelerated pace, they will run out of math curriculum before they reach high school.

This myth is mentioned when considering the possibility of a student accelerating, even at a young age. It is important to think about the long-term impact of acceleration, even when a student is in the early grades. For students who skip one or more years of mathematics, it is true that they might not have any more courses to take in their high school when they reach 11th or 12th grade. However, there is always more mathematics to study (ask any college mathematics professor). Students, educators, and parents might need to be flexible and creative to ensure that students are receiving the appropriate mathematics course(s). For example, a student might study mathematics with a mentor in 4th grade, study high school geometry while in 6th grade, and take a calculus course on a college campus while in 11th grade. With the increasing availability of computers and Internet-based courses, students in rural areas no longer have to be left out of these opportunities. Chapters 5 and 6 and the "Resources" section provide information about the many options for students.

Myth 12: Students—even those who are mathematically talented—shouldn't study algebra until eighth or ninth grade.

One of the reasons for this myth includes the fact that most of the administrators and policy makers in today's schools experienced a traditional sequence of mathematics courses. In a traditional sequence, algebra is not formally introduced until ninth grade or, at best, eighth grade. In addition to the historical component to this myth, there has also been a concern that students younger than grade 8 may not be developmentally ready for the formal, abstract reasoning required by algebraic principles.

The work of Julian Stanley and his colleagues have discounted the developmental aspect of this myth. For over 30 years, Stanley and his colleagues (Benbow & Lubinski, 1996) have been discovering students who are ready for algebra well before grade 9 and many who are ready as early as grades 5 or

6 (and a few are ready well before grade 5). Stanley's work with the Study of Mathematically Precocious Youth (SMPY) at Johns Hopkins University has had a far-reaching effect, and, as a result, many students have been accelerated into algebra.

While the mathematically talented students who were discovered were quite content to be exposed to formal algebra when they were cognitively ready (rather than waiting until they were chronologically ready), mathematics educators reacted negatively to this accelerated programming. This attitude was initially reflected in the professional document developed by mathematics educators, the Curriculum and Evaluation Standards for School Mathematics (National Council of Teachers of Mathematics, 1989). The 1989 version contained strong statements against acceleration and promoted the notion that

> all students can benefit from an opportunity to study the core curriculum specified in the Standards. This can be accomplished by expanding and enriching the curriculum to meet the needs of each individual student, including the gifted and those of lesser capabilities and interests. (p. 253)

Throughout the 1990s, mathematics educators continued to fine-tune the curriculum standards, and this antiacceleration approach was a component of this refining process. By the end of the decade, antiacceleration reached a peak. One section of the working draft of the Principles and Standards for School Mathematics (NCTM, 1998) titled "Fostering Algebraic Competence Without Acceleration or Specialization" began:

> In recent years in the middle grades there has been a trend toward acceleration and specialization related to algebra. Students in grade 8, or even in grade 7, are increasingly taking courses that focus exclusively on algebra and that are organized in a manner similar to the traditional algebra course in high school. This

trend represents a well-intentioned response to what many perceived to be a lack of quality and challenge in the mathematics program for middle school students. However, such acceleration and specialization can have negative consequences for students. One negative consequence is that students are likely to have less opportunity to learn the full range of mathematics content, especially topics in geometry and data analysis, that are expected in the middle grades. (NCTM, 1998, p. 214)

Fortunately, this antiacceleration philosophy did not make it into the new version of the Principles and Standards for School Mathematics (NCTM, 2000a). The current philosophy promotes algebra as a strand in the curriculum that begins in kindergarten or before. The current standards for middle school students (grades 6–8) recommend that all students should study significant amounts of algebra and geometry in sixth, seventh, and eighth grade so that, by the end of eighth grade, they will have a good understanding of foundational algebraic and geometric ideas.

This approach is a challenging alternative to the practice of offering a select group of middle grades students a one-year course that focuses narrowly on algebra or geometry. All middle grades students will benefit from a rich and integrated treatment of mathematics content. Instruction that segregates the content of algebra or geometry from that of other areas is educationally unwise and mathematically counterproductive. (NCTM, 2000a, p. 213)

In the paragraphs above, we have indicated how and why the myth that algebra should not be studied until eighth or ninth grade has been propagated. The new standards (NCTM, 2000a) should help to dispel this myth. But, with the new standards come two additional concerns with respect to developing programs for mathematically gifted students. First, it takes a great deal of time to implement the standards (change of this magnitude may take 5–10 years). Consequently, this is too late for students who are currently in upper elementary or middle school. Additionally, the new standards still do not address programming that promotes appropriately challenging coursework that allows mathematically talented students to progress through the formal mathematics curriculum at a depth and pace that is intellectually stimulating.

## Conclusion: What Should Be Done?

In this chapter, we have briefly presented and discussed the 12 major statements that we hear most often as reasons not to differentiate programming for mathematically talented youth. These statements have taken on a mythical quality with the power to shape the worldview of the educational culture. Broadly speaking, this worldview reflects a naïve perspective that ignores individual differences among students. We have indicated why we consider these statements to be fiction, and we have introduced facts to refute the myths. The remaining chapters of this book will elaborate on these issues.

There is, however, one overarching myth that we did not specifically address. This is the myth that it's best not to do anything that is different from the regular programming. For parents of mathematically talented students, this can be a particularly frustrating situation that poses a dilemma for them regarding whether or not they should advocate for their child. Advocacy is the subject of the following chapter.

# 2 Advocacy

---

## Key Points

- Parents are their children's primary advocates. In advocating for their children, parents are not "pushing" their children.

- Effective advocates maintain a positive attitude of cooperation with the school throughout the process. This includes becoming informed about the characteristics and needs of mathematically talented students.

- Objective information is critical for effective advocacy. Effective advocacy results from matching this objective information with the available resources within a school. Many times, advocacy will result in acceleration of a student.

- Change is neither easy nor immediate; there is typically tension between parent desire and school policy. We advise parents to concentrate on adapting the current situation so that their child's needs are met in a timely manner, rather than trying to overhaul the school system. However, parents should also look to the long term and recognize that their efforts at advocacy may have a positive impact on programs provided for mathematically talented students in future years.

*Advocacy: The "act of pleading or arguing in favor of something, such as a cause; active support."*
—*American Heritage Dictionary, 3rd ed. (1993, p. 20)*

TWO KEY WORDS IN THE definition of *advoacy—pleading* and *support*—summarize why we devote a whole chapter to the notion of advocacy. We continuously receive pleas for help, usually from parents, as they strive to encourage their children who are frustrated by the underchallenging regular mathematics curriculum. Thus, a primary focus of this chapter is the parental role as advocate for talented students. One of our specific goals is to advise parents about approaching their child's educators to generate a supportive partnership between home and school. Because parents are well informed about their children's out-of-school learning experiences, personality, and general level of social-emotional development— in other words, they know their children best—parents are in the best position to notify educators about their child's academic interests and needs. Educators, on the other hand, are in the best position to provide curriculum and instruction. Although the teacher sometimes initiates and advocates for a change in the student's educational program, usually the parent is in the position of advocating for an accommodation that will result in more challenging programming and curricula.

The individuals involved in making decisions about changing a student's educational program may have very different ideas about what the student needs and what resources should be made available to him or her. We can't guarantee that parents' efforts at advocacy will be nonadversarial; but, we can help parents and educators understand the advocacy process with respect to attitudes, interactions, and information, and that is the primary purpose of this chapter.

## A Model of the Impact of Attitude on Interactions Between Home and School

A useful model for understanding the impact of attitude on the interactions between parents and educators of gifted children was delineated by Colangelo and Dettman (1982; see also Colangelo, 2003). Although the Colangelo and Dettman model was developed for school counselors, we think it is relevant for understanding any parent-educator interaction. The model, described below, has four interaction types and is based upon parent- and school-perceived level of activity and attitude about each other.

1.  *Type I (Cooperation)*: Both parents and educators have the attitude that action is needed and wanted; the focus is on providing the appropriate programming for the student. Whether parents or educators initiate the request is irrelevant to the process.
2.  *Type II (Conflict)*: In this scenario, parents actively seek challenges for their student, but the attitude of school personnel is passive.
3.  *Type III (Interference)*: The interactions of Type III also result in conflict, but the attitudes are the reverse of Type II. In Type III, parents are passive while school personnel are more active in initiating and promoting a programming change for the child. Readers of this book may wonder whether or not this situation actually exists! It does; however, in our experience it is not as common as Type II or Type IV.
4.  *Type IV (Natural Development)*: Parents and educators both believe that the current school curriculum, even if it is underchallenging, is adequate and, if the talent is there, it will eventually develop without intervention. This situation reflects agreement by both parents and educators; therefore, the approach and attitude on the part of both groups is passive.

The type of interaction that best serves the student is *Type I: Cooperation*. School personnel and parents view each other as partners and meet to discuss common concerns on behalf of the talented child. Parents look to the school for guidance in educating their child, yet encourage the child to question work that does not appear challenging or meaningful. Likewise, school personnel attempt to respond to requests from parents and are flexible in meeting the needs of gifted children.

From our perspective, *Type II: Conflict* is the most difficult for both parents and educators, and it takes a serious toll on the student, as well as the parents and educators who are in direct conflict. Typically, parents believe that their child needs special programming in order to be sufficiently challenged in mathematics, whereas school personnel maintain that the school curriculum is adequate for meeting the needs of the mathematically talented student. In this situation, school personnel may adopt the attitude that action is not necessary because of the (erroneous) belief that parents are pushing their youngsters and that the parents do not support the school. Parents may be so frustrated that they hold this school situation responsible for fostering their child's feelings of boredom and frustration.

Determining the exact type of interaction between parents and educators is not as important as understanding how accurate information about the child's academic needs can inform both parents and educators. Advocacy involves providing information that is designed to inform/change attitude and is heavily dependent on objective information gained through appropriate assessment, including test scores, portfolios, and specific information about strengths and weaknesses in mathematics, as well as other subject areas (e.g., writing and reading). Effective advocacy results in—and is a result of—matching this information with the available resources within a school or district.

## How Do Parents Make a Change in Their Child's Educational Program?

Most parents who contact us are looking (pleading) for assistance because they are in a *Type II: Conflict* situation. Parents seek a programming change for their student, but the attitude of the school personnel is passive, resistive, or both to the parent-requested change. Because of our work with mathematically talented students, parents contact us because they generally assume that we will be able to transfer our "power" to their school and "change" their child's school system so that it has a more cooperative attitude toward programming for their mathematically gifted child. If we could, we would!

When the teacher or principal turns down their request, parents are usually very disappointed, and they often change their focus from trying to change the practices of an individual teacher to changing school policies. This is a perfectly logical direction in which to turn; it is typical for parents to assume that, if they place their concerns about their child within larger more general educational concerns, then they will have a better chance of having those concerns addressed and changed. However, anyone who has participated in either broad or narrow efforts at educational change can attest to the fact that, simply put, it is never easy.

One of the most informative and readable books about educational change is *The New Meaning of Educational Change*, by Michael G. Fullan with Suzanne Stiegelbauer (1991). This book contains so many important points that it is hard to select only a few. We have chosen to highlight the four points below because they are most relevant to our discussion of advocacy:

1. "the typical situation of teachers is one of fixity and a welter of forces keeping things that way." (p. 35)
2. "there is little room, so to speak, for change. When change is imposed from outside, it is bitterly resented." (p. 35)
3. "Even when voluntarily engaged in, change is threatening and confusing." (p. 36)
4. "there is a strong tendency for people to adjust to the 'near occasion' of change, by changing as little as possible—either assimilating or abandoning changes that they were initially willing to try, or fighting or ignoring imposed change." (p. 36)

In other words, change within the educational system is extremely difficult, and teachers and administrators resist it for many reasons. Even for the most mathematically talented student, making accommodations within the educational system may seem to be nearly impossible.

Take for example the kindergartner who enters school with academic skills comparable to those of a third grader. Many third graders are comfortable with addition, subtraction, and multiplication. However, many kindergartners do not know their numbers beyond 10. Since many kindergarten teachers consider a major focus of the kindergarten curriculum to be socialization, they will be reluctant to address the learning needs of the mathematically talented kindergartner out of concern that his or her social/emotional developmental needs will be compromised. This is an illustration of the inflexibility that will be more fully elaborated in "A Journey of Advocacy: As Told by Alexis's Mother" later in this chapter.

### If change is so difficult, what's a parent to do?

Our response begins with a caveat: Do not demand that a school district establish a special class for a group of students as a way to address your child's needs. This type of request requires policy and systemwide changes that can rarely—if ever—be implemented within a time-frame that accommodates a child's immediate needs. A more effective approach is to focus on the child's specific needs and find a way to match the curriculum to the learner. Options might include moving the student up a grade for mathematics class, having the student participate in a distance-learning program, or matching the student with a mentor.

The goal should be the development of a plan to challenge the student in a consistent, systematic manner. One of the best ways to do that is through a program such as that described in Chapter 4 on Diagnostic Testing➤Prescriptive Instruction. But, how can that program (or any other) be implemented and what is the interaction between parent and school? There are at least four possibilities:

1.    Bypass the school. The child works privately with a mentor. The arrangement is between parent and mentor.

2.  Bypass the school. The student works privately with a mentor under the administrative expertise of a third party (e.g., university-based programs; see references in chapters throughout this book).
3.  Inform the school. The student works privately with a mentor—outside of the school day; however, the school is advised of the activity so the student can receive credit for this work. This communication also promotes long-term planning for the student's programming throughout his or her school years.
4.  Implementation within the school: For example, a program such as Diagnostic Testing→Prescriptive Instruction (DT→PI) described in Chapter 4, is administered by the school and the student receives credit and placement. Any resources or expenses are not the responsibility of the parents.

Although all four scenarios are possible, the third and fourth are the most conducive to cooperation. These options require program and curricular changes for an individual child or small groups of very talented students. Change at the individual or small-group level is easier to implement than the systemwide change that is so desired by parents and often dictated by law or policy.

### What legal options are available when parents perceive that school policy does not match their child's academic needs?

A federal definition of giftedness and talent was produced in the early 1970s (Marland, 1972). In 1993 the federal Office of Education generated the National Excellence Report (U.S. Department of Education, 1993), which decried the general lack of gifted programming. Despite this federal influence on definitions and programs, there is no federal government mandate requiring school districts to provide special programs for gifted students (Karnes & Marquardt, 2003). The National Association for Gifted Children (NAGC), a national organization composed of teachers, K–12 educators, university educators, and parents, supports mandating services to meet the unique needs of gifted and talented children.

> Numerous studies . . . have documented that needs of our nation's gifted and talented students are not being met. . . . The needs of gifted and talented students have been well-documented by research and federal studies. To educate all our children and allow America to compete in a global economy and all fields of human endeavor, the nation must provide an environment in which gifted and talented students, along with all of our children, can reach their full potential" (NAGC position paper, "Mandated Educational Opportunities for Gifted and Talented Students," reprinted in Karnes & Marquardt, 2003).

Although this is a laudable document, the fact remains that gifted children are not a constitutionally protected group of individuals.

Even though there is not a federal mandate protecting gifted students, there is a variety of approaches to providing services for them throughout the individual states. For example, some states have a mandate for the provision of gifted education, whereas others only "permit" gifted education. That is, the school district may provide gifted education, but it is not required to accommodate the gifted child. To determine if their state has a statutory mandate requiring special instruction for the gifted, parents can ask an official in their state's Department of Education directly, or they can refer to a publication from the Council of State Directors of Programs for the Gifted, which is published on a biennial basis. Parents who attempt a legal solution from a state without a mandate have little chance of legal recourse.

Parents who enter the legal process in a state with a statutory mandate for the provision of gifted education have somewhat of a chance in the legal system. An interesting case in Pennsylvania, a state that mandates gifted education, is discussed in Karnes and Marquardt (2003; see also Karnes &

Marquardt, 1988). In this case, *Centennial School District v. Commonwealth Department of Education* (1988), parents of a boy identified as intellectually gifted and having outstanding abilities in mathematics and reading requested that the school district provide instruction to serve his special talents in the regular classroom. At the time, the student was receiving gifted education services through a resource approach—a pull-out program —which allocated 90 minutes per week. The district claimed that this was the only economically feasible approach. The family requested a due process hearing, and an impartial officer ruled in favor of the student. This ruling was upheld through two appeals by the school district. Ultimately, the school district appealed to the Pennsylvania Supreme Court, who also ruled in favor of the student by determining that the resource program did not provide the individualized instruction required under state law (i.e., an individualized educational plan [IEP] that tailors the instruction to the student). However, the court went on to say that the individualized instruction need not "maximize" the child's abilities. Thus, the school district was required to provide an individualized, appropriate curriculum to its gifted children, but it did not have to allocate additional resources to do so.

School districts in Pennsylvania were therefore required to serve the needs of their gifted students using instructional staff and curricula the school district already had in place. "The case provides a judicial precedent that gifted education proponents can use to support the demand for individualized, appropriate education for gifted students, particularly in states statutorily mandating that districts provide gifted education" (Karnes & Marquardt, 2003).

The tendency of educators to resist change can be extremely frustrating, and the seemingly intractable position of schools may even result in the pursuit of legal recourse by both parties (e.g., the Centennial School District appealed *three* times a ruling that favored individualized programming for a student in the district). However, this choice of action is not expedient, and informal or quasi-formal resolutions are preferable to those that involve the courts (Karnes &

Marquardt, 2003). In fact, Karnes and Marquardt recommended that the resolution of educational issues begin with the "source" (i.e., teacher or gifted education coordinator) and, if necessary, proceed through negotiation, mediation, due process, administrative review and, as a last recourse, the courts.

Figure 2.1 illustrates this process of resolving educational issues by starting with informal means, including parent-teacher conferences, child study team, and negotiations within the school. If the interactions with the teacher, gifted education coordinator, or principal do not result in the desired change, parents might move on to quasi-formal means, including mediation, administrative review, and due process, in which the parents present the situation to a representative from the state's Department of Education. The exact procedures may vary from one state to another. Again, if the results aren't satisfactory, parents may pursue the court system, with its many roadblocks and delays. Obviously, we recommend that differences be resolved in the informal manner, so that changes can be made quickly and efficiently for the child. The final option, the courts, is the least desirable option.

The responsibility of finding appropriate programs with adequate challenges for mathematically talented students ultimately falls on the parents. In fact, Rogers (2002) culled hundreds of research articles, summarized her dozens of interactions with parents, and overtly deduced, "it is unlikely that the schools will suggest a uniquely individualized educational plan. So, if a plan is going to be implemented, you must be the one to initiate it, to collect the data, and to design the initial plan. This isn't all bad; after all, you are the one who knows your child best" (p. 8).

This responsibility is especially significant for parents because compounding a school's general resistance to change is the fact that many educators have little or no training in gifted education. At the elementary level, teachers of mathematics may also have, at best, minimal training in identifying mathematically talented youth (National Commission on Teaching and America's Future, 1996). (What may be even

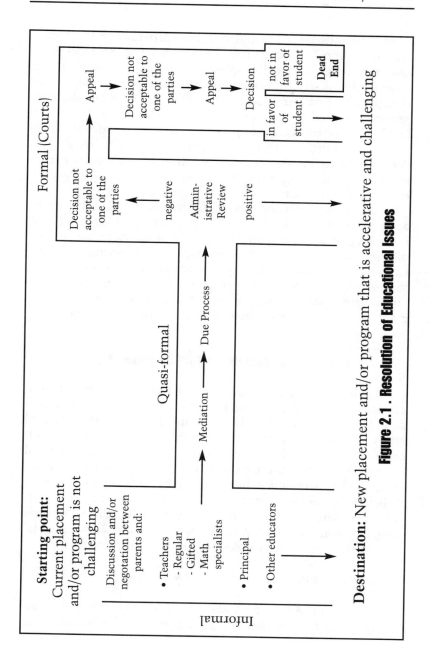

**Figure 2.1 . Resolution of Educational Issues**

**Destination:** New placement and/or program that is accelerative and challenging

more frustrating for parents is that mathematics teachers—although there are exceptions—seem to have little desire to discover mathematically talented youth!) It is also not unusual for district-level coordinators to have little formal training on identifying and programming for gifted students in general (Council of State Directors of Programs for the Gifted, 1999; Tomlinson, Coleman, Allan, Udall, & Landrum, 1996; Ward & Landrum, 1994) and mathematically talented students in particular; however, it is often the gifted education teacher who will assist the parents in their efforts at advocacy for challenging math.

Teacher-preparation programs rarely emphasize differentiating mathematics for talented youngsters, and little training for current teachers is offered by school districts concerning differentiating for mathematically talented youth. Consequently, teachers and school administrators might think that simply offering a few enrichment activities might be adequate, rather than making an effort to have a systematic program or plan in place for mathematically talented students.

## A Journey of Advocacy: As Told by Alexis' Mother

In an ideal educational world, a challenging accelerated curriculum would exist and parents would not need to advocate. However, we can only strive for the ideal. As discussed above, when advocating for their child, parents cannot concentrate on the problems with the system. Rather, they need to work to change their child's program. This is the parents' job and, as in so many other parent jobs, only a parent can do it. Below is a detailed account of the efforts of one set of parents (primarily the mother) as they traveled the sometime smooth, sometimes bumpy, road of advocacy. (Alexis' mother's comments are indented and in a different font.)

### Kindergarten: The Path From Cooperation to Natural Development

When she entered kindergarten, Alexis was the only student in her class able to read. Fortunately, her teacher was very supportive and gave Alexis every opportunity to read and write on her own. At the end of the year, a few additional students were able to read and write, and the teacher shared with me her philosophy that there is a wide window in which children develop reading and writing skills and other children will "catch up."

Parents of gifted children are often told that other children will "catch up." Of course, the vast majority of students do master reading and writing by grade 2. However, the individual differences that are apparent among students at the beginning of kindergarten remain even as children mature as part of the natural process of development. Average students do not catch up with precocious students. In fact, research supports our observation that the gaps between gifted and average children observed during the primary grades only get wider as children progress in school (Waxman, Robinson, & Mukhopadhayay, 1996b).

Alexis was both verbally and mathematically talented. She was first identified as being exceptional because of her talent in the verbal area. Although this is something for which her parents will continue to advocate, the struggle for curricular change focused on mathematics because Alexis' educators were very resistant to any proposed change in this area.

### Grade 1: The Bumpy Road From Natural Development to Conflict

When Alexis entered first grade, her reading skills far exceeded the other students in her class and she was dreadfully bored during the reading period. I got the first indication of the difficulties to come when I consulted with Alexis' teacher. I suggested that she give Alexis a writing assignment to occupy her time and to help her hone her writing skills. I was informed that the teacher was not permitted to give anything but a reading assignment during the required reading period. Fortunately, she agreed to allow Alexis to choose a book to read when she had completed the class assignment. The degree of difference between Alexis' reading ability and that of her peers was still not clearly apparent to us. In retro-

spect, one indicator of the difference was that her classmates did not recognize Alexis' Halloween costume when
she dressed as Pippi Longstocking.

When I picked Alexis up on the last day of first grade, her
teacher told me that she had asked each student to set a
goal for second grade and that Alexis had said that she
wanted to learn division. Her teacher commented, "You know,
she already knows multiplication." Well, I hadn't known.
"Should I teach her division?" I asked. "No," her teacher
responded. "If you teach her division, she will be bored when
she learns it in third grade."

Educators often suggest that gifted students not study a
new topic (even though the student is ready for the topic)
because they anticipate boredom when it is formally introduced in a higher grade or they are concerned that future
teachers "won't have anything to teach them." Many teachers
do not realize that gifted students have often learned a topic
well before they arrived in the classroom and are ready for
even more advanced topics (Reis et al., 1993).

## Grade 2: The Exit to Cooperation is Missed

Even though students were ability-grouped for math and
reading and some students were in a talented and gifted
(TAG) program, which met weekly for 2 hours, things were
actually worse. The high-ability groups in reading and math
were operating at a level that was lower than what was
needed to keep Alexis engaged. When I suggested to Alexis'
reading teacher that Alexis might need some enrichment,
she responded that she taught the highest level, therefore
Alexis could not possibly require enrichment. In addition, the
teacher suggested that Alexis' immaturity might be the reason for her dissatisfaction with the curriculum. But, I wasn't to
worry, she told me. Alexis is young for the class and will eventually catch up. I observed Alexis' "immaturity" on parent
observation day. There, in the presence of her classmates'
parents, as well as her classmates and teacher, Alexis spent
the entire lesson balancing pencils on her ears. Alexis'

behavior was very surprising to me since she was typically more attentive than most children her age (e.g., she could sit through long programs of classical music).

Alexis allied with another bright student and, together, they walked slowly to reading so they would miss part of the class. Alexis complained bitterly about school. The only day she did not resist going to school was on the day she went to the TAG program. By May, Alexis requested that I speak with her principal about her level of unhappiness in school. However, I thought that perhaps Alexis was just having a difficult year and maybe there was a teacher-student mismatch. I decided to wait until third grade.

Concerns about social/emotional development are often cited as a reason for holding students back academically (Assouline, Colangelo, Lupkowski-Shoplik, & Lipscomb, 1998). Unfortunately, students often act out when they are bored, and these behaviors are perceived as immature. In reality, this is a teacher's way of abdicating the responsibility of addressing the academic reasons for the bright student's acting-out behaviors. Immaturity is a pretext for a "wait and see" approach. Later, parents regret the lost time because the situation rarely improves independently of intervention.

### Grade 3: The Road of Agreement Gives Way to Conflict

Because Alexis had an absolutely wonderful teacher whom she adored, the year started out great. This upbeat beginning obscured from us the difficulties we would encounter as we traveled through a fog of passivity on the now-rough road of educational advocacy. The first sign of a need to advocate appeared during the parent-teacher conference when Alexis' teacher indicated that Alexis' intellectual ability was far beyond other students in her class. She commented that Alexis had many interesting things to say, but most went over her classmates' heads. Around the same time, I began to notice that Alexis was having a much easier time of her schoolwork than other bright children, even other children in her gifted class. She was selecting books to read that other children in her high-level reading group couldn't read and would not have selected.

Even though Alexis was very advanced verbally, most of her complaints were directed toward the math class. However, when I discussed these concerns with her teacher, she refused to give Alexis additional work on the pretext that it would be perceived as special treatment. However, she encouraged Alexis to do the "challenges" that she provided for any student who had finished his or her work. Furthermore, she suggested that I send additional work for Alexis, as long as it did not go beyond the material being covered in class. However, Alexis told me she didn't want to do the challenges or the work being sent from home because it was just more of the same stuff she was bored with in the first place. She said she would rather daydream. But, she also stated she still wanted to learn division and wanted to know why she hadn't learned it since she had been told it would be taught in third grade.

Alexis' teacher felt she had done all she could, and we agreed that the next step was to talk to the principal about the situation. The principal was unavailable, but suggested that we meet with the assistant principal. Little did we suspect that this was part of an administrative strategy to interfere with our attempts to advocate. At that meeting, the assistant principal seemed very understanding. My husband and I suggested a number of possible resolutions, but all were politely declined for one reason or another. The assistant principal recognized that Alexis was very bright, but told us that many children in the school were very bright. She suggested that Alexis had a behavioral problem stemming from an attitude of entitlement and that she felt superior to the other students. This could not have been farther from our (or her teacher's) observation of Alexis. In fact, Alexis had many friends at all levels of ability. We perceived that Alexis was well liked and highly regarded by her friends and that they all knew she was smart—or it was not important to them. At that point, we decided to get a professional opinion.

*Detour for the evaluation.* The idea of seeking a professional opinion from a psychologist who specialized in evaluating gifted students was reinforced by an e-mail discussion with other parents of gifted students. Essentially, I had stumbled upon an e-mail list for parents of gifted students called TAGFAM (see http://www.tagfam.org). Until discovering this list, I was unaware that there were different levels of giftedness and that there were different approaches to teaching gifted students. My brief participation on this list made me consider that perhaps my daughter needed more than her high-ability reading and math grouping or the TAG pull-out class could provide and that a licensed psychologist could help in obtaining this information.

My first encounter with Dr. Lance, the psychologist specializing in working with gifted students, was via telephone. I recall how shy I was about using the word gifted and how I was even more reluctant to assign this description to my child. I told Dr. Lance that I was not sure that I needed to have Alexis evaluated, but was considering the possibility that Alexis' problems in school might stem from her needing more academic challenges, not from the possibility that Alexis had emotional problems. After telling the psychologist more about Alexis and the school environment, she concurred that further evaluation would be helpful.

The first part of the evaluation consisted of a series of surveys to complete, an interview with me and my husband, and a portfolio assessment of Alexis' work. Dr. Lance then administered to Alexis an IQ test and an achievement test. From these results, Dr. Lance suggested an additional IQ test, which was administered at a later date. The results of the tests and evaluation were compiled into a report that was shared with the school. Among other things, the achievement tests indicated that third grader Alexis was already performing computational math at a sixth-grade level (her lowest achievement test score). So, she apparently had learned division, although it had never been taught to her formally.

*Yield for a meeting with the school.* After sending the psychologist's report to the school, we scheduled another meeting with the principal. When we arrived, we were told that the principal had, unfortunately, been called away. The assistant principal greeted my husband and me and politely suggested that the psychologist, who had accompanied us, wait in the hall during the meeting. In our city, it is the law that a parent can bring anyone he or she likes to a meeting with the school. I insisted that Dr. Lance was necessary if there were anything in the report that needed explaining. The assistant principal indicated that there would not be a need for an explanation and we were on "her turf" now. However, Dr. Lance insisted on being present and was included in the meeting.

Our goal for this first meeting was to improve Alexis' attitude toward school. Even with an exciting, stimulating teacher, Alexis was growing increasingly dissatisfied. She was reluctant to go to school and overtly expressed that she was not learning anything in school and that she could barely tolerate sitting through class. In addition, her work began to show signs of tuning out; for example, sometimes she could not answer homework questions because she had daydreamed through a lesson. The assistant principal suggested that these problems were due to behavioral/emotional problems, not academic problems. She went on to say that the school was one of the best in the city with some of the brightest students, thus the school was already providing for academically gifted students. It was suggested that perhaps we were not doing enough for Alexis outside of school.

During that meeting, every suggestion we generated was shot down for one reason or another. In particular, we suggested that Alexis move to a higher grade for math. We were told that was not possible because then she would have nowhere to go when she got to sixth grade. However, the assistant principal agreed to excuse Alexis from math class. This decision was based upon evidence that Alexis had perfect or near-perfect scores on several tests that the class had been taking as practice for an upcoming standardized test. So, Alexis was excused from math and would instead work with the TAG teacher on a writing assignment. Everyone was in agreement—the assistant principal, the classroom teacher, the TAG teacher, Alexis, and us (her parents). After Alexis worked on the writing assignment for 3 days, I got a call from the principal. She indicated that I had misunderstood and that Alexis couldn't be excused from math because Alexis, like all the other students, needed to practice for the standardized math test. This was very demoralizing for Alexis. In fact, after this incident, Alexis became a reluctant writer. She had gotten the message that her writing was "bad," mostly because the TAG teacher wouldn't work with her on the project.

The principal also indicated that she would not discuss adjustments for Alexis until receiving Alexis' standardized test scores. She reasoned that those scores, more than the scores from the psychologist's evaluation, would indicate Alexis' ability.

*Further meetings with the principal are dead-ended.* One day before Alexis' test scores came back, the principal called me at work to express her concern that I had provided Alexis with inappropriate reading material. I was shocked and asked for clarification. The principal had observed Alexis' class when the students were completing an assignment. For the assignment, students were to choose a play and select a scene to perform in class. The principal observed Alexis perform Amanda's monologue from Tennessee William's *The Glass Menagerie*, a play she deemed inappropriate for a third grader. I responded that my recollection of the play did not include sexual content, foul language, or violence. I also made it clear that Alexis had selected the play herself. "But," the principal replied, "her presentation to the students will not endear her to them." I used the opportunity to suggest that perhaps now she understood the problem and might work with us to adjust Alexis' education appropriately. Instead, she suggested that I read David Elkind's book, *The Hurried Child*, although she acknowledged that she had not read it.

The second meeting, which was to have been scheduled after the district-administered test results were in, was never scheduled.

*The end of the road.* We had, by this point in time, decided that Alexis could not return to this school in September because it was a "toxic" environment for her. Even if we were able to get the school to agree to some sort of academic adjustment, we had the impression that the environment would be too unpleasant, difficult, or both for Alexis to continue in that school. So, we started the application process to private schools. In addition, Alexis had gotten some relief from the imposed academic boredom by enrolling in the Education Program for Gifted Youth (EPGY) through Stanford University (see "Resources" for more information about this distance-learning opportunity).

However, I was very angry. It did not sit well with me that I was supposedly sending Alexis to the best public school in our city, but that her needs couldn't be met there because she was too smart. So, while we considered private school, I continued to advocate for Alexis in public school.

Alexis had been in this school for almost 4 years (K–3). My husband and I were very active members of the Parents' Association and we participated in school activities in ways that were helpful. We thought we had developed positive relationships with parents, teachers, the assistant principal, and the principal. It seemed to us that Alexis' "profile" was ideal. She was a socially well-adjusted child who was liked by other children and her teachers. She was generally well behaved and performed well academically. In our perception, there were really no negative aspects to her behavioral, academic, or social record in school. So, it was especially surprising to us that the school was so recalcitrant to making adjustments and so antagonistic to us in general. I will add that we never demanded anything in particular. We regarded the faculty and administrators of the school as experts in education and treated them with respect. What we really wanted, initially, was for them to advise us on how to best accommodate Alexis so that she would remain happy in this "excellent" school.

The roadblocks described above are, regrettably, not uncommon. Neither are excuses such as, "But, there are other bright students in this school," or "If we do it for your child, we'll have to do it for all of the children." One of the most dangerous roadblocks is found in the reluctance of school officials to recognize the results from tests other than school-administered tests. Parents must keep in mind that they are making a reasonable request: match the curriculum to the abilities and achievements of the child. In order to do this, Alexis' family continued to gather and document:

- specific information about Alexis' abilities,
- expert opinions about Alexis' educational needs,
- research pertinent to Alexis' situation, and
- information about the experiences of other families of gifted children.

### Skipping Grade 4: The Legal Bumps on the Road of Conflict

Throughout that year, I tried to meet with the district superintendent, who did not return my calls. I also researched the educational laws, statutes, and policies for Alexis' school, school district, city school system, and state. My goal was to find written indications of policies that would help in our quest to get Alexis' needs met. I found out that it was not immediately obvious where one might find help. Surprisingly, I got the most sympathy and information from people who had dealt with the educational rights of students with physical, mental, and learning disabilities. These individuals seemed to know the laws and how to implement them within the system. However, the laws that apply to students with disabilities do not apply to gifted students in my state.

I consulted three lawyers, all of whom told me that there were no legal provisions for gifted students in my state and city and, therefore, they could not help me. I called every educational administrator I could think of, including my district office, the chancellor's office, and the state Department of Education office. I called the education editors of the major newspapers in my city. I called the offices of my local, state, and federal representatives. None could help, although many suggested that they would "look into the matter" by calling the district superintendent. Several called me after talking with someone at the district. So, at the least, the district superintendent was getting calls from these various officials or their representatives.

Although most students in our city attend their zoned middle school after elementary school, there is a special magnet middle school in our city that draws students from a number of zones. I knew of this middle school and was planning for Alexis to apply there when the time came. One of the big attractions for us was that this school has a philosophy of attending to the individual needs of all their students. It occurred to me that I could resolve this by grade acceleration to fifth grade so that Alexis could begin middle school at this particular school.

I started by suggesting this to the principal of Alexis' elementary school, who made it clear that she would never approve of grade acceleration for Alexis, even though it would mean getting rid of us! So, I tried to bypass the principal. Although the receiving middle school was favorably disposed to this idea and was willing to consider Alexis as a "special case," they could not make the grade acceleration. Another individual in a high-level position in the district wrote a letter on Alexis' behalf, indicating the district's support; however, she could not make the grade acceleration either. In fact, the only person with the authority to make the acceleration was the one person who refused to consider it: the principal of Alexis' school.

The scores on the standardized tests taken in school indicated that Alexis received perfect scores on all four tests (city reading and math; state reading and math). I called to remind the principal that a meeting was to be scheduled upon receipt of the standardized test scores. Not only did she refuse to meet with us, but she was verbally abusive to us. I immediately called the district office to report our conversation. About 10 minutes later, I received an apologetic phone call from the principal. Nonetheless, she made it clear that, since she would not grade accelerate Alexis, there was no reason for her to meet with us and she would not take the time to do so. I sent a letter to the school chancellor, documenting our experience.

At the end of the school year (grade 3), the district superintendent called to say he would meet with us to discuss our situation and consider a transfer of Alexis to a different school. I invited the district official who had been sympathetic to our situation and the psychologist to attend that meeting. I asked Alexis' teacher to write a letter (to me) describing how she experienced Alexis in her classroom. Much to my chagrin, the principal's views of Alexis had influenced the teacher, and her letter stated things diametrically opposed to her previous comments and observations. Among other things, the teacher's letter to us indicated that Alexis refused to do the class "math challenges." In my opinion, the teacher had not accurately (or honestly) described Alexis.

We prepared carefully for the meeting with the superintendent. I had documentation of my meetings with the assistant principal at Alexis' school, which included written correspondence. I brought a few articles about acceleration and gifted children and all the official documentation of educational policy that applied to Alexis' situation. I also carefully selected samples of Alexis' work that showed high ability and indicated her boredom with school. I had the tests from the EPGY work Alexis was doing. I also included evaluations of Alexis and her work in the teacher's handwriting. In addition, I brought some of the "math challenges" the teacher provided and similar work Alexis had done at home. I met with the psychologist in advance of the meeting to plan how we would make our presentation. I was concerned because it had come up in meetings with the assistant principal that Alexis' short stature would become an issue. Fortunately, I was able to obtain a letter from a parent on TAGFAM (an e-mail list for parents of gifted children; see http://www.tagfam.org) describing the successful acceleration of her short-statured son.

The district superintendent was receptive to what we had to say, although he expressed concern about Alexis' emotional health. My husband made it clear to him that we were also concerned with Alexis' emotional health and our only reason for seeking an adjustment to her academic situation was to ensure her emotional well-being. The district superintendent expressed concern about Alexis' short stature. I produced the letter from the TAGFAM parent. The district superintendent expressed concern about the fact that Alexis refused the more challenging work the teacher had provided. I showed him the "challenges," then I showed him similar, but more complex work Alexis was doing at home and told him that Alexis refused the "challenges" because they were not interesting to her. When he looked at the work Alexis was doing at home (they were complex logic puzzles), he expressed surprise and understanding. We left the meeting with an agreement that he would help place Alexis in a different school with a more receptive principal who would give Alexis a trial period in the fifth grade—a one-grade acceleration.

The results of the standardized testing were informative, but so were specific examples of the student's work and evaluations of Alexis' work by the teacher. The decision to accelerate Alexis took place before the availability of the Iowa Acceleration Scale (Assouline, Colangelo, Lupkowski-Shoplik, & Lipscomb, 1998), which would have been a significant aid in the acceleration decision-making process.

### Grade 5: The Smooth Ride on the Road of Cooperation

The decision to skip grade 4 was made after the close of the school year, so we were unable to meet with the principal of the new school. We decided to take a chance on this arrangement, with the idea that, if it didn't work out, we would still have the option of private school.

About a week before the start of school in September, I was able to bring Alexis to visit the school and meet with the principal. The difference in the principal's attitude, compared to the principal of the previous school, was astounding. This principal talked directly to Alexis. He told her that it was important to him to see that she was happy in school because only then would she become a lifelong learner. He called her prospective classroom teacher into his office, and she brought Alexis to the classroom for a visit. During Alexis' visit to the classroom, we talked with the principal about our concerns regarding the acceleration; we wanted him to remain flexible with academic adjustments for Alexis without penalty. We wanted the ability to opt out if, for any reason, we felt it was not right for Alexis. Moreover, we wanted the school to do everything possible to ensure the success of the acceleration. I had known of students who were accelerated, only to have the situation undermined by a difficult teacher or administrator or by a lack of sensitivity to problems that might ensue. Both the principal and the teacher were very agreeable.

The acceleration went without a hitch. In fact, there were even fewer problems than I had anticipated. Alexis made friends rather easily, performed well academically and was liked by her classmates and teachers. By October, she was able to invite as many friends from her new school as from her previous school to her birthday party.

At the beginning of the academic year, I tried to convince Alexis that she didn't need to continue the EPGY distance-learning program for math. My reasoning was that she would be in a math class more closely matched to her ability, and I was reluctant for her to have the extra burden of an additional math assignment each day. But, Alexis insisted on continuing EPGY, although she didn't want anyone to know about it.

A few months into the fall, Alexis decided that she didn't want the extra work and stopped the EPGY program. However, by March, she was asking to do EPGY again. This time, however, she wanted to do EPGY instead of math in school and instead of the math homework assigned by the teacher. I suggested this at the spring parent-teacher conference and was absolutely flabbergasted when the teacher responded that it would be okay and all that was needed was to do this without jeopardizing Alexis' relationships with her classmates. I asked if she needed to talk to the principal about this. She indicated that she did, but it would not be a problem. After working out a few details, Alexis started EPGY, this time through Johns Hopkins University. We decided that the best way to do this was for Alexis to do the computer-based lessons at home and bring the paper-based homework to do in the classroom during the scheduled math lesson. We also agreed that, if for any reason the teacher felt it necessary for Alexis to participate in a math class or do some of her assigned homework, Alexis would. In addition, Alexis would have the option of choosing to participate in the math class and do the assigned homework any time she wanted to. For the remainder of the year, there were only three homework assignments the teacher asked Alexis to do. I understood from Alexis and the teacher that Alexis participated in the math class about once a week, usually when they did some sort of group work. Also, I sent the EPGY reports into the teacher so that she could monitor Alexis' progress and performance.

The transfer to this school, within the same district, seemed to make all the difference in the world. I am firmly convinced that finding a school that is the right fit for your child is more important than any one thing a school could provide. In our case, we needed a school whose teachers and administrators recognized that Alexis' giftedness required some academic adjustments. In addition, we needed Alexis to be in a school that would be willing to exercise flexibility in applying those academic adjustments. An indication that this school would be flexible came when the principal indicated at our first meeting that, if grade acceleration didn't work out, we would try something else.

Even when things are going smoothly, attention to the child's program is still required. There is still a need to monitor progress and plan for the future.

### Deciding About Grade 6: A Crossroads

Acceleration from grade 3 to grade 5 was successful and included additional subject acceleration in math through the distance-learning program. However, as fifth grade was nearing conclusion, I knew I had to explore an appropriate placement for middle school. We had a couple of options for public school: (1) Alexis could remain at her current school through sixth grade and go to the middle school it fed into for seventh grade; or (2) she could go the special magnet middle school starting in sixth grade. We discussed our options and concerns with the principal of Alexis' school, who urged us to keep Alexis at his school. He also suggested we speak with the principal of the middle school she would go to as a seventh grader. Because the principals knew each other well, Alexis' current principal was willing to explain the situation and discuss the need for accommodation and flexibility.

However, the response of the middle school principal was discouraging. He did not want to talk with me because it conflicted with his policy of not talking to parents until after the child is enrolled in his school. But, I was insistent. I explained that the principal had urged me to call him to discuss our "special case" and that I needed to talk with him in order to make a decision. He reluctantly let me explain Alexis' situation to him over the phone, after which he told me that it appeared as though I had a very smart daughter who would likely be placed in honors classes just like every other bright student. I inquired as to how math would be handled, as Alexis had already completed seventh-grade math in fifth grade and was likely to progress more in sixth grade. "She will be placed in honors seventh-grade math," he said. He then explained that they didn't differentiate the curriculum for their students in seventh grade, no matter what. High-ability students were just placed in honors classes. In eighth grade, however, high-ability students could be subject-accelerated one grade in math and science (this was a state requirement).

I then decided to call the special magnet middle school and was connected to one of the guidance counselors. I received a similarly lukewarm response. "You say your child is gifted," the counselor said. "Every year I get calls from parents who tell me they have a gifted child and want to know if their child will be getting enough homework." He made it clear that the school was not a school for gifted children. They had heterogeneously grouped classes, no gifted programs, and no honors classes. I told him that I was aware of the mission and philosophy of the school and that I would be more than happy if Alexis never got any homework. However, she was grade-accelerated one year and subject-accelerated in math by several years. I wanted the opportunity to show him Alexis' evaluation and to discuss whether they could accommodate her.

After reviewing Alexis' evaluation, the counselor indicated that he believed Alexis could be happy in his school as long as I wasn't looking for special gifted programs or honors classes. He said that he would make Alexis' teachers aware of her abilities. As far as math was concerned, he specified his understanding that Alexis could not go into a regular sixth-grade math class without having some adjustments made. Although he did not know the specifics, he assured us there would be an accommodation based upon her needs.

We decided that Alexis would go to this school. I must admit that I was a bit nervous leaving that meeting without a specific commitment. On the other hand, I knew of too many parents who pushed for specific accommodations for their child only to have their child locked into an untenable situation they had to make work, much to the detriment of the child. The truth of the matter was that I didn't even know at that time what to ask for. I couldn't anticipate what grade level of math Alexis would be ready for at the start of the next academic year. I also didn't know if Alexis would be better suited to—or if the school could better accommodate—single-subject acceleration, grade acceleration, EPGY instead of math in school, or a differentiated curriculum.

With each school year, Alexis and her family had several options for school placement. In this case, living in a large city was an advantage for them. However, for some families, there will be geographic constraints. The choices may include making changes within the regular classroom, accelerating the student, or removing the student from the class for distance-learning or homeschooling.

Back on the Road of Cooperation: Grades 6–9

Before the start of sixth grade, I met again with the guidance counselor to review the need for math accommodations. The counselor showed some of the math teachers Alexis' EPGY work. Also, I conferred with the people at EPGY with regard to what they thought appropriate for Alexis. We discussed possibilities including subject acceleration and the use of EPGY instead of classroom math. But, Alexis felt strongly that she wanted to be in a classroom.

Within the first few weeks of school, the guidance counselor discussed with Alexis her math placement, and she was placed in Sequential I Math, the subject-accelerated math class for qualifying eighth graders (this is normally a ninth-grade class). Their rationale was that starting Alexis out at the highest level would give them the option to move her down if it didn't work out. They believed this would be easier than moving her up to an advanced class.

We impressed upon the guidance counselor that we wanted this to be a trial; if Alexis were uncomfortable with this arrangement for any reason, she could opt out. As in her previous school, however, we wanted this situation optimized so that it had every chance of success. We expressed our concerns about a number of factors: ease of leaving and returning to class; level of support of the home teacher; and, most importantly, would Alexis be accepted in a class of students several years older and much larger than she? Everyone involved was positive about this arrangement, and it ended up working out quite well.

The math placement was close to perfect for Alexis. The most difficult problem for Alexis was getting used to showing her work. This was not a skill she had honed through the distance-learning math. She did many of the steps in her head, and she didn't have a good sense of what parts of the work she needed to show in order for the teacher to glean her work process and in order to prevent careless errors.

With the appropriate math placement, the mismatch between Alexis' ability level and the curriculum in the other subjects was less important. Even Alexis expressed that she was not concerned when she was not challenged, but only when she was bored. Moreover, the other classes were interesting for the most part, and Alexis appeared to be receiving instruction at an adequate level. In areas in which she excelled, she did more on her own and there was a lot of room for that kind of flexibility. This school had heterogeneously grouped classes that spanned a rather wide spectrum in terms of student abilities. That first year, in sixth grade, Alexis' class included a girl who read at the 1st-grade level, Alexis, who read above the 12th-grade level, and students at every level in-between. Yet, Alexis' academic needs seemed to be well satisfied. I know that other parents of students at all ability levels felt their child's needs were satisfied, as well.

There also didn't seem to be any envy that we experienced at the first elementary school. There are usually several parents who resent that you are seeking a special service for your child or that your child is getting special treatment. Those attitudes were nonexistent at this school, probably because most parents felt their own child was getting what he or she needed. Indeed, the treatment of Alexis—that she was put into the advanced math class—was not really viewed as a special service. The guidance counselor told me that, when he invited Alexis to participate on the math team (which only included eighth graders), he got some questions from other students and parents. But, he said he handled it by explaining that Alexis was qualified for the team.

As the end of the year approached, I knew we had to work out a new solution for the following year. The school did not offer a math course beyond Sequential I Math. Alexis' math teacher offered to teach Sequential II Math to Alexis one on one. In addition, I gathered information about distance-learning classes. But, Alexis really wanted to be in a classroom. I spoke with the guidance counselor, and he suggested that I call high schools to see if any offered the appropriate class at a time Alexis could attend and whether they would allow her in the class. I called the math department chairperson at the three high schools closest to our home or the middle school. The only math chairperson who was receptive to the idea was the one at a specialized school for high-ability students. They would offer the appropriate class early in the morning, and Alexis was welcome to attend on a trial basis. She would have to miss homeroom and part of first period at her middle school 4 days a week. Also, I would have to provide transportation. The guidance counselor at Alexis' middle school was very supportive. He was not concerned that she would miss part of her first period 4 days a week. He expressed that she could easily make up the work. So, we went ahead with this arrangement and found that it worked out quite well.

As an entering ninth grader, Alexis would have completed Sequential III Math and would be ready for precalculus. A major consideration in selecting a high school was whether there would be enough math to keep Alexis challenged for 4 years.

As Alexis' mathematics program moved into the secondary level, more educators, the school counselor, department chairs, teachers, and Alexis herself became involved in the decision-making process.

## Roadblocks to Advocacy

Alexis' case illustrates some important attitudinal barriers parents encounter as they advocate for their child. Table 2.1 summarizes these philosophical obstacles that often translate into physical roadblocks preventing action on behalf of the learner. The adjacent column suggests responses to eliminate these roadblocks.

### Recommendations for Advocates

Advocacy is hard work. The need to advocate often emanates from educator resistance to a parent-proposed curricular or programmatic change to accommodate a learner's advanced needs. Because change is so difficult, advocacy requires sustained effort to obtain the desired result. In the best of situations, the parent's efforts result in an immediate program accommodation that never requires another meeting with the school. The more common scenario for parent-advocates, as detailed in Alexis' case, involves many parent-

## Table 2.1
## Roadblocks on the Road of Advocacy

| Roadblocks | Responses |
|---|---|
| There is not a clear indicator as to which educator—the teacher, principal, or superintendent—should be approached first. | Begin at the source. If there is a situation in the classroom that needs to be addressed, talk to the teacher. If you are making a placement decision, talk to the principal. If you have exhausted both of these options, talk to the superintendent. |
| Key administrators cannot (or do not) attend scheduled meetings. | Call in advance to make sure the principal and other necessary members of the decision-making team (for example, the current and receiving teachers, school psychologist, and school counselor, if possible) will be present. After-school meetings are preferable to before-school meetings. |
| Educators are concerned that, "If a student works on advanced material in this grade, the teacher in the next grade won't have anything new to teach." | A student who needs advanced material in one grade will continue to need advanced material in subsequent grades. |
| The classroom teacher suggests, "The student is immature and doesn't seem ready for more advanced material." | Educators often use social/emotional concerns as a reason for holding students back academically. Unfortunately, students often exhibit immature behaviors when they are bored. |

| | |
|---|---|
| The administrator indicates, "There are other bright students in this school and they all need enrichment." | Enrichment might be appropriate for some students, but don't let this concern divert the focus on the individual child's needs as determined by performance on advanced material and tests. Document, record, and save work samples. |
| The parents' concerns are dismissed as a natural desire for all parents to think their child is gifted. | All children are special, but not all children have the same academic needs. |
| Results from professional assessments are not considered valid, and therefore are not used in program planning. | It is important to communicate with the child's teacher prior to the assessment. When the assessment is complete, review with the psychologist the best way to disseminate the results. |
| Many educators equate parents' efforts on behalf of their gifted child with the "pushy" parent syndrome. | One research study asked gifted students if they thought their parents were pushy. Over 90 percent of respondents perceived their parents' involvement in their education was "about right." If anything, students want to see their parents more involved. |
| Students who finish assignments more rapidly than their peers can help their classmates. | Students who are having trouble with an assignment need special assistance from a teacher, not from a fellow student. Only the teacher has the appropriate pedagogical background to help students who don't understand a concept. |

teacher conferences, consistent and continual awareness of the curriculum, an educational assessment, and annual meetings with teachers and administrators. The pointers below should be helpful to parents as they prepare to advocate for their children.

1.   *Become an informed advocate.* Find out what options might be appropriate for your child now and in the future. What resources are available to you? Become informed about organizations, individuals, books, and programs that focus on mathematically talented youth. Reading this book is a great start! Recognize that you may have greater expertise with respect to the needs of mathematically talented students than your child's classroom teacher or principal, but also understand that you cannot use this expertise to demand change. A parent's knowledge is best used to plan a program cooperatively.

2.   *Obtain an objective assessment of your child's abilities and achievements.* This objective assessment will be essential to help you discern what types of programs and curricula will be appropriate for your child and what local resources you have. This assessment might be completed by your school district's psychologist or by a private psychologist in your community. The next chapter will be helpful as you begin this process.

3.   *Set the tone for a positive partnership between parent and teacher.* At the beginning of the school year, think about what you can do as a parent to ensure your child has a good year in school. Get to know your child's teacher early in the school year and create a spirit of positive cooperation. Regularly attend parent-teacher organization meetings, open house nights, and parent-teacher conferences. Volunteer in your school. Help your child to solve problems in class him- or herself, rather than always calling the teacher. Go to the teacher first if there is a problem, rather than approaching the principal or superintendent (DeVries, 1996).

*4. As it becomes apparent that you need to request a change, approach the activity optimistically, as well as realistically.* Optimistically, you should assume that your child's teachers and administrators have the best interests of the student at heart. They are fundamentally concerned with their students; therefore, they are vitally interested in your child and all of the children in their classes. They believe they are doing the best job they can with their students—and most teachers are. Realistically, then, most suggestions for change result in a defensive stance from the educator. When educators respond "No" to your suggestion, they are operating under the assumption that they have good reasons to defend the status quo. Do not react to this defensiveness.

Recognize that the policy supporting the teacher's negative response to your request is unjust for your child, but that you will not single-handedly implement a policy change to benefit him or her. Concentrate on providing information that demonstrates the degree to which your child is underchallenged. Gently inform your child's educators about current research evidence about the harm of an underchallenging curriculum. We find it is most effective for parents to approach the school with an attitude that "We're all in this together," not the adversarial approach of "You should be doing this for my child!"

*5. Include your child in the decision-making process.* Find out what the options are and discuss them with your child. Of course, the younger the child, the more you will need to make the decisions for him or her. However, by the time the student is in sixth or seventh grade, he or she can be a fairly active participant in decision making. When the child is involved in these discussions, it is imperative to present a positive attitude toward the school. The student doesn't need to hear you saying, "Andrew's teacher doesn't know anything about math!" Parents can model advocacy by providing an open environment where children feel comfortable coming to them to address concerns. Parents can show their children how to approach their teachers and begin the process of shifting from parent-led advocacy efforts to student-initiated advocacy.

6. *Make requests in writing and keep good records.* Take good notes, keep copies of letters, and maintain a record of what has happened and the conversations and agreements you have had. Keep records of test results (standardized and teacher-made tests) and also save samples of your child's work (dated, with your child's age).

7. *Consider that your efforts to make changes for your own child may have a long-term beneficial impact on younger students.* You want to take care of your child's needs for appropriate challenge as expediently as possible. At the same time, consider that your efforts may improve the programs, curricula, and teacher training for future students. As we have already discussed, it is easier to effect change in a specific class with a specific teacher. It is much more complicated to make a systemwide change.

For example, Arthur's parents advocated conscientiously for their son to be sure that he would be challenged in mathematics. They paid for a mentor to work with him, and they spent many hours discussing his case with school personnel. Several years after Arthur had moved on to middle school, his parents could look back and see that the elementary school was now making adjustments for students who came after Arthur. They realized that their efforts had resulted in positive changes for many other students for whom the school was more willing to make accommodations. Arthur's parents paid for an individualized program that eventually became an accelerated class for mathematically talented students.

8. *Walk the fine line between not being a nuisance and not waiting too long to intervene.* Be concerned about earning the reputation as the parent who is always unhappy with the school, but balance it with advocating appropriately for your child. One parent realized that her mathematically precocious daughter hadn't learned much over the past year while she was waiting for school personnel to respond to her many requests for changes in her daughter's educational program. The mother regretfully reported that, since her daughter had

mastered so much of the grade-level material, she was allowed to leave the classroom to go to the library where she did most of the data entry to change the library from a card-catalogue system to a computer-catalogue system. The mother reflected, "Well, she did learn a lot about computers this year." However, she also expressed regret that she hadn't been more vocal in articulating that the program accommodation should have matched the student's academic strengths.

*9.  If all else fails, find out about your options for due process.* What are the proper channels in your district and your state for requesting a change to your child's educational program? When requesting a change, start with your child's teacher and principal. If you are not satisfied, contact the school district superintendent and state Department of Education with your questions. Your state may have a system in which a parent can request a meeting with a third party (a mediator) who will assist the parents and school personnel in coming to an agreement about an appropriate program for the student.

*10. Contact outside experts for assistance.* Again, the state Department of Education may be helpful. Also find out about local, state, and national gifted education advocacy groups (see Resources). They generally have members who have "been there" and can give you valuable advice and information about specific resources. Also seek information from universities that offer programs for gifted students (e.g., Carnegie Mellon or the University of Iowa).

*11. If you choose to change schools, write a letter to the school board explaining why.* The central administrators of a district need to be aware of your concerns and actions.

*12. Be willing to compromise.* This is also known as "choose your battles." You won't get everything you want right away for your child.

*13. Sometimes, things won't go your way.* Sorry to say, but we often don't get exactly what we think we want when we want it. For a variety of reasons, students may not be stimulated or engaged by the curriculum every minute of every math period. Parents will not be able to make everything perfect for their child in school, and it will not harm the child if a parent does not react every time a child says he or she had a boring day in school. Decide where and when it's important for you to intervene and when it's acceptable that your child is in a less-than-ideal situation.

*14. Find and recognize positive developments.* One family we know reacted to a parent workshop we gave by writing the letter in Figure 2.2. We appreciate their recognition of a positive situation, and we're sure their school personnel did, too.

## How Does Advocacy Compare With the Regularly Scheduled Parent-Teacher Conference?

Most schools have regularly scheduled parent-teacher conferences in which the teacher shares information about the child's progress with the parent. These conferences are fairly circumscribed, and the information typically flows from teacher to parent. During the conference, parents may receive information precipitating the need to advocate for a change in their child's curriculum, but time constraints of the parent-teacher conference usually mean that a separate meeting will need to be scheduled. Meetings that are scheduled as a part of a parent's efforts to advocate often have educators and administrators in attendance and may have the information flowing from parent to educator as the parent explains the need for a change in the curriculum.

The following suggestions (adapted from DeVries, 1996) will help parents and teachers make the most effective use of the conference time. The goal is to achieve a positive partnership between home and school.

Before the meeting, parents need to prepare themselves (see Figure 2.3). Make a list of the points you would like to discuss. Consider practicing what you will say. Gather samples of your child's work to take with you. You might consider inviting someone else to come with you, such as another person who has responsibility for the welfare of the child.

On the day of the conference or meeting, arrive on time. Enter the conference confidently and positively. As you speak with the teacher, be specific about your concerns and give specific examples of your child's behavior. Explain what you have tried at home. Ask for suggestions on ways "we" (parent and teacher) can work together to improve the situation. When the teacher speaks, listen actively. Show through your comments and your body language that you are listening to what the teacher has to say. During the conference, try to achieve consensus on a plan of action.

If you are uncomfortable or dissatisfied with a suggestion, offer that you would like time to reflect and think about the implications. Send a follow-up letter, make a phone call, or have a second conference.

After the conference, send a thank-you note to the teacher for taking the time to discuss your child's educational progress with you. Make arrangements for a follow-up phone call or another conference, if needed.

## How Common is the Need to Advocate?

As detailed above, advocacy requires significant effort. With that in mind, one might wonder just how common is the need to advocate? Recently, 3,000 parents of elementary students received a questionnaire prior to their child's participation in the University of Iowa's Elementary Student Talent Search (see Chapter 5 for an extensive discussion of talent searches as an educational opportunity). Nearly 2,500 parents (80%), predominantly from Iowa, but also from Florida and Illinois, responded to the questionnaire, which included the question: "Have you contacted school personnel to request special academic accommodations for your child?" Parents could select one of four responses (see Table 2.2). We think the percentages of parents responding to the

Dear Mr. D.:

Recently, we attended a workshop entitled, "Parenting Mathematically Talented Youth" at Carnegie Mellon University. Ann Lupkowski-Shoplik, Director of C-MITES (Carnegie Mellon Institute for Talented Elementary Students) presented the program. Our son "Logan" meets the criteria as mathematically talented via school psychological testing and the results of the Iowa Tests of Basic Skills administered in the second grade. We entered the workshop wondering whether we as a family and his educational team were addressing and meeting his needs. We were delighted to conclude the afternoon realizing that our school district has addressed our concerns and is well on its way to meeting the unique academic needs of our son.

As Dr. Lupkowski-Shoplik outlined many options and discussed the positive and negative consequences, it became clear that our school district has taken the steps to allow Logan's advancement and success. As we listened to horror stories from other families which ran the gamut from poor curriculum to a student given the math book for the next grade and directed to a desk in the hall, we realized how truly blessed we have been. We would like to commend Logan's entire team for its insight and willingness to push for Logan's advancement.

Mrs. V. M. recognized his talents and "started the ball rolling."

Ms. C. T. performed initial testing and coordinated the effort.

Mrs. S. F. performed diagnostic testing and pushed for a unique educational approach.

Mrs. M. S. consulted and provided her insight for working with students with special needs.

Mr. M. K. implemented the DT→PI (Diagnostic Testing→Prescriptive Instruction) Model using our district's choice of curriculum to allow Logan to accelerate to a level that better meets his needs.

Mrs. M. B. and Mrs. C. S. cooperated on scheduling and are helping to meet his educational and social needs.

Mr. A. B. recognized our concerns as parents and worked to make the entire process possible.

Mrs. L. Y. assured a curriculum that is intentional and challenging and addresses both computation and theory.

More challenges await Logan's education and our attempts to assure the best possible programming, but we are comforted knowing that we are on the right track and surrounded by competent and caring professionals.

Sincerely,
    Mr. and Mrs. L.

## Figure 2.2. Letter to Superintendent

1. Bring samples of the work your child has done and be prepared to discuss why these samples demonstrate a need for more advanced material. Include work your child has done in school and outside of school. Consider bringing:

   - examples of "recreational math" books your child has used,
   - computer software your child has used at home,
   - information about outside-of-school programs he or she has attended, and
   - information about other outside-of-school activities in which he or she has participated.

2. Gather test results and be prepared to discuss why the test results demonstrate a need for more advanced material.

3. You might need to discuss the child's attendance in school (e.g., child has excellent attendance) and how that might have an impact upon programming/curricular decisions.

4. Be prepared to keep the tone of the meeting positive. For example, start off the meeting with a positive comment ("My daughter really enjoyed the group activity in math class last week").

5. Make a list of points you would like to discuss at the meeting. For example:

   a. "I'm concerned that my son isn't working up to his potential in your class. For example, in the summer program he attended this past year, he loved the prealgebra work he was doing."

   b. "My daughter is reluctant to go to school in the morning because she is frustrated with the repetition of simple computations."

   c. "I have found some really interesting math materials that my child might enjoy working on. How can we fit them into his program?"

   d. "In what ways might we work together to keep him challenged?"

### Figure 2.3. Getting Ready
### for the Conference or Advocacy Meeting

four options are informative. (Note: We categorized parents according to their child's math aptitude based upon test scores. Boys and girls who were designated "Superior Math Aptitude" had earned a score in the top quarter of the group on the talent search test. When completing the questionnaire, the parents had not yet received their child's scores indicating their child's math aptitude. Also, we do not know if parents actually used these scores to advocate for their child—we hope they did!)

What can we conclude from Table 2.2? From this sample of parents of elementary talent search participants, many parents either requested an accommodation for their child or thought an accommodation was necessary. The aptitude and gender of the child did seem to have a bearing on the percentage of parents who responded to the various options.

1. In the bottom right corner of Table 2.2, we see that 60% of the parents who responded "No accommodation was requested because it was not necessary" were the parents of the girls whose math was "good," but not considered "superior" compared to other bright students.
2. Nearly twice as many parents of boys with superior math aptitude (29%) than parents of girls with good math aptitude (15%) had asked for an accommodation and thought the accommodation was successful.
3. There was very little difference between the percentage of parents of girls with superior math aptitude and parents of boys with superior math aptitude who requested an accommodation and had a satisfactory result. Also, an identical percentage (16%) of parents of boys with superior math aptitude and girls with superior math aptitude requested accommodations and were *not* satisfied with the result.

## Conclusion

The content of this chapter has been directed mainly at parents because they are the primary advocates for their chil-

### Table 2.2
### Percentage of Parents Responding to a Question Asking if They Had Contacted School Personnel to Request Special Accommodations

| Gender and Math Aptitude of Student | Yes: Accommodation Requested/ Result Satisfactory | Yes: Accommodation Requested/ Result Not Satisfactory | No: Accommodation Not Requested, but Necessary | No: Accommodation Not Requested and Not Necessary |
|---|---|---|---|---|
| Boys With Superior Math Aptitude | 29% | 16% | 12% | 43% |
| Girls With Superior Math Aptitude | 26% | 16% | 10% | 48% |
| Boys With Good Math Aptitude | 20% | 13% | 14% | 53% |
| Girls With Good Math Aptitude | 15% | 12% | 13% | 60% |

dren. Parents have the right and the obligation to pursue those educational avenues that will result in a differentiated curriculum for their mathematically talented child. Thorough and objective information regarding the child's progress is essential in advocating appropriately for children.

It is difficult to make changes, especially in a system. It is much easier to make a change at the classroom level and to make modifications for a child within a classroom, rather than changing a school's approach to educating students. Therefore, it is important for parents to differentiate between issues that concern their child and issues that concern the larger school system.

Even though the road to effective advocacy for gifted children can be long and sometimes rocky, remember: If you don't advocate for your child, who will?

# 3 Educational Assessment

## Key Points

- Thorough and objective information obtained through an educational assessment is essential in advocating, identifying, and programming for mathematically talented students.

- Testing is one of four components of an educational assessment. The other three components include interviews, observations, and informal assessment.

- The purpose for an assessment drives the decision-making process with respect to selecting tests.

- Within the vast testing industry, there are thousands of tests and well-articulated theories underlying the development of these tests. In this chapter, we have distilled the most relevant information for parents and educators who need to select, administer, and interpret the results from tests as part of their work with mathematically talented students.

- The major points of the chapter are presented in a sample report about a mathematically talented student.

*At the beginning of the 21st century, there were 2,939 commercially available tests.*
    *—Murphy, Impara, & Plake, Tests In Print V*

THE LARGE NUMBER of tests available to psychologists and educators presents an interesting paradox comparable to that faced by the shipwrecked person stranded at sea. Even though there is plenty of water all around, without the proper knowledge, that individual doesn't know how to obtain potable water. With nearly 3,000 tests available to educators, it is as though we are swimming in a sea of tests, yet we are stranded in this sea without the skills for distilling information to better understand and plan for mathematically gifted students. In this chapter, we present several different types of tests, thereby giving the reader enough information about each to make informed choices for a particular student or group of students.

It would be a challenge to find a parent, student, or teacher for whom the word *testing* does not evoke strong feelings. Frequently, the feelings are negative and have a negative impact on behaviors and attitudes. For example, if an educator's personal experiences with assessment and testing have not been positive, then the educator may have little confidence in the information that is obtained from an assessment and may choose to disregard it or may not even recommend that the student's learning needs be assessed. In this worst-case scenario, teachers prefer subjective information and opinions in lieu of the objective information discernable from tests. This is ironic because standardized tests were developed to remove bias and subjectivity from decisions.

One of the best descriptions of standardized tests and their purpose originates from Green (1981):

A standardized test is a task or set of tasks given under standard conditions and designed to assess some aspect of a person's knowledge, skill, behavior, or personality. A test provides a scale of measurement for consistent individual differences regarding some psychological concept and serves to compare people according to that concept. Tests can be thought of as yardsticks, but they are less efficient and reliable than yardsticks, just as the concept of verbal reasoning ability is more complex and less well understood than the concept of length. A test yields one or more objectively obtained quantitative scores, so that, as nearly as possible, each person is assessed in the same way. The intent is to provide a fair and equitable comparison among test takers. (cited in Sattler, 2001, p. 4)

While we can't change past personal experiences that resulted in certain behaviors and attitudes, we can influence the present and future by detailing our professional experiences that lead us to assert that a good assessment is the first step in advocating for an educational program for gifted students. This will mean selecting appropriate tests for obtaining the necessary information. This chapter reviews a variety of instruments that are used to test mathematically talented students, purposes of testing, and the use of test results in generating recommendations for programming.

## Major Considerations in Assessing Mathematically Gifted Students

No matter what the impetus for testing, there are certain considerations that should be addressed in order to make the best possible use of test information in an assessment. However, before we proceed, we want to make a brief statement about the relationship between *testing* and *assessment*. These words are often used interchangeably and that will sometimes be the case throughout this chapter. However, there are subtle distinctions between the two terms that are important to mention. According to Sattler (2001), *standardized testing* is one of the four pillars of assessment. The other three pillars include *interviews*, *observations*, and *informal assessment procedures*. Popham (2002) also differentiates between assessment and testing:

> Assessment is a broader descriptor of the kinds of educational measuring that teachers do—a descriptor that, while certainly including traditional paper-and-pencil tests, covers many more kinds of measurement procedures. . . . Educational assessment is a formal attempt to determine students' status with respect to educational variables of interest. (p. 4)

These considerations include the following questions and are answered throughout this chapter:

1.  What is the purpose for testing? In other words, what are the "variables of interest"? Determining which variables are of interest is important because they will help the psychologist/educator determine which instrument(s) to use. For example, will a teacher-made test sufficiently measure a student's progress in a certain subject? Is there a question about the student's general level of academic ability? Should the assessment include an aptitude test, an achievement test, or some combination of these instruments?
2.  What professional is needed for test administration and score interpretation? Is the individual a psychologist who has training in administering and interpreting individual IQ tests? Is the individual familiar with the variety of aptitude and achievement assessments available? Which tests, if any, can an educator, with little to no specialized training in test administration, administer?
3.  In order to make the most knowledgeable recommendations about programs and curricula, how can information based upon standardized testing from an individual assessment be combined with (a) standardized testing information from group assessments and (b) nonstandardized information (e.g., portfolios, teacher observations, past academic performance)?

## Principal Tests for Assessing
## Mathematically Gifted Students

Testing should be driven by a question. For example, "What is a student's level of intellectual development?" The results from an intelligence test, which measures general ability, can provide the best answer to that question. Parents and educators might also ask, "Does the student who is, overall, very academically talented have a specific aptitude for mathematics?" The results from a specific aptitude test would be most effective in answering that question. Finally, educators, students, and parents all need to know how effective instruction has been, which is typically demonstrated by the results on achievement tests.

Tests that measure ability, aptitude, and achievement have many similarities, but also some important differences. A review of *Measurement and Assessment in Teaching* (Linn & Gronlund, 1995) highlighted how easy it is for the "experts" to use the terms, especially *ability* and *aptitude*, interchangeably. For example, when we turned to the index to look up ability tests, the entry indicates that the reader should, "See Aptitude tests" (p. 549)! Nevertheless, Linn and Gronlund (1995) have provided some informative distinctions based upon a continuum of test type determined by the extent to which the content of the items are dependent on specific learning experiences. On their test-type continuum, familiarity with specific subject content, as taught in an educational setting, is at one end and problem solving of items unrelated to school learning is at the other.

Linn and Gronlund's (1995) continuum is represented in Figure 3.1. As can be seen, since achievement tests are very much based upon the student's familiarity with specific subject-matter content, these tests are at the far right of the continuum; aptitude tests that measure problem solving in specific content areas taught in school (e.g., math, reading, and vocabulary) are in the middle of the continuum; and general problem-solving tests that are unrelated to school learning are at the far left of the continuum.

| Ability Tests | Aptitude Tests | Achievement Tests |
|---|---|---|
| ← | | → |
| General problem solving not related to school learning (e.g., Cognitive Abilities Test [CogAT]) | Problem solving of school-related content, not taught in school (e.g., School and College Ability Test [SCAT]) | School-based learning of specific content (e.g., Iowa Tests of Basic Skills [ITBS]) |

**Figure 3.1. Continuum of Tests**

## Ability Tests

Ability tests were designed to measure general intelligence. This is easier said than done because general intelligence is an elusive concept. McGrew and Flanagan (1998) have suggested that

> Attempts to define the construct of intelligence and to explain individual differences in intellectual functioning, attempts which have spanned decades . . . have been characterized by much variability. . . . To a large extent the variability between theories of intelligence can be accounted for by differences in underlying research traditions in psychological measurement that have developed largely independently of one another. (pp. 1–2)

The history and debates surrounding the various theories of intelligence and how those theories have—or have not— been translated into tests and assessments is intriguing. However, it is not the purpose of this chapter to go into detail in those areas; rather, we hope to equip readers with information to help them make effective assessment choices that will result in appropriate programming decisions based upon assessment information.

Tests of general ability can be categorized in many ways. For our purposes, we start with two very broad categories: group-administered and individually administered. Group-administered tests are paper-and-pencil tests designed for administration to more than one person at a time. Even if a group-administered test is administered in an individualized setting, it is not considered to be an individually administered test. Individually administered tests are designed for administration in a one-on-one setting and do not rely heavily on paper-and-pencil tasks.

The most reliable measure of general ability is obtained by administering an individual ability test. These tests are most commonly referred to as *intelligence tests*, or *IQ tests*. It is important for parents and teachers to understand the similarities and differences between the major individual intelligence tests, so we will highlight commonly used individual intelligence/general cognitive ability tests and briefly discuss the origins and uses of each.

### Individually Administered Ability Tests

*Stanford-Binet Scales.* The Binet Scales have a long and fascinating heritage that began in the 1890s in Paris. In 1905, after years of testing school-aged children, Alfred Binet and Theodore Simon developed a 30-item test intended to measure judgment, comprehension, and reasoning (Binet and Simon, 1905, as cited in Sattler, 2001). The Binet-Simon Scales came to the United States in 1908, but the first U.S. version of the test did not appear until 1916. The scales began to acquire their present-day look with the 1937 revision, conducted by Lewis Terman and Maud Merrill, who named the test the Stanford-Binet. In 1960, the Stanford-Binet was revised by selecting the best items from the two 1937 forms and combining them into one form titled the Stanford-Binet (Form L-M; Terman & Merrill, 1960). Although the Stanford-Binet (Form L-M) is no longer available for purchase, some psychologists—those who work primarily with gifted youngsters—continue to use it because they consider it to be a reliable and valid instrument for use in predicting academic success. However, we concur with Robinson's (1992) recommendation that gifted educators discontinue the practice of using the Stanford-Binet (Form L-M) and replace their testing kits with the most current version, the Stanford-Binet Intelligence Scale: Fourth Edition (Thorndike, Hagen, & Sattler, 1986a).

The Stanford-Binet Intelligence Scale: IV (SB:IV) was published in 1986 after 10 years of development and is the revision of the Stanford Binet (Form L-M). It is appropriate for people ages 2 through adult and therefore covers approximately the same age range as the Stanford-Binet (Form L-M). The SB:IV maintained much continuity with the Stanford-Binet (Form L-M) by keeping many of the items the same. Instead of the Stanford-Binet (Form L-M) age-scale format (one of the primary reasons some psychologists who work with gifted youngsters continue to use it), the Stanford-Binet IV is comprised of 15 subscales that yield an overall score measuring general cognitive functioning (for more specific information about the SB:IV, see Thorndike, Hagen, & Sattler, 1986b). The fifth edition of the Stanford-Binet, the Stanford-Binet 5, is scheduled for release sometime after 2003.

*Wechsler Scales.* David Wechsler was born in 1896, about the time that Alfred Binet and his colleagues were busy testing children with questions that eventually resulted in the 1905 Binet-Simon Scale. Wechsler became involved in intelligence testing as a U.S. Army private during World War I when the Army was conducting its large-scale testing program. This introduction to the measurement of intelligence resulted in Wechsler eventually developing an intelligence test that would take into account factors contributing to a global (i.e., general) concept of intelligence. Wechsler was the author of the original and revised editions of the Wechsler Preschool and Primary Scale of Intelligence (WPPSI; Wechsler, 1967); the Wechsler Intelligence Scale for Children (WISC; Wechsler, 1949); and the Wechsler Adult Intelligence Scale (WAIS; Wechsler, 1955). The WPPSI was first published in 1967 and was revised in the late 1980s and published in 1991 as the WPPSI-R. The WISC, first published in 1949, was revised as the WISC-R in 1974 and revised again in 1991 as the WISC-III (Wechsler, 1991). The WISC-IV is scheduled for release in 2003. The WAIS was first published in 1955; a revision, the WAIS-R, was completed and published in 1981, and another revision, resulting in the WAIS-III (Wechsler, 1997), was completed and published in 1997.

The WPPSI-R was designed to measure the intelligence of children ages 3–7; the WISC-R and WISC-III were designed to measure the intelligence of children ages 6–16; and the WAIS-R and WAIS-III measure the intelligence of individuals aged 16 to adult. Because of the nature of the Wechsler scales, very bright children often are not sufficiently challenged by the items on the test designed for their age, and their ability is not fully measured. For example, the WISC-III does not have enough difficult questions for brilliant elementary students; therefore, they should be given the WAIS-III in order to have a more accurate estimate of their abilities. In other words, the tester needs to "shift to a test which is appropriate for an individual of the estimated mental age, rather than chronological age, of the person being tested" (Robinson & Janos, 1987, p. 40). Robinson and Janos suggested using a test designed for older students as an adjunct measure that enhances the information obtained from measuring the student's performance with the test designed for his or her age.

*Differential Ability Scales (DAS).* The Differential Ability Scales (DAS; Elliott, 1990) is an individually administered battery of 17 cognitive and 3 achievement tests for children and adolescents ages 2 years, 6 months, through 17 years, 11 months. The DAS is a revision and extension of the British Ability Scales (Elliott, 1990). With a publication date of 1990, the DAS is a relatively new instrument and reflects recent (i.e., since the mid-1960s) thinking about theories of intelligence and cognitive abilities. During the development phase of the DAS, newer theories of intelligence (e.g., Gardner's 1983 Theory of Multiple Intelligences and Sternberg's 1986 Triarchic Theory of Intelligence) were emerging; therefore, it is not surprising that Elliott adopted the position that, because "notions of intelligence and IQ have become very popular with the general public but have also been subject to widespread misunderstanding . . . that it may be useful to avoid the terms" (Elliott, p. 20). The DAS overall composite score is referred to as a General Conceptual Ability (GCA). Elliott considers the GCA to be a "purer" measure of an individual's ability to perform complex mental processing than IQ.

Sattler's (2001) review of the DAS suggests that it is a well-standardized test with good administration procedures. Sattler stated that only the WISC-III, WPPSI-R, WAIS-III, Stanford-Binet Intelligence Scale: IV, and the DAS are recommended for the assessment of a student when a special education placement decision must be made. In general, the DAS appears to be a positive addition to the academic field of measurement, but it is too soon to tell what its contribution will be to the understanding of academically talented students. We think that it is noteworthy that a primary limitation of the DAS is the fact that the subtests differ considerably depending upon the age of the student.

*Kaufman Assessment Battery for Children (K-ABC).* In the mid-1980s, a new individually administered intelligence test, the Kaufman Assessment Battery for Children (K-ABC; Kaufman & Kaufman, 1983) entered the measurement arena and provided a useful alternative to the more traditional Wechsler or Binet Scales. The K-ABC was designed to measure the intelligence and achievement of children ages 2 years, 6 months, to 12 years, 5 months. It defines intelligence as the ability to process information to solve unfamiliar problems and focuses on two types of problem-solving strategies: (1) Sequential Processing, where the child mentally manipulates stimuli one at a time in a stepwise manner, and (2) Simultaneous Processing, where the child must integrate many stimuli at once to come up with a solution. From an administration of the K-ABC, the child earns four scores: Sequential Processing, Simultaneous Processing, Mental Processing Composite (combining Sequential and Simultaneous Processing Scores), and Achievement. The K-

ABC is a useful instrument for quickly assessing a student's ability and achievement; however, because of its limited age range, it may not have enough ceiling for extremely talented elementary-aged students.

*Kaufman Adolescent and Adult Intelligence Test (KAIT).* The Kaufman Adolescent and Adult Intelligence Test (KAIT; Kaufman & Kaufman, 1993) was designed for individuals ages 11 to adult. Many psychologists see the KAIT as an advancement in the field of cognitive assessment (Flanagan, Alfonso, & Flanagan, 1994) because it measures the individual's ability to solve new problems. However, with respect to measuring the intellectual functioning of gifted individuals, Flanagan et al. have asserted that "validity studies with individuals with gifted abilities and mental retardation are necessary to substantiate further the psychometric rigor of the KAIT as well as its clinical usefulness for assessing the intellectual functioning of these populations" (p. 516).

*Woodcock-Johnson III Tests of Cognitive Abilities (WJ III COG).* The Woodcock-Johnson III Tests of Cognitive Abilities (WJ III COG; Woodcock, McGrew, & Mather, 2001) is an individualized measure of general ability. Although both regular and special educators recognize the Woodcock-Johnson Psychoeducational Battery–Revised (Woodcock & Johnson, 1989) because it is routinely used as a measure of achievement in special educational assessments, most educators are unfamiliar with the WJ III COG. For special education placement decisions, the school psychologist will typically administer one of the individually administered ability tests discussed above (i.e., the SB:IV, the WISC-III, or even the DAS), as well as the reading, math, and writing sections of the achievement tests from the Woodcock-Johnson III Tests of Achievement. Because the training of most school psychologists is in the use of a Wechsler or Binet test as an individualized measure of ability, few psychologists use the WJ III COG. Nevertheless, administering the WJ III COG is practical for educators of gifted students because the training involved in administration and interpretation is less extensive than that for the Wechsler or Binet. The WJ III COG can only be computer-scored by the publisher. This may be a significant advantage for educators because it avoids errors. However, educators will need to allow sufficient time to have the scores and interpretation returned. Additionally, the WJ III COG was based upon a psychological model known as the information-processing model and may provide educators with diagnostic information, as well as "classification," or "placement" information.

*Slosson Intelligence Test (SIT).* The Slosson Intelligence Test (SIT) was originally published in 1963 and was renormed in 1981 and 1985. A revised version, the Slosson Intelligence Test–Revised (SIT-R), was normed in 1991 (Slosson, Nicholson, & Hibpsham, 1991) and renormed in 1998 (Slosson, 1998). The test is orally administered and takes 10–30 minutes to administer. We concur with Sattler's (2001) comments regarding use of SIT-R:

> The Slosson Intelligence Test–Revised might have some merit as a screening device. . . . However, it is a questionable practice to report age equivalents that go beyond the age groups in the standardization sample. The SIT-R should not be used as a substitute for the Stanford-Binet: IV, the WISC-III, WPPSI-R, or DAS, especially in assessing children with disabilities. (p. 566)

In other words the SIT-R is more appropriate to consider as a screening test, rather than an actual measure of intelligence. The scores from the SIT-R are not appropriate for use in placement or programming, although they might be an indicator that additional testing, using one of the recommended tests described above, is warranted.

### Group-Administered Ability Tests

For special education services, individual intelligence tests are usually mandated. However, for general educational purposes, including screening for gifted programs, group tests of intelligence are used far more extensively than are individually-administered intelligence tests because they are more cost-effective. Two tests widely administered to groups of students are the Otis-Lennon School Ability Test (OLSAT) and the Cognitive Abilities Test (CogAT).

*Otis-Lennon School Ability Test (OLSAT).* The seventh edition of the Otis-Lennon School Ability Test (OLSAT) was published in 1996 and is the most recent in the Otis series of ability tests that was first published in 1918 (Otis & Lennon, 1996). The OLSAT-7 was designed for use as a group-administered ability test and yields a total score, a verbal score, and a nonverbal score. The OLSAT-7 was concurrently normed with two achievement tests, the Stanford Achievement Test and the Metropolitan Achievement Tests. According to Goldman (2001), the major limitation to the OLSAT-7 is its relative lack of validity data demonstrating the relationship between its scores and school grades. DeStefano (2001) also listed the lack of validity data as one of the most serious limitations of this instrument. She concluded her review as follows: "If test users acknowledge the limitations of the test . . . and accept it as one of a variety of instruments that could be used for screening purposes . . . then the technical characteristics of the OLSAT qualify its use for this limited role" (p. 205).

*Cognitive Abilities Test (CogAT).* The newly revised Cognitive Abilities Test Form 6 (CogAT-6; Lohman and Hagen, 2001a) is a psychometrically, psychologically, and educationally excellent group-administered test. It measures important reasoning abilities in three domains: verbal, quantitative, and nonverbal (or figural). Lohman and Hagen (2001a) have argued persuasively that measuring reasoning abilities (especially inductive reasoning abilities) remain central to the identification and nurturing of gifted youngsters. They show that only about half of the students who would be identified as gifted by using both a good achievement test and the CogAT-6 will be identified by either measure alone. The discrepancy between reasoning ability and achievement is even stronger for minority students on the Nonverbal battery.

One of the most useful features of the CogAT-6 is the "Ability Profile" that is reported for each student. The authors argue that the profile of reasoning abilities is more indicative of how to teach than prescriptive of what to teach. Information about a student's performance on the CogAT-6, when combined with other information (e.g., results of an achievement test such as the Iowa Tests of Basic Skills [ITBS]), can help educators discover the unique learning needs of their students and can help inform decisions about instruction. This information is provided both in the manuals that accompany the test and on the Web for teachers who do not have access to the interpretive guides.

Also unique to Form 6 of the CogAT is the computation of confidence intervals for each score that are based on the consistency of the student's responses to the items and subtests that make up the score. This is particularly helpful when testing young students who might be confused about the directions for one of the subtests or have difficulty using a machine-readable answer sheet when tested out of level. Finally, tables reported in the research handbook (Lohman & Hagen, 2001b) give explicit guidance on how to use expected errors of measurement at different score levels to select the best level of the test for above-level testing of gifted children.

Results from group-administered tests can help educators understand the general nature of the ability levels of the students in their class. However, by their nature, group tests of intelligence require limited interaction between the tester and student. In addition, the scores are designed for group use, therefore, most of the emphasis is placed on the score. Group ability tests are most appropriately used for initial screening purposes, and the results should not be used in isolation to make a programming decision about an individual student. Results from a group-administered test should be supplemented by an individually administered test that is appropriate for placement/classification decisions. More specific tests of aptitude and achievement should be used when detailing programming.

## What Do General Ability/Intelligence Tests Measure?

Parents and teachers are often apprehensive about having an intelligence test administered to a student. This apprehension usually stems from a lack of familiarity with the nature of individual intelligence tests and from a concern that scores from these tests will be misused. It remains the examiner's responsibility to put these concerns to rest by providing information about the test and its intended use in placement and programming.

Whereas the above-mentioned tests each have unique features, they all try, in some fashion or another, to measure verbal comprehension; language development; attention, concentration, and memory; quantitative reasoning; perceptual organization; and visual motor coordination. Each test typically has a balance of activities requiring verbal and nonverbal responses. Most tests include vocabulary as one way of measuring verbal comprehension. Short-term memory is often measured by asking students to repeat a series of numbers. The tests vary in their methods of assessing these abilities, however, and some measure other abilities in addition to those previously mentioned. Each test kit includes a technical manual that provides details about the constructs and also explains scoring procedures and other technical information about the development and administration of the test.

In our experience, most students enjoy the administration of an intelligence test, especially one that is individually administered. They like the individual attention and are usually eager to attempt the tasks. In many ways, the administration of such a test is a structured interview that lasts 1–2 hours, and much can be learned about the student both during the administration time and from the results.

## What Does an Intelligence Test Score Mean?

The common term for the score obtained from an intelligence test, an Intelligence Quotient (IQ), derives from the notion of a ratio of mental age to chronological age. IQ was introduced by Terman and his colleagues in 1916 when they introduced the Stanford-Binet Scales (Sattler, 2001). Shortly thereafter, it was realized that IQs for different ages were not comparable, that is, the ratio of mental age to chronological age has a different meaning for different ages. This problem was solved by introducing the Deviation IQ.

Our point in presenting this terminology is that the score obtained from an intelligence test is sophisticated and has significant implications about a student's general ability to succeed in a school setting. An IQ is also informative to educators and psychologists because an IQ has a statistical conversion to a percentile ranking. A percentile ranking allows educators and parents to understand the student's position relative to the other students who were part of the testing sample; this is important information.

IQs obtained from administering the tests described above all have an average score of 100 (Sattler, 2001). As mentioned, the actual score from an assessment may be most meaningful when it is converted to a percentile ranking, as this allows the student, parent, or educator to know how an individual's performance compares with that of others his or her age. If a child earns a score of 100 on an intelligence test, his or her percentile rank is 50. This means that the child scored as well as or higher than 50% of the children in the comparison group. As the child's score goes over 100, the percentile ranking goes above 50, indicating that the performance surpasses that of a larger percentage of the child's agemates. For example, a child earning a score of 132 on the WISC-III would have a percentile ranking of 98, thus indicating that this child's performance surpassed that of 98% of children his or her age.

Percentile rankings can be misleading, however, for the upper range of scores. For example, all scores between 133 and 155 on the WISC-III are at the 99th percentile, yet the performance of the child who earns 133 differs remarkably from that of the child who earns 155. Also, 155 is the highest IQ that can be earned on the WISC-III; however, it may not accurately reflect just how exceptionally capable a student is. It is always important to go beyond the IQ and look at how the child performed on specific subtests, as well as the pattern of those scores.

How Effectively Do General Intelligence Tests Predict Math Aptitude?

A general intelligence test is most effective in determining the pacing of curricular material. For example, we have known since the 1930s (Hollingworth, 1942) that students with an IQ at the 98th percentile or above need classwork that is at least 2 years beyond the work typically given to their agemates. However, for specific information about programming in mathematics, one needs to go directly to assessments of mathematics achievement and aptitude.

## Aptitude Tests: General and Specific

As discussed above, there are several tests that measure general ability that are typically referred to as tests of general intelligence or IQ tests. Individually administered IQ tests are effective in illustrating an individual's general ability to succeed in a school setting (Sattler, 2001). However, because an individualized IQ test such as the WISC-III or the Binet IV must be administered and interpreted by a trained professional (e.g., a psychologist), an individual administration is not always convenient, and educators may choose to rely on a general measure of aptitude that can be administered by someone other than a psychologist.

General Aptitude Tests

Two general aptitude tests are discussed below. They both serve as important indicators of cognitive functioning, and can be helpful in understanding components of a student's ability to reason in lieu of a more comprehensive individualized intelligence test.

*Raven's Progressive Matrices (RPM).* This nonverbal test (i.e., examinee responses do not require use of any language) is an excellent test for measuring abstract reasoning. The Raven's Progressive Matrices (RPM; Raven, Raven, & Court, 2000) include three forms: the Coloured Progressive Matrices (developed for primary children), the Standard Progressive Matrices (developed for children ages 6 through 13), and the Advanced Progressive Matrices (developed for above-average adults). The nonverbal nature of this instrument makes it a culturally fair assessment of children who do not speak or have limited skills in English. When taking the RPM, the student is presented with meaningless figures and asked to discern the nature of the pattern for each figure and complete the relations. Although it should never be used alone for placement, we strongly recommend the RPM as a measure of abstract reasoning ability and recommend that talented elementary students be given the Standard Progressive Matrices as a measure of "intellectual reasoning" based upon figural reasoning. The connection between mathematics and figural reasoning skills are obvious, and the RPM is a particularly useful instrument in determining the sophistication of the student's cognitive ability. A student who earns superior scores on an individual intelligence test and also on the RPM will most likely have the necessary cognitive structures for studying math at more advanced levels (Lupkowski & Assouline, 1992).

*School and College Ability Test (SCAT).* The School and College Ability Test (SCAT) is a scholastic aptitude test developed in 1955 by the Educational Testing Service (ETS) and marketed by Publishers Test Service in Monterey, CA. The original SCAT was revised to the SCAT-II in 1966 and the SCAT-III, the most recent form, in 1979. There are three levels of SCAT-III: an elementary level (grades 3.5–6.5), an intermediate level (grades 6.5–9.5), and an advanced level (grades 9.5–12.9). Each level has two forms. The tests at each level have approximately 100 items and take approximately 40 minutes to complete.

The SCAT was designed to measure the verbal and quantitative abilities of students in the third grade through senior year in high school. Therefore, it is useful as an above-level test for talented elementary students. A few elementary talent searches use the SCAT-III as their talent search instrument (see Chapter 5).

A student's performance on the SCAT-III is a helpful guideline for determining the need and direction for further assessment. In one review (Ahmann, 1985, p. 1315), the SCAT III was described as a sophisticated aptitude test that uses two types of test items: verbal analogies and quantitative-comparative test items. Ahmann's review indicated that the greatest strength of the SCAT-III was that student performance on it could be compared with student performance on STEP III (see page 86 of this chapter for a brief description of STEP III). This comparison is also the major point used in the validation of SCAT-III. Passow's review (1985, p. 1317) concurs with Ahmann's; however, Passow offered a caveat concerning the paucity of the technical manual's information regarding the validity of the test.

## Specific Aptitude Tests

Some mathematically talented students have much better verbal ability, mechanical ability, spatial relations ability, or nonverbal reasoning ability, than do others. These abilities are best measured by specific aptitude tests. Aptitude tests are distinguishable from general ability (intelligence) tests mainly because the content of an aptitude test is more specific. General ability tests are designed to measure an individual's ability to do general problem solving that is not specifically related to school learning. Aptitude tests are like general ability tests in that they measure problem solving; however, the problem-solving activities are typically associated with school-related content, although it is not expected that the student has been exposed to that content. Aptitude tests are different from achievement tests, which are dependent upon mastery of specific content to which the student was exposed in the past. Unlike achievement tests, which measure past exposure to content, aptitude tests measure the potential for future performance. Some aptitude tests are designed to measure one specific aptitude (e.g., mechanical reasoning), whereas other aptitude tests measure multiple areas. When measuring the aptitude of extraordinarily talented students, it is often necessary to use a test that was designed for older, more advanced students.

*Differential Aptitude Tests (DAT).* One useful instrument for measuring multiple aptitudes is the battery known as the Differential Aptitude Tests (DAT; Bennett, Seashore, & Wesman, 1947), which has undergone four revisions since its original publication in 1947. The most recent revision, the fifth edition (published in 1990), assesses eight aptitudes in eight different tests: Verbal Reasoning, Numerical Reasoning, Abstract Reasoning, Perceptual Speed and Accuracy, Mechanical Reasoning, Space Relations, Spelling, and Language Usage. There are two levels for each test in the DAT. Level 1 is intended for students in grades 7–9, and Level 2 is intended for students in grades 10–12. The DAT is appropriate for some gifted students younger than age 12 because it has items that are sufficiently challenging. The more exceptional the child, the younger he or she might take the DAT. Results obtained from testing young children with the DAT might be useful in educational programming, even though scores cannot be compared to norms for the youth's age group. It may not be appropriate, however, for children younger than 9.

When using the DAT, an examiner may choose to use one or any combination of the eight tests to assess a student's strengths and weaknesses. Three DAT subtests that are particularly useful when assessing aptitudes of students already known to be talented mathematically are Abstract Reasoning, Mechanical Reasoning, and Space Relations. Results from these three subtests can help educators program relevantly for both math and science classes such as junior high physical science and high school physics (Stanley, 1984).

*Iowa Algebra Aptitude Test (IAAT).* The Iowa Algebra Aptitude Test (IAAT) was developed in 1931 by the University of Iowa testing program. The purpose of this test is to predict the performance of students in Algebra I. Since 1931, the IAAT has gone through numerous revisions, the most recent of which was in 1993 (Schoen & Ansley, 1993), which uses the

1989 Curriculum and Evaluation Standards for School Mathematics developed by the National Council of Teachers of Mathematics (1989). The IAAT has four subtests focusing on the following areas:

1. interpretation of mathematical information such as graphs and technical writing,
2. translation to symbols,
3. finding relationships, and
4. using symbols.

The reviews of the IAAT (Fleenor, 1995; Monsaas, 1995) have been positive. Additionally, the test has several useful features including two equivalent forms, self-scoring answer sheets, and a well-written technical manual that provides useful information with regard to curriculum planning.

*Orleans-Hanna Algebra Prognosis Test.* The Orleans-Hanna Algebra Prognosis Test evolved from the 1928 Orleans Algebra Prognosis Test (Orleans & Orleans, as cited in Hanna, 1998), which was developed to predict the success of students in a first-year algebra course. It is a 50-item test with the most recent standardization being in 1996. As a measurement instrument, it has an interesting design: There are five "lessons," each of which is followed by six test questions based upon the lesson. The final section of the test is comprised of 20 "review" items that include topics linked to the 1989 NCTM Curriculum and Evaluation Standards for School Mathematics as they relate to the middle school mathematics curriculum (Hanna). Previous editions of the Orleans-Hanna included a self-report questionnaire about grades, achievement, and the student's self-prediction about success in algebra; however, the 1996 edition only includes four questions about past grades, and the responses do not figure into the scores. There are reviews of the 1982 edition of the Orleans-Hanna in the *Ninth Mental Measurement Yearbook*, and both reviewers, Kuchemann (1985) and Secolsky (1985) identified it as valid for predicting success in algebra. The comprehensive manual for the 1996 edition (Hanna, 1998) includes complete descriptions of the validation studies of the redesigned new edition, and the interested reader is directed to that manual for more details.

*Test of Mathematical Abilities for Gifted Students (TOMAGS).* The Test of Mathematical Abilities for Gifted Students (TOMAGS) was developed by Susan K. Johnsen and Gail R. Ryser in alignment with the National Council of Teachers of Mathematics standards (NCTM, 1989) and published in 1998. The descriptive information for TOMAGS states specifically that this test is not intended for diagnostic purposes. Rather, it serves as a screening instrument for the assessment of mathematical talent in children ages 6–12 years.

*Test of Mathematical Abilities–2nd Edition (TOMA-2).* The Test of Mathematical Abilities–2nd Edition (TOMA-2), developed by Brown, Cronin, and McEntire (1994), includes four core subtests: Vocabulary, Computation, General Information, and Story Problems. It was developed for use with students ages 8–18. Sattler's (2001) review indicates that the TOMA-2 has limited use. This is true for the general student population, but even more so for the mathematically gifted student population.

*Test of Early Mathematics Ability–2nd Edition (TEMA-2).* Sattler's (2001) review of the Test of Early Mathematics Ability–2nd Edition (TEMA-2) is equally cautionary, primarily because of the poor standardization. TEMA-2, developed by Ginsburg and Baroody (1990), was designed as a screening instrument for children between the ages of 3 and 8. Because it is essentially a screening test and is not intended to be used with children who are 8 years or older, it is of limited use for mathematically gifted students.

### Achievement Tests as Diagnostic Tests

Achievement tests differ from aptitude and intelligence tests by specifically measuring what a student has learned.

These results can be used to compare a student's progress with the progress of others and can serve as a baseline when measuring future progress. Sometimes, achievement testing is used for placement into programs. In addition to informing parents and educators regarding placement decisions, achievement tests may also be useful in a diagnostic capacity, as their results may play a critical role in helping teachers and parents plan the student's academic program. Although achievement is measurable in all curricular areas, we focus on the measurement of achievement in mathematics only. Several commonly used tests are discussed below.

*The Stanford Diagnostic Mathematics Test–4th edition (SDMT-4).* Like its predecessors, the Stanford Diagnostic Mathematics Test–4th edition (SDMT-4). was designed as a diagnostic test, not an achievement test (Harcourt Brace, 1996). It was designed to be administered to groups of students, but can easily be administered individually. No special training other than familiarity with the instructions is required to administer it. Each level has two different assessment formats: multiple choice and free response. The SDMT-4 is closely aligned with the 1989 NCTM Standards.

The SDMT-4 has several features that make it a useful instrument for educational programming. First, there are two forms for each of the test's six levels. The first level (Red) is designed for use with grades 1–2; the Orange Level is for grades 2–3; the Green Level is for grades 3–4; the Purple Level is for grades 4–6; the Brown Level is for grades 6–8; and the Blue Level is for grades 9–12. A student's score can be content-referenced with progress indicators on an individual diagnostic report and it can be norm-referenced (i.e., percentile ranks and grade equivalents can be obtained). Since each level has two forms, it lends itself to pre- and posttesting.

We concur with Poteat's (1998) summary of his extensive review of the SDMT-4:

In summary, the SDMT-4 is an impressive instrument. It is primarily designed to be a diagnostic test

. . . as a diagnostic instrument, it provides a great deal of information and the free-response format will allow for a more detailed analysis of students' mathematical skills. . . . I would recommend the SDMT-4 for use in grades 1 through 8. (p. 938)

When working with mathematically talented students, it is critical that an examiner use above-level tests. Often, the examiner will start with the level that is equivalent to a student's grade, but will then move through the materials until the student reaches a challenge level that can be diagnostically useful for programming. These ideas are described comprehensively in all of the chapters following this and especially in Chapters 4 and 7.

*Sequential Tests of Educational Progress (STEP).* The STEP battery of achievement tests assesses achievement in reading, English, mathematics, science, and social studies. STEP tests differ from typical end-of-year comprehensive tests by encompassing broader, more general goals for each achievement area measured.

The STEP tests are available exclusively through Sylvan Technology Centers, which administer the tests through Prometric, a worldwide distribution network for computer-based testing services. (Their Web site, http://prime.prometric. com, indicates that they have more than 2,500 testing centers serving 180 countries.) Students/parents may register online for testing, but students need to go to a Sylvan Technology Center to test. Eventually, testing may be available through the Internet. Although distance-testing, like distance-learning, has the allure of eliminating geographic barriers, it comes with many disadvantages, not the least of which is the frustration involved in navigating through a cyber-system.

*Comprehensive Testing Program IV (CTP-IV).* CTP-IV tests (Educational Records Bureau, 2002), designed primarily for members of the Educational Records Bureau (ERB) and marketed by ERB, have been available since 1992. This battery of tests measures achievement for grades 1–10 in vocabulary, reading comprehension, mechanics of writing, writing concepts and skills, and mathematics (including an end-of-course test in Algebra I). The CTP-IV battery also measures verbal reasoning ability for grades 3–10, and there is a measure of quantitative reasoning ability for grade 3. The usefulness of the CTP-IV tests for the talent search population has not yet been well documented. However, the tests were intentionally designed for students in schools where achievement is above average, therefore it may be useful in curricular planning for students who typically score in the upper end on grade-level standardized tests of achievement.

*Key Math–Revised.* The Key Math–Revised (Connolly, 1997), published by the American Guidance Service, has become familiar to educators because it is commonly used to diagnose students who have a specific learning disability in mathematics. For that purpose (i.e., diagnosis of a mathematics learning disability), it is an excellent instrument and is highly recommended by reviewers (see Sattler, 2001). However, as a diagnostic instrument for mathematically talented students, the Key Math–Revised falls short. Even though it is individually administered and is designed to provide a broad picture of a student's understanding and application of important mathematics concepts and skills, it is too broad to provide information that is specific enough to develop a program for the mathematically gifted child. For example, it can indicate mastery of basic computation operations (i.e., addition, multiplication, subtraction, and division), but it cannot provide more substantial programming information.

*Woodcock-Johnson III Tests of Achievement.* The Woodcock-Johnson III Tests of Achievement (Woodcock, McGrew, & Mather, 2001) reflects the most recent revision of this individually-administered battery of achievement tests for individuals between the ages of 2 and 90. In all, there are 22 tests, and various clusters of the tests measure the general content areas of reading, language, writing, and mathematics.

Many psychologists rely on the Woodcock-Johnson as an indication of an achievement/ability discrepancy representing a specific learning disability in reading, mathematics, writing, or any combination. Similarly to the WJ III COG, the Woodcock-Johnson III Tests of Achievement can only be scored by using a computer. Although it is an excellent achievement-test battery, especially for diagnosing learning disabilities, the information from the achievement tests of this battery is typically not specific enough to develop programs for mathematically gifted students.

## How Can Test Results Provide More Than a Score?

A student's test score has little meaning if it is not referenced to scores obtained by other students. Scores earned by a normative group (comparison group) are called *norms*. The most useful comparison score is a percentile ranking. This number tells what proportion of the student's agemates scored lower than the student. For example, a student earning a score at the 50th percentile performed better than 50% of his or her agemates in the norm sample. The 50th percentile represents an average score.

When comparing a talented student's performance to the normative group, it is critical to use norms above the student's current grade placement because the purpose of testing is to measure mastery of the material, as well as to document the student's advanced achievement when compared to advanced students. For example, if a mathematically precocious 8-year-old third grader takes the Purple Level (designed for grades 4–6) of the Stanford Diagnostic Mathematics Test the progress indicators for each skill could be compared to fourth, fifth, or sixth graders.

With all tests, one can derive much useful information by closely attending to the manner in which the student approaches the test-taking task and carefully analyzing the pattern of correct and incorrect answers. For example, on an administration of the Raven's Standard Progressive Matrices (RPM), one student demonstrated her anxiety in test-taking situations by taking an excessive amount of time (i.e., 50 minutes) to complete the test. Although the test is untimed, most students complete the test in 30 minutes or less. However, this fourth grader worked methodically through each item and earned a score that was equivalent to the 99th percentile when compared to 13-year-old students. Based upon observations of her behaviors while completing the RPM, the examiner was able to structure the environment for the administration of the Iowa Algebra Aptitude Test (IAAT), which is a timed test.

On the IAAT, this same student earned a score at the 45th percentile. She was not able to complete three of the four IAAT subtests within the required time frame. However, when allowed to complete the unfinished items, she earned a score that placed her at the 92nd percentile. Clearly, the results of the RPM and the IAAT suggest that she will soon be ready for prealgebra and algebra. However, because she was also demonstrating signs of perfectionism, it would be extremely important to monitor her anxiety level, as well as her progress in mathematics.

The assessment should be useful immediately for planning the educational program and should also provide information that will be helpful in long-term planning, such as when considering the possibility of whole-grade acceleration. The examiner can make important initial observations concerning the student's social and emotional development, as well as the development of fine and gross motor skills. All of this should figure into the recommendations for the student's program.

## Curriculum-Based Assessment

The tests described above were norm-referenced. In other words, a student's performance is compared to the performance of others on the same test. Measurement of mastery of a particular set of skills from specific curricular materials is referred to as Curriculum-Based Assessment (CBA). Oftentimes, the publisher of a textbook series will have done this for the teacher in the form of chapter and unit tests, or the teacher may choose to generate the test items based upon the specific curriculum being employed.

In contrast to assessments used for classification purposes, curriculum-based assessments may provide a stronger connection between what is tested and what is taught. There are two advantages to this method. First, it gives the instructor a baseline against which progress can be measured. Second, since the items are derived from the curriculum, instruction is directly linked to the results. Thus, the risk of omitting instruction in a certain area is avoided; the teacher and student need not worry about gaps in the student's background.

Although CBA is not new, it has the appeal of a "novel" approach to assessment and, at first blush, may seem more relevant to a specific learning environment. However, a major caveat regarding CBA is the tendency by some educators to develop items that emphasize lower order thinking (e.g., basic facts), rather than higher order thinking (e.g., mathematical applications or problem solving). Also, for some educators, CBA has become the answer to the perceived "competition" associated with norm-referenced measures. In reality, students in a class know almost intuitively who are the more able students. The best use of CBA is as a complement to the standardized measures that comprise an assessment. The same is also true of the standardized measures presented above. Results from standardized tests are most useful when combined with other information about the student, including curricular information.

## What Professionals Are Available for Completing the Assessment?

The central office or centralized educational service centers of many school systems are usually equipped to provide individual intelligence testing, as well as aptitude and achievement testing, but parents may have to insist that an assessment be done. Typically, there will be a wait of several weeks or months before the assessment can be accomplished. Otherwise, private, certified psychologists (who should usually have a Ph.D. or a Psy.D. degree) may be needed. An assessment by a private psychologist may seem expensive in the short-run (these assessments can cost several hundred dollars and may cost $1,000 or even more). But, the costs of not knowing and choosing not to act are more expensive in the long run. The information from an assessment by a psychologist who is suitably trained and appropriately experienced can help parents and educators develop an individualized educational plan.

## How Are Gifted Education and Special Education Connected?

Educators who have entered the profession since 1975 have been able to witness a remarkable event in education, namely the required provision that children with disabilities must have an appropriate education. In 1976, this act was called the Education for All Handicapped Children Act, but, since 1990, when it was updated, it has been known as the Individuals With Disabilities Education Act (IDEA). Since then, it has been reauthorized and amended (1997), and, in 1999, regulations implementing IDEA '97 were issued. We will comment briefly on three general results of this legislation.

The first result is that educators are more familiar and comfortable with a variety of tests that are used to understand the unique learning characteristics of students whose disabilities run the gamut from mildly to profoundly challenging. This has led to the second result, a greater appreciation for individual differences. Many educators are familiar with the power of testing for placing students into programs, as well as using that information to determine programming. Indeed, special education and gifted education are flip sides of the coin of individual differences.

Third, the heart and soul of IDEA is the individualized education plan (IEP). In many states, especially those where gifted education is mandated, an individualized plan may be manifested as the personal education plan (PEP), or as a gifted individualized educational plan (GIEP), or an IEP (see Chapter 9, Case Studies, for an example of a PEP). The law mandates development of an IEP for students who qualify for special educational services. Although there is not a similar federal mandate for students who are identified for gifted and talented programs, the trend in many states is to create such a plan. The psychoeducational report, typically written by a psychologist who has administered the tests and thus is reporting the results, is pivotal in developing a student's personalized plan for programming.

## What Does a Good Psychoeducational Report Look Like?

A psychologist's report provides official documentation of the results of an assessment. In addition to reporting test scores, a report should reflect the psychologist's interpretation of the child's behavior during the educational assessment in conjunction with information provided by the parent and teacher. All reports should serve as a means of informative communication. However, the length of the report may be misleading with respect to information. For example, a 10-page document that goes into great detail with irrelevant background information and makes unfounded predictions concerning the child's future is unsuitable. Equally unsuitable, but at the other extreme with respect to length, is a two-sentence document that states, "Johnny earned an IQ score of 145 on the WISC-III. This score indicates that Johnny is gifted and should be placed in a program."

A good report starts with some brief demographic information about the student and then briefly explains the reason for referral. The initial reason for referral to the psychologist dictates the type of assessment (i.e, which tests are used). The tests used determine the information included in the report. During an assessment, the psychologist should spend an adequate amount of time getting to know the child and parents in order to develop an appreciation for the child's history as it pertains to the present situation. Because intelligence test scores have so often been used as the principal source of information for placement, classification, or both, they are often regarded as an end in themselves. It is our position that a useful assessment should provide diagnostic information that may result in a placement recommendation. The ultimate goal of an assessment should be to develop written recommendations that will guide the child's educational program.

During the assessment, the skilled psychologist will carefully observe how the child approaches different types of problems, attend to the level of language used by the child, look for indicators of impulsivity and stress, and interpret the child's general attitude in that type of setting. This information should be used anecdotally in discussing recommendations for the educational program.

The section of the report labeled "Recommendations" is actually the crux of the report and should serve as the foundation for any individualized educational plan being developed. The recommendations are action-oriented and suggest programming, as well as future assessments and evaluations of the student. This plan should include a description of the educational setting and materials that will be necessary for the student's success. It should always include a method for follow-up, which does not necessarily need to be conducted by the psychologist. However, the psychologist should aid the teacher and parent in identifying the appropriate personnel for follow-up. Figure 3.1 shows an example of a psychoeducational report generated after the assessment of a mathematically talented child. In the report, the first test mentioned is EXPLORE, which was used as a talent search instrument. EXPLORE and other talent search tests such as the ACT Assessment and the SAT I are discussed extensively in Chapter 5.

## Consumer Guidelines: What Do I Need to Know About Educational Assessments?

In this chapter, we have presented the benefits of an academic assessment. Below are "consumer guidelines" for parents and educators who have students with exceptional talents. Included within these guidelines is a table (see Table

## Psychoeducational Report

Student:               Kayla (D.O.B.= 3/15/91)
Assessment:            Abstract Reasoning
                       and Algebra Aptitude
Assessment Dates:      September 16, 2000
                       and November 12, 2000
Report Date:           November 16, 2000

### Background

Kayla is a fourth-grade student at an elementary school in a mid-sized university community in the Midwest. When Kayla was in third grade, she participated in the Elementary Student Talent Search and took EXPLORE. Her scores were outstanding and indicative of the need for a very challenging curriculum. Mathematics is a content area that appears to be particularly strong for Kayla. Her parents have sought additional opportunities for challenging experiences outside of the school setting, including mentoring.

### Reason for Referral

The assessment that was completed in September and November was part of a diagnostic assessment to determine Kayla's cognitive strengths and to identify specific content objectives for the mentor.

### Tests Administered/Reviewed

EXPLORE

The Raven's Standard Progressive Matrices (RPM)

The Iowa Algebra Aptitude Test (IAAT)

**Results**

**EXPLORE**

The results of Kayla's performance on EXPLORE (taken in January of grade 3) were as follows:

| Test | Standard Score | Grade 8 Percentile | Grade 3 Talent Search Percentile |
|------|---------|-----------|-----------|
| English | 12 | 38th | 67th |
| Mathematics | 13 | 46th | 91st |
| Reading | 15 | 60th | 91st |
| Science Reasoning | 16 | 71st | 90th |
| Composite | 14 | 54th | 89th |

**Raven's Standard Progressive Matrices (RPM)**

Kayla worked quickly and accurately and completed the RPM in 23 minutes. This is an untimed test. She earned a total score of 54 (out of 60); this score is at the 99th percentile compared to students aged 12.5 years. The 99th percentile for students age 9.5 years is a score of 48.

The Raven's Progressive Matrices is an excellent measure of abstract reasoning. Obviously, Kayla is an outstanding abstract reasoner, and her abstract reasoning skills are superior even when compared to students who are chronologically much older than she.

**The Iowa Algebra Aptitude Test (IAAT)**

The primary purpose of the IAAT is to predict a student's future success in Algebra I. There are four sections to this test, and each section is timed, with a total of 36 minutes allowed to complete the test. Kayla earned a total score that was at the 95th percentile. She missed the most items on Part 1, "Interpreting Mathematical Information," which measured the interpretation of graphs and technical writing. Two of the items missed on this section were not completed. She only missed one item on the second part, "Translating to Symbols"; she specifically missed an item that measured a simple expression with a variable. Kayla did not miss any items on the third part, "Finding Relationships," and she missed three items on the fourth part, "Using Symbols." One of the items missed on this section measured the application of symbolic representation, and the other two items missed measured the skill of identifying relationships among variables in a formula.

## Summary and Recommendations

Kayla is an extraordinarily able student. Her parents are to be commended for seeking additional challenges that allow her to progress systematically through the prealgebra curriculum. We recommend the following:

1.  Share the above results with Kayla's teachers. Kayla's scores on the tests indicate that she performs better than the majority of fourth graders on these tests. Kayla's talents in mathematics are exceptional for her age. She compares well to her age group and to older mathematically gifted students. She would benefit from moving through the mathematics curriculum at a fast pace (even more quickly than the typical gifted fourth grader).
2.  Kayla would benefit from an instructional program in which she is grouped with other mathematically talented students. Most likely she will need to be grouped with mathematically talented students 1–3 years older than she.
3.  As demonstrated by her performance on the IAAT, Kayla is ready for Algebra I. If she is not readily accommodated at her school, her parents will need to identify a mentor who can delineate a program allowing her to progress at her pace.

4.  Kayla might enjoy participating in the Mathematical Olympiads for Elementary and Middle Schools (MOEMS) contest. This would give her the opportunity to interact mathematically and socially with other talented students. Kayla also would benefit from appropriate mathematics enrichment activities such as problem-solving, classroom math games, playing computer games, and computer programming.

5.  Kayla would also benefit from programs for talented youth such as the summer classes offered by the school system or university-associated academic programs. These programs offer both academic and social benefits.

6.  Future testing should include the EXPLORE test as a fifth grader. When Kayla enters grade 6, she will be ready for the Scholastic Assessment Test (SAT-I), and, as a seventh or eighth grader, she will be ready for the ACT Assessment.

### Figure 3.2. Sample Psychoeducational Report

3.1) that summarizes the tests discussed in this chapter, the constructs measured by these tests, the qualifications for the administrators of these tests, and the age level of the student. We have also indicated those tests that we recommend for programming for the mathematically talented students. By design we have omitted the major tests of the elementary and middle school talent searches (e.g., EXPLORE, PLUS, ACT Assessment, and SAT I) because these tests are extensively discussed in Chapter 5.

*1. Know what question guides the assessment.* This is the first issue to address. The question that guides the assessment is the one that helps us to choose the appropriate test and drives the recommendations. Parents should play a part in formulating this question. Examples of questions include:

## Table 3.1
## Summary of Tests

| Test (publisher) | Construct Measured | Age of Student | Who Can Administer | Setting |
|---|---|---|---|---|
| Stanford-Binet Scales (Riverside) | General intelligence | 2–adult | Certified or licensed psychologist | Individually administered |
| Wechsler Scales (Psychological Corporation) | General intelligence | 3–adult | Certified or licensed psychologist | Individually administered |
| Differential Ability Scales (Psychological Corporation) | Intelligence and achievement | 2–17 | Certified or licensed psychologist | Individually administered |
| Kaufman tests (American Guidance Services) | Intelligence and achievement | 2–adult | Certified or licensed psychologist | Individually administered |
| Woodcock-Johnson III Tests of Cognitive Abilities (Riverside) | Intelligence as general intellectual ability and specific cognitive abilities | 2–90+ | Psychologist or specially trained/ certified educator | Individually administered |
| Slosson Intelligence Test–Revised (Slosson Educational Publications) | Verbal Intelligence | 4–65 | Psychologist or educator | Individually administered |

| Otis-Lennon School Ability Test (Harcourt Brace Educational Measurement) | General intellectual ability | Grades K–12 | Psychologist or educator | Group administered |
|---|---|---|---|---|
| Cognitive Abilities Test (Riverside) | Verbal, quantitative, and nonverbal ability | Grades K–12 | Educator | Group administered |
| Raven's Progressive Matrices (Oxford Psychologist Press) | Nonverbal test of abstract reasoning | Primary to above-average adults (6 to 65) | Educator | Group administered |
| School and College Ability Test* (Available only through computerized testing at Prometric Testing Centers) | Verbal and quantitative aptitude | Grades 2–12 | Prometric Testing Centers | n.a. |
| Differential Aptitude Tests* (Psychological Corporation) | Verbal, numerical, abstract, and mechanical reasoning; space relations; and others | Grades 7–12 | Educator | Group administered |

*continued on next page*

## Table 3.1 continued

| Test (publisher) | Construct Measured | Age of Student | Who Can Administer | Setting |
|---|---|---|---|---|
| Iowa Algebra Aptitude Test* (Riverside) | Diagnostic/ predictive test of success in algebra | Grades 7–8 | Educators | Group administered |
| Orleans-Hanna Algebra Prognosis Test* (Harcourt Brace Educational Measurement) | Diagnostic/ predictive test of success in algebra | Grades 7–11 | Educators | Group administered |
| TOMAGS (PRO-ED) | Screening instrument to assess math reasoning and problem solving | Grades K–6 | Educators | Group administered |
| Stanford Diagnostic Mathematics Test–4th ed.* (Harcourt Brace Educational Measurement) | Diagnostic mathematics test | Grades 1.5–13 | Educators | Group administered |
| STEP* (computerized testing at Prometric Testing Centers) | Achievement test battery | Grades 2–12 | Prometric Testing Centers | n.a. |

| CTP-IV* (Educational Records Bureau) | Achievement test battery | Grades 1–12 | Educators | Group administered |
|---|---|---|---|---|
| Key Math (American Guidance Service) | Diagnostic for students with learning difficulties | 5–22 | Educators | Individually administered |
| Test of Mathematical Abilities–2nd ed. (TOMA-2) (PRO-ED) | Achievement screening | 8–18 | Educators | Group or individually administered |
| Test of Early Mathematics Ability–2nd ed. (TEMA-2) (PRO-ED) | Achievement test battery | 3–8 | Educators | Individually administered |
| Woodcock Johnson III Tests of Achievement (Riverside) | Specific curriculum taught in school, developed by textbook publisher and/or class-room teacher | 2–90 | Psychologist or specially trained/ certified educator | Individually administered |
| Curriculum based assess-ment* (Teacher developed and/or cur-riculum developed) | | All grades/ ages | Educators | Group administered |

*Note.* *Authors' recommended tests for programming for mathematically talented students.

- What is my child's level of mathematical talent and what is the appropriate level of instruction?
- Is my child eligible for the gifted program?
- Will Algebra I be too hard (or too easy) for my sixth grader?
- If my fourth grader skips into fifth-grade mathematics, will there be gaps in his or her mathematical background?

2. *Know what tests are appropriate and useful for obtaining the needed information.* We don't expect parents to be able to select specific tests for the assessment because most parents don't have the professional background to do so. However, parents should be aware that a general ability test won't give enough specific information about a child's mathematical ability to determine placement in a mathematics class. They should also be aware that a grade-level achievement test probably will not give enough information about what a student has learned, as well as what the student is ready to learn.

3. *Confirm that the person conducting the assessment has appropriate training* (see Table 3.1). Some tests can be administered by a teacher who is familiar with the directions. Other tests require extensive training and the person administering them usually has an advanced degree.

4. *Reaffirm the importance of effective communication among parents, educators, and the assessment expert about the results and recommendations.* Test results should be reported in written form. This report should include the actual test scores, which should be presented within an educational context. The score by itself is of little value.

5. *Verify that the report will include several specific recommendations individualized to the child who was tested.* A photocopied list of recommendations is not acceptable. The report should include a system for follow-up.

6.  *Reports should be completed and sent in a timely fashion* (i.e., within one month after the assessment has been completed). Parents should be notified of any delays.

7.  *What is the delivery system for the assessment?* In other words, are the tests individually or group-administered? Is the test electronically completed, does the student respond orally, or does he or she use paper and pencil to respond to test items?

8.  *How much should this type of assessment cost?* At one end of a cost continuum, testing might be done through the school district at no cost to parents. At the other end, parents might pay several hundred dollars, especially for a thorough assessment that includes an individualized intelligence test.

## Conclusion

The main purpose of this chapter was to familiarize the reader with the notion of a psychoeducational assessment for gifted children. We want parents and educators to think of a psychoeducational assessment as a way to learn more about a child's cognitive characteristics (e.g., ability, aptitude, and achievement). The tests that are used in an assessment should be determined by the purpose for which the assessment is being conducted, and the information from tests is meaningful within a context. A good psychoeducational assessment is the first step in advocating for an educational program. The next step is implementation of the program based upon the information obtained from the assessment. This is the model referred to as Diagnostic Testing➤Prescriptive Instruction, which is described in the next chapter.

# 4

# The Diagnostic
# Testing→Prescriptive
# Instruction Model

- The Diagnostic Testing→Prescriptive Instruction (DT→PI) model is a five-step procedure designed to tailor instruction to a student's learning needs. The design of the instructional plan is based on a series of diagnostic testing.

- Using tests developed for older students (above-level assessment) is an important component of the DT→PI process.

- Techniques for pretesting and posttesting are presented and the critical nature of this activity is discussed.

- The chapter presents examples of how to use the DT→PI process and offers suggestions for implementing it successfully.

*Avoid trying to teach students what they already know.*
—*Julian Stanley, 2001, p. 298*

THE PURPOSE OF this chapter is to explain the Diagnostic Testing→Prescriptive Instruction model as developed by Julian Stanley for use with mathematically precocious students. This model is useful in working with exceptionally talented students to ensure that they study mathematics that is appropriately challenging, but that they do not skip important concepts or have "gaps" in their backgrounds. This chapter illustrates in a step-by-step manner the DT→PI model and includes examples of students who have used it.

The notion of diagnostic testing and prescriptive instruction has its roots in special education (Lerner, 1976). The approach is founded on a system of testing students "out of level." In special education, a test below the grade level of placement is used. One of the first researchers in gifted education, Leta Hollingworth, who wrote the first textbook in gifted education and is sometimes referred to as the "mother" of the gifted education field, recognized that this idea of out-of-level testing could also be useful for gifted students who could be assessed using tests designed for older grade levels (Hollingworth, 1942; for more information about Hollingworth and her work, see the special issue of *Roeper Review*, Volume 12, No. 3, March 1990.). Julian Stanley extended Hollingworth's ideas in the late 1960s and early 1970s (Stanley, 1990, 2001) and developed the Diagnostic Testing→Prescriptive Instruction model to identify mathematically talented students' strengths and weaknesses and to pinpoint areas in which they needed work.

A key component of the DT→PI model is the systematic, objective approach to determining the most appropriate curriculum for mathematically talented students (Benbow, 1986; Lupkowski, Assouline, & Stanley, 1990; Stanley, 1978, 1979a, 1991, 2001; Stanley & Benbow, 1986). In the field of gifted education, Stanley's adaptation of the DT→PI model is especially useful for exceptionally mathematically talented students. Since it is an individualized approach, it can be adapted easily for individual students, but it also can be used with a small group of students who demonstrate varying degrees of mathematical talent.

The DT→PI process begins by administering an above-level aptitude test to a talented student (see the previous chapter for an extensive discussion of above-level aptitude testing). Students who do well on this initial screening measure may then participate in above-level achievement testing, where their strengths and weaknesses on particular topics are pinpointed. After this, students work with a mentor on the topics they did not understand. Once they have mastered a topic, they take a posttest and then reenter the process at the next higher level of achievement testing. In reading through the description of the Diagnostic Testing→Prescriptive Instruction process, it may seem as though students are taking many tests. Although this is the case in the initial phase of DT→PI, the purpose of the testing is to tailor instruction, and the percentage of time spent on testing is much smaller than the overall percentage of time spent on instruction.

## Above-Level Assessment

Most regular classrooms use an on-grade-level curriculum that is designed to be implemented by a teacher who is not necessarily a mathematics educator, and the curriculum is not oriented to the individualized implementation required by diagnostic testing with prescribed instruction. Typically, the gifted student in the regular classroom will have demonstrated mastery of the grade-level curriculum (often through home-instruction, self-instruction, or both). In other words, gifted students know much, if not most, of the curriculum for their grade. When these students take a standardized test that was designed for their grade level, their responses to all or most of the items are correct, thus reaching what psychologists call the test's "ceiling." For these students, the grade-level test does not adequately measure their talents because answering all of the items correctly informs us that they performed well compared to other students in their grade. However, we don't know the extent of their talents due to the ceiling effect of the test. In the DT→PI model, the talented students simply take a test that was designed for older students, which has been shown to be extremely effective with talented students (Benbow, 1992a; Benbow & Arjmand, 1990; Benbow & Lubinski, 1996; Benbow & Stanley, 1983; Keating, 1976; Stanley, Keating & Fox, 1974).

As a case in point, when a student scores at the 95th percentile or above on a grade-appropriate mathematics test, the test may not have measured a student's full achievement in that area (see Chapter 3 for a detailed explanation of a percentile). This is an example of a student hitting the ceiling of a test. What is needed is a more difficult test that contains more advanced items. A more challenging test allows students to demonstrate what they know and what they don't know in mathematics. Above-level tests spread out the scores of able students, helping us to differentiate talented students from exceptionally talented students. This information is extremely helpful for good educational planning (see Chapter 5 for more information about above-level testing).

The DT→PI model, designed with precocious junior high school students in mind, has been adapted for use with younger students (see Lupkowski & Assouline, 1992; Moore & Wood, 1988, Stanley, 1978). Each step of the model is detailed in Figure 4.1.

## Steps in the DT→PI Model

### Step 1: Determine Aptitude

The purpose of this step is to determine the mathematical aptitude of students who are performing well on grade-level mathematics. For example, elementary school students who have scored at the 95th percentile or above on a nationally standardized test such as the Iowa Tests of Basic Skills (ITBS) are eligible to participate in above-level testing. Students do not have

## Table 4.1
## Tests Recommended for Aptitude Testing

| Grade | Above-Level Test | Contact Information* |
|---|---|---|
| 2–4 | SCAT | CTY (Johns Hopkins) |
| 3–6 | EXPLORE | Belin-Blank Center (The University of Iowa), C-MITES (Carnegie Mellon), CTD (Northwestern), TIP (Duke) |
| 5–6 | PLUS | CTY (Johns Hopkins), RMTS (University of Denver) |
| 1–6 | Select the level of a standardized achievement test that is at least two grade levels above the student's current grade. Standardized achievement tests include: Iowa Tests of Basic Skills, Stanford Achievement Test, or Metropolitan Achievement Test. Using an above-level achievement test serves as a measure of aptitude. | Local school district |
| 7–9 | SAT I, ACT Assessment | State, regional, or university-based talent searches listed above as well as in "Resources" |

*Note.* *Addresses and phone numbers can be found in "Resources."

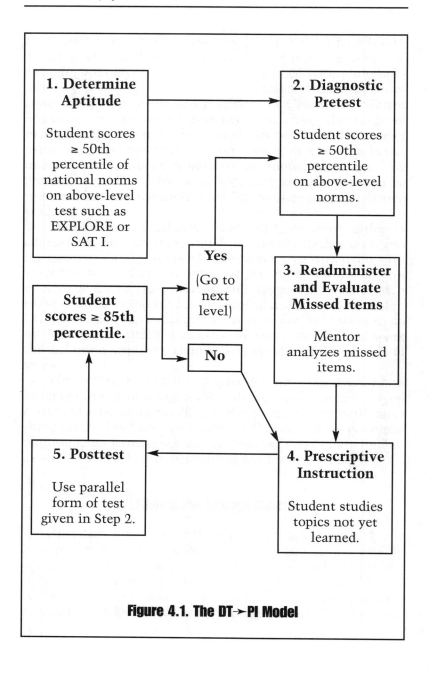

**Figure 4.1. The DT→PI Model**

to score at the 95th percentile on the overall test, but a score at the 95th percentile is strongly recommended on the mathematics subtests (e.g., Mathematics Concepts or Mathematics Problems and Applications) as a launching point for determining more precisely the student's aptitude in mathematics.

The 95th percentile cutoff is a guideline; it does not need to be adhered to rigidly. If a student scores slightly below the cutoff, but school personnel and parents have other evidence that the student has exceptional mathematics ability, then he or she may be eligible for above-level testing (see Ebmeier & Schmulbach, 1989; Lupkowski-Shoplik & Swiatek, 1999).

We strongly recommend the use of a standardized, nationally-normed test in this phase of the DT→PI process. Extensive research has demonstrated that useful above-level measures of aptitude for students younger than seventh grade include the PLUS, School and College Ability Test (SCAT), EXPLORE, and Comprehensive Testing Program (CTP); (Institute for the Academic Advancement of Talented Youth, 1997; Lupkowski & Assouline, 1994; Lupkowski-Shoplik & Swiatek, 1999; Mills, Ablard, & Stumpf, 1993; Mills & Barnett, 1992). We also recommend that school personnel consider using the quantitative sections of nationally standardized achievement tests they may already have available, such as the Iowa Tests of Basic Skills (ITBS), Stanford Achievement Test (SAT), or Metropolitan Achievement Test. If school personnel use one of these readily available tests, it is important to select one that is at least two grade levels higher than the student's current grade placement (see Table 4.1).

It is important to use above-level tests, not grade-level tests. Mathematically talented students may know advanced material that is not typically included on the grade-level test. The point of administering an above-level assessment is to determine what a student doesn't know so that instruction can be based upon filling in their knowledge gaps. Standardized tests are especially effective for this purpose because they provide corresponding instructional objectives. Now the task becomes deciding how far above level to go. We recommend the following:

- Kindergarten–Grade 2: Use a standardized test such as the Iowa Tests of Basic Skills (ITBS) or Stanford Achievement Test. However, select a level that is two grades above the child's current grade. For example, a first grader would take the third-grade form of the Stanford Achievement Test.
- Grades 3–5: Have the students participate in an elementary student talent search (see Chapter 5 for extensive information about talent searches) and take a test such as EXPLORE, or select a level of a locally administered standardized test that is two or three grades above the child's current grade.
- Grade 6: Have the child participate in one of the elementary talent searches and take a test such as EXPLORE.
- Grade 7: Have the child participate in one of the middle school talent searches and take the SAT I.
- Grades 8–9: Have the child sit for one of the middle school talent searches and take the ACT or the SAT I.

When Step 1 is completed, the scores will determine whether or not the student will go on to Step 2. Scores earned by talented students should be compared to scores for students in the above-level grade for which the test was designed. For example, scores earned by fifth graders who take EXPLORE are compared to scores earned by the eighth-grade comparison group because EXPLORE was designed for eighth graders.

Standardized tests were developed with the 50th percentile as a key indicator of average performance for the grade level of the test. Therefore, when talented students earn scores at or above the 50th percentile on an above-level test, it is a good indication that their performance is comparable to average students at that grade level. With that in mind, we recommend that talented students who earn scores at the 50th percentile on the test administered in Step 1 move on to Step 2 of the DT→PI. To illustrate:

Helena, a third grader, earned a total mathematics score at the 98th percentile when compared to third-grade norms on the locally administered Metropolitan Achievement Test. Her teacher realized that this high percentile ranking did not provide sufficient information about where to begin instruction so that Helena was introduced to new concepts. The teacher then administered the fifth-grade level of the Math Subtests of the Metropolitan Achievement Test. Helena's Math subtest scores were at the 65th percentile when compared to fifth graders, therefore, she (and her teacher) were ready for Step 2 of the DT→PI.

We do not recommend that talented students who score below the 50th percentile on the above-level test continue with the DT→PI process. Instead, we encourage curricular adjustments such as enrichment or problem solving activities (see Chapters 6 and 7 for more information). Some students may have the opportunity to participate in planned enrichment activities in mathematics through their gifted program or through extracurricular activities such as Mathematical Olympiads for Elementary and Middle Schools (listed in "Resources").

### Step 2: Diagnostic Pretest

In Step 1, Determine Aptitude, the goal was to discover mathematically talented students, those who demonstrated exceptional mathematical ability and would benefit from an individualized, advanced program. This was achieved by giving the students an above-level aptitude test. Based upon this testing, a select group of students is identified for further testing and specialized programming. This testing is part of Step 2, the purpose of which is to measure talented students' mathematical achievement and determine where to begin instruction. In Step 2, we administer achievement tests, starting with the grade level that approximates the above grade level of the aptitude test used in Step 1.

In this step of the DT→PI model, we start by using an above-grade-level achievement test. Why not use the grade-level end-of-course test for the student's current grade level as a beginning point? Although this might seem to be a good idea for "proving" to school personnel that the student has no content gaps, it doesn't really have much pedagogical advantage for programming. The goal is to determine what talented students know and do not know so that instruction can be tailored to their needs. Standardized achievement tests, as well as chapter tests and final exams provided by textbook publishers, are typically used in Step 2. If a standardized achievement test is used, it is helpful to have two parallel forms of the test because the second form of the test can be used in Step 5 (Posttest). Tests recommended for this phase of the DT→PI model are listed in Table 4.2.

The diagnostic pretest of Step 2 is administered under standardized conditions (e.g., the test proctor follows the instructions for administration as described in the test manual and observes time limits). One exception is made: Students are encouraged to answer all questions, but are told to indicate those items about which they are uncertain by writing a question mark to the left of the item number on the answer sheet. When the testing time has elapsed, the examiner takes the test materials from the student, scores the test, and determines the percentile rank of the student's score.

There are three possibilities for students in this step of the model, and only the second results in moving on to Step 3:

- They do very well on the diagnostic pretest (85th percentile or above). These students should take a more difficult version of the test.
- They do moderately well (earning scores between the 50th and 85th percentiles). These students should move on to Step 3, Readminister Missed Items.
- They do not do well (the scores are below the 50th percentile). These students should exit from the model and receive enrichment instruction in specialized mathematics topics.

| Table 4.2 | | |
| --- | --- | --- |
| **Tests Recommended for Diagnostic Pretest** | | |
| **Grade** | **Above-Level Test** | **Contact Information*** |
| 2–8 | Stanford Diagnostic Tests of Mathematics | Harcourt Brace Educational Measurement |
| | Comprehensive Testing Program IV (CTP-IV) | Educational Records Bureau |
| | End-of-year tests | Available through the text-book publisher |
| 4–6 | Iowa Algebra Aptitude Test | Riverside |
| 4–6 | Orleans-Hanna Algebra Prognosis Test | Harcourt Brace Educational Measurement |

*Note.* *Addresses and phone numbers can be found in "Resources."

In the first of the above three possibilities, the highest scoring students, those who score at the 85th percentile or above when compared to the normative group on a standardized test, have demonstrated mastery even though they might not have perfect scores. Therefore, students earning scores at the 85th percentile or above should take the next level of the test.

In the second possibility, students who score between the 50th percentile and 85th percentile when compared to the appropriate normative group on the standardized test are ready to move on to Step 3, Readminister Missed Items (Stanley, 1979a). Those students who earn scores between the 50th and 85th percentiles are likely to learn the material quickly.

The final possibility, the student earns a score below the 50th percentile on the diagnostic pretest, results in the student exiting from the DT→PI model. These students still need exposure to advanced topics in mathematics through enrichment instruction in specialized topics (e.g., tessellations, statistics and probability, or Fibonacci Sequences).

Here are three examples representing the scenarios described above:

> Kim, a talented fifth grader, earned a score above the 50th percentile (when compared to eighth graders) on EXPLORE Mathematics (a test developed for eighth graders). Step 2 involved the administration of the Iowa Algebra Aptitude Test, a measure of readiness for algebra. On this test, he earned a score at the 99th percentile even though he had no formal instruction in algebra. Therefore, he was administered an algebra test to determine which algebraic concepts he needed to learn.

> In Step 1 of the DT→PI model, Helena, a gifted third grader, earned a score at the 65th percentile on the fifth-grade level of the Metropolitan Achievement Test. As part of Step 2 of the DT→PI model, Helena's teacher administered Level D of the Comprehensive Testing Program (CTP) Mathematics Test (Level D was designed for grades 4–6). She earned a score at the 57th percentile when compared to fifth graders, and therefore went on to Step 3.

> Shawn, a fourth grader, earned a score at the 55th percentile on the Mathematics Total of the sixth-grade level of the Iowa Tests of Basic Skills. In Step 2, he was administered the sixth-grade level of the Stanford Diagnostic Test of Mathematics. On this level of test, his score was at the 35th percentile, indicating that his mathematics instruction could be provided outside of the DT→PI model. However, he still needed exposure to special enrichment topics in mathematics.

### Step 3: Readminister and Evaluate Missed Items

The purpose of Steps 1 and 2 of the DT→PI model was to identify students ready to move on to Step 3. The purpose of

Step 3 is to gain a more complete understanding of what topics the student does and does not know so that instruction can focus on new material.

The first activity of Step 3 is to return the test booklet to the student and have him or her rework missed or omitted items or items marked with a question mark. Unlike Step 2, when the student and instructor must adhere to published time limits, there are no time limits to Step 3. The examiner does not return the original answer sheet to the student or tell the student how the items were missed the first time. The student reworks the items on a separate piece of paper, showing all work.

At this point, the mentor becomes involved (although, in some cases, the examiner and mentor are the same person). The items are checked again, and the mentor evaluates the concepts not understood by the student. These concepts are related to predetermined goals and objectives provided by the test or textbook publishers. The mentor bases instruction upon this information.

In Helena's case, she correctly answered (within the time limit) 41 items out of 100 on Level D of the CTP Mathematics Test. She did not attempt 29 of the items because she ran out of time; 30 others she marked incorrectly. She put question marks next to four additional items (which had been answered correctly). The total number of items that she was asked to retry was 63. She was told to show all work and was given unlimited time. Based upon a careful analysis of the content of each item and Helena's responses to the 63 items, Helena's teacher determined that she was ready for instruction in numerous aspects of prealgebraic mathematics typically taught to fifth and sixth graders. These aspects included properties of geometric shapes, geometric formulas for volume and circumference, formulating equations from word sentences, charting information to find an unknown, algebraic notation, sequencing steps in a multistep problem, making tree diagrams, solving problems of chance, and spatial problem solving.

The final activity of Step 3 is identifying who will best serve as the instructor for Step 4.

## Step 4: Prescriptive Instruction

The purpose of the DT→PI process is to arrive at Step 4. The prescriptive instruction of Step 4 is based on a thorough analysis of the testing results obtained in Steps 1–3. Prescriptive instruction may or may not be provided by the classroom teacher, but it is critical that whoever does provide it have an excellent background in mathematics. This person is referred to as a *mentor*.

The mentor designs an instructional program based upon the diagnostic testing. The mentor carefully determines what principles the student does not yet understand and the areas in which the student needs further practice. The mentor also questions the student in order to gain more insight into what he or she does and does not understand.

In this important phase of the model, the mentor works with the student on the concepts—not the items—he or she does not understand. Very little time is spent on the topics about which the student has demonstrated mastery. We recommend that the mentor design problems to help the student study a topic. Textbooks are also useful resources for practice problems.

The goal of prescriptive instruction is to master each topic before moving on to the next, not to work through every page of the textbook. Students do not repeat topics they have already learned. The DT→PI model also permits students to study concepts in greater depth than is typically possible in the regular classroom. They are given new material, which helps them to learn challenging mathematics at an appropriate pace. The goal for the student is to gain a rich, solid foundation in mathematics that will serve him or her well when studying more advanced mathematics.

The mentor scheduled 12 weekly 2-hour sessions in a study room at the local public library over a 3-month period. Helena was still placed with third graders for the mathematics period at school, but she was not required to do all of the work the third graders were doing. Helena worked on her mentor-assigned homework while the other students worked on the daily lesson. In the evenings, Helena's parents checked to see if her homework was completed (they were not expected to check for accuracy). The regular classroom teacher was supportive of Helena and the completion of the mentor-assigned homework, and she encouraged her to ask any time she had questions concerning the homework. If she completed her mentor-assigned homework before the other students completed their daily work, she was permitted to read, work on the computer, or do other homework. Helena's teacher also made sure to include Helena in the classroom games and other group activities in mathematics.

The mentor developed the curriculum from a fifth-grade mathematics text that was part of the local district's curriculum. If Helena had questions about the homework, she was encouraged to contact the mentor via e-mail. Throughout the prescriptive instruction step of the DT→PI model, the mentor evaluated and documented Helena's progress. This information was helpful in future planning.

### Step 5: Posttesting

The final step in the DT→PI model is posttesting to determine if students have mastered the content. After completing the prescriptive instruction, students take a parallel form (equivalent in difficulty, but with different items) of the same test used for pretesting.

On the posttest, students who score above the 85th percentile for the appropriate above-level norms are considered to have mastered the material. Students who score below the 85th percentile require additional instruction and practice with the material. Even those who score at the 85th percentile, but earn less than perfect scores on the test, require work on the topics they do not yet understand. After the student has demonstrated mastery and the mentor is satisfied that he or she has adequately filled in any knowledge gaps on that particular topic, the student reenters the process at Step 2, using achievement tests and materials for the next level or topic. Thus, the student studies the mathematics topics in a systematic, sequential fashion, demonstrating mastery before moving on.

To measure Helena's mastery of the material, the mentor administered a parallel form of the CTP Mathematics Test, Level D. Compared to fifth graders, Helena earned a score at the 95th percentile. (Remember, prior to the mentor-paced instruction, Helena's score on Level D of CTP Mathematics was at the 57th percentile compared to fifth graders.) The mentor went back and reviewed with Helena the concepts measured by the items she had missed on the test. This reassured the mentor that Helena had mastered those concepts. Helena reentered the DT→PI process at Step 2 by taking the end-of-book test for the sixth-grade book.

## Putting the DT→PI Model Into Practice

In the preceding sections, we have described how students are selected for a mentor-paced program. The remainder of the chapter focuses on how the model is implemented. Consideration needs to be given to who, when, where, and for how long the mentor and student(s) meet, how students are evaluated compared to the other students in their grade, and how issues of credit and placement are resolved.

The DT→PI process with elementary-age students has been used extensively in programs at Carnegie Mellon University, Johns Hopkins University, the University of Iowa, and the University of North Texas. Based on our experiences with these programs, we have listed our responses to issues encountered by parents, teachers, and other school personnel. Also, we explain some of the details of developing the programs (see also Lupkowski, Assouline, & Vestal, 1992).

Forms included in this book, such as the one presented in Figure 4.2, were adapted from forms used in these university-based programs.

## Who Participates in Mentor-Paced Programs?

The DT→PI model has been used successfully with mathematically talented students as young as first graders. Standardized testing does not begin until second grade in many schools, so the need for this type of program for young students is not documented. Because of the nature of standardized testing and the identification component for the gifted program in most schools, it is more common for the majority of students to start participating in the DT→PI model when in third grade or later.

Students must not only demonstrate a high level of aptitude and achievement in mathematics, but they should also be mature and highly motivated. Participation in this type of program is best when students are eager to study more mathematics. The program demands a great deal of time and effort on the student's part. It is critical for children who participate in such a demanding program to do it because they want to do it, not because it is something their parents or teachers choose for them to do.

## How Important is the 50th Percentile Guideline?

Using the 50th percentile as a recommendation for including a student in a mentor-paced program means that the student has performed as well as the average student who has already completed that course. The talented student (who earned a score at the 50th percentile before being exposed to the curriculum) is a likely candidate for being able to complete the course quickly and well. This 50th percentile guideline has been used extensively by university-based programs for talented youth because it successfully provides direction for programming (Bartkovich & Mezynski, 1981; Benbow & Lubinski, 1997; Stanley, Keating, & Fox, 1974).

Teachers should use their professional judgment with a student who falls slightly below the recommended 50th percentile. A student who scored slightly below the 50th percentile could still continue on with the DT→PI process. This won't "hurt" the student since it is a highly individualized process and the model will self-correct. In other words, a student who has difficulty with the material will be given more time by the mentor to master the material. For students who fall well below the 50th percentile, however, placing them in a mentor-paced program might not be the best use of resources. If a student's percentile ranking is around the 40th percentile, consider evaluating him or her at a later date (perhaps next term) and look for other indicators that he or she may need a challenging mathematics curriculum (e.g., advanced cognitive reasoning skills and a high level of motivation).

### What Is the Role of the Mentor?

Stanley (1979a) described the mentor's role as follows:

> For the "prescriptive instruction" one needs a skilled mentor. He or she should be intellectually able, fast-minded, and well-versed in mathematics considerably beyond the subjects to be learned by the "mentee(s)." This mentor must not function didactically as an instructor, predigesting the course material for the mentee. Instead, he or she must be a pacer, stimulator, clarifier, and extender. (p. 1)

Who makes the best mentors? It is not necessary for the mentor to be a trained mathematics teacher. In addition to high school math teachers, engineers, college professors, undergraduate math majors, and graduate students in mathematics have been successful mentors. It is critical that the mentor have a good understanding of both the mathematics the student is currently studying and the mathematics he or she will study in the near future. Although we have worked with numerous mentors who were not teachers, we have found that some schools will recognize a student's work with a mentor only if the mentor is a certified teacher.

We do not recommend that parents mentor their children, even if they have the appropriate background in mathematics. Parents may demand too much of their own child or may be unable to get enough cooperation from their child. They also may be too ego-involved in the mentoring situation, or they simply may not have credibility with the school.

Sometimes, it is also suggested that a high school student might be a mentor. Our experience has been that high school students are busy with their own academic work and extracurricular activities and, therefore, would have difficulty managing the responsibilities of planning for mentoring sessions and meeting consistently on a weekly basis.

The mentor-to-student ratio is often 1:1. However, a skilled mentor can work successfully with up to five students (Moore & Wood, 1988; see also the North Hills School District program described in Chapter 6). Students at approximately the same level of understanding of mathematics can be grouped and it is not necessary for them to be of the same age. The Center for Talented Youth (CTY) at Johns Hopkins University offers "Young Students Classes" based on the DT→PI model. Based on the students' performance on diagnostic tests, they are placed in small groups of two to five (Mills, 1992; Moore & Wood, 1988). The benefits of this approach include both appropriate placement within the mathematics curriculum and the opportunity to interact with intellectual peers.

### How are the Mentoring Sessions Conducted?

In a typical school, mathematics class usually takes place every school day for about 45 minutes. When using the DT→PI process, however, the learning is much more highly concentrated. Therefore, daily instruction is not necessary. We recommend that the mentor and student meet for a total of 2 hours per week. For students in fifth grade and older, it may be best to meet once a week for 2 hours. Because younger students may be more easily fatigued, we recommend shorter, more frequent sessions (twice a week for an hour each time). One school system that was extremely eager to have a student participate in the mentor-paced program allowed the mathematics mentor to go into the classroom twice a week for an hour each time to work with the student. Between meetings, the mentor assigned the student homework. It is also helpful if the mentor is accessible to the student via telephone or e-mail to answer questions that arise between meetings.

During their meetings, the mentor works with the student on the principles (not the specific test items) the student didn't understand. Textbooks are used as resources, but mentors often devise their own problems. As this is a highly individualized process, assignments are tailored to a student's specific strengths and weaknesses. Students must demonstrate mastery of one topic before moving on to the next, but they are not required to work through every page of a text. This process is in sharp contrast to the spiral approach of most mathematics textbooks, where students are not expected to master a concept because they will be exposed to it the following year. If a textbook is used as a resource, students may not need to work through every page of the text because they will already have mastered much of the material (see Chapter 7).

### What Happens Between Meetings?

Homework completed on a daily basis (4–5 days per week) is essential in a mentoring situation because the student does not meet with the mentor every day. However, the homework should not take more than 20 minutes to complete each day. Students with questions about the homework may contact the mentor by phone or by e-mail. It is critical for the mentee to take responsibility for his or her own learning; this means doing homework carefully in a timely manner. Students participating in the mentor-paced program should be self-motivated and self-disciplined. Parents remain actively involved by supervising the completion of homework.

> Homework is an essential aspect of any fast-paced mathematics program. The material is covered in class so quickly that it must be reinforced by extensive homework assignments. The amount of homework should not be so great that it places a burden on the student or becomes repetitive or busy work. Nevertheless, homework can help a gifted youth make the most of his or her abilities. Students . . . must develop good study habits in order to space out the homework over the interval between classes. The discipline of pacing themselves through the homework assignment also leads to better recall of the material. (Bartkovich & George, 1980, p. 21)

Although parents of younger students might need to supervise homework sessions closely to make sure the work is completed on time, we want to emphasize the importance of self-motivation. The student needs to be interested in participating in the DT→PI process, not just doing it to please his or her parents. The mentor (and the parents) should try to make it an interesting experience; ideally, the student will find participation in the DT→PI process more challenging and fun than regular math classes in school.

### Parent, Student, Mentor, School: How Do They Get Along?

The answer to this question depends on how the DT→PI model is implemented (see the discussion about parent-school partnerships in Chapter 2). In some cases, the DT→PI model is implemented privately by parents who hire mentors to work with their children outside of school, with or without receiving school credit for the work completed by the student. On the other end of the spectrum is the situation in which the school develops its own mentor-paced program, systematically screens and serves students in this program, and has a plan for their placement in mathematics after the program is completed.

In our experience, many schools are eager to have their students participate in DT→PI programs, even if it is an external program that the parents have brought to the attention of school personnel. Educators understand that these types of programs supplement what the schools are able to provide. Cooperation is assured through communication: Letters explaining the program and reports of the student's progress, as well as meetings among parents, mentors, and school personnel facilitate communication and cooperation (see Figure 4.2, an adaptation of a form used in a university-based math mentor program).

Many school personnel demonstrate their support of mentor-paced programs through their cooperation. Sometimes, teachers are the first to recognize talent and encourage parents to contact program administrators. In other cases, parents investigate the program first. We always encourage parents to provide school personnel with information about their children's academic activities (e.g., test reports) and to discuss educational options for their child. Teachers find it helpful when parents share pertinent articles.

### Who Should Administer the Achievement Tests That Assess the Students' Progress?

We recommend that an achievement test be administered by the mentor or in collaboration with school personnel to ensure that it is conducted according to the directions provided in the manual. Achievement test results are useful in determining appropriate credit for work the student has completed since that work is not a part of the regular curriculum (Lupkowski & Assouline, 1992).

Results of the testing should be presented in a written report that also includes a description of the child's behavior during the testing and recommendations for prescriptive instruction based upon the results. In addition to giving the report to the parents, the examiner should also share it with the school principal, counselor, teachers, and other appropriate school personnel (Lupkowski & Assouline, 1992). More information about this type of report is found in Chapter 3.

## Is It Better to Use Standardized Tests or Teacher-Made Tests in Step 2?

Standardized tests are usually accompanied by specific instructional objectives, which is a distinct advantage. This allows a mentor to link test results directly to prescriptive instruction, therefore making standardized tests very useful in the DT→PI process. Teacher-made tests have a great deal of face validity, however, and teachers often feel more comfortable with their own tests. Unfortunately, most teacher-made tests are not well designed (Popham, 2002), and, in some cases, they have been developed as a way of "getting back" at a mathematically talented student. In addition, information from these tests is often misused, and teachers may not apply a reasonable level of mastery to the situation. For all of these reasons, we prefer standardized tests, but we recognize that the best-case scenario would include both standardized tests and teacher-made tests.

## Will Students Participating in the Mentor-Paced Program Have Less Opportunity to Interact With Others About the Material Being Studied?

The environment of a mentor-paced setting differs dramatically from the environment in a regular classroom. One of the most notable differences is that students in a mentor-paced program spend a great deal of time working individually. However, the student is not studying mathematics in isolation. He or she can easily exchange ideas with the mentor about the material being studied because of working in a small group or one on one. An additional benefit of working with a mentor is that he or she can provide more accurate answers to questions than peers can. The mentor also has the knowledge and ability to extend the student's questions or to ask new questions of that student.

Sometimes, educators and parents are concerned that students in a mentor program will have fewer opportunities to interact with their peers and may even be isolated from them by participating in the mentor-paced process. Although they may not be working with their peers in mathematics class, students in a math mentor program may be in the regular

To:        Educator and Administrator of Student's School
From:      _____, Math Mentor Program
           Coordinator or Math Mentor

The purpose of this letter is to inform you that _____ (name of student) is eligible to participate in the Math Mentor Program. The goals of the program are discussed below. Your assistance is needed to help the student succeed in this program.

The Math Mentor Program was developed for select students who demonstrate exceptionally high aptitude and achievement in mathematics as well as high motivation for studying mathematics. Mentors who work with these students have a strong background in mathematics. Mentors may meet with students up to two hours once a week in the evening or on weekends. Mentors may work individually with the student or with small groups of up to five students. Students are required to complete mentor-assigned homework before the next meeting.

The primary goal of the Math Mentor Program is to keep students challenged by providing advanced material. This means that the mentor will determine what areas of mathematics the student needs to study. This is accomplished through the Diagnostic Testing→Prescriptive Instruction approach, which is accelerative in nature. Students study advanced material at an appropriate level and pace for their exceptional aptitude in mathematics. This results in students studying material that is several years beyond their grade level.

To encourage students' successful participation in this selective program, educators and administrators are asked to do the following:

1.  Excuse Math Mentor Program students from regular math class activities. Progress through the Math Mentor Program will be determined through an assessment procedure implemented by the mentor. Student progress will be assessed routinely by mentors via mentor-made tests and mentor-generated homework.

2.  Allow students in the Math Mentor Program to complete mentor-assigned homework while students in the regular mathematics classroom are completing teacher-assigned work. This mentor-assigned work should be in lieu of regular math class work.

3.  Encourage students in the Math Mentor Program to partic-
    ipate in enrichment activities including mathematics
    games, competitions, or work on the computer.

The mentor will:
*   work with school personnel to evaluate the student's per-
    formance,
*   recommend a grade for the student based upon work com-
    pleted within the Math Mentor Program, and
*   communicate with school personnel to address placement
    decisions for future study of mathematics.

Communication among the mentor, educator, and parents is
essential for this program to be a success. Below are the names
of the mentor and the Math Mentor Program coordinator and
their phone numbers. Please contact us with any questions you
may have.

Math Mentor:
Name _____    Telephone number _____
Math Mentor Program Coordinator: _____
Name _____    Telephone number _____

Please check the appropriate category and sign below:
___ We will permit the student to work on mentor-assigned
    homework during the regular math class and facilitate the
    student's participation in the Math Mentor Program.
___ We are not yet prepared to make this commitment. (Please
    note that the Math Mentor Program Coordinator will call
    you to answer your questions if you check this box.)

_____        _____
Teacher         Date           Principal        Date

Thank you for your interest and involvement in the student's
progress.

### Figure 4.2. Math Mentor Program Information Form for Schools

*Note.* We suggest that individuals implementing this program also
attach articles, chapters, or summaries explaining the DT➤PI process.

classroom for their other subjects. Participation in mathematics clubs and contests (e.g., Mathematical Olympiads for Elementary and Middle Schools; see "Resources" and Appendix) will give students a chance to interact with other students in a mathematical and social context. In addition, we encourage them to participate in both unstructured play and more structured activities such as sports, music, and scouts. These varied activities will give them an abundance of opportunities to spend time with their age peers.

However, it is not necessary for students to spend every spare moment interacting with peers. This time should be balanced by adequate time alone. This time alone, which many talented students prefer, allows them the opportunity to think about what they have learned and experienced. The time can be used to formulate new questions and to investigate them. Thus, what is sometimes perceived as isolation by adults actually has many positive aspects (Lupkowski & Assouline, 1992).

### What Should Students Who Participate in the Mentor-Paced Program Do While Their Classmates Are in the Regular Math Class?

This important question should be addressed before a student begins a mentor-paced program. While other students are in the regular math class, the student might work on mentor-assigned homework, read, work on the computer, or go to the library. We recommend that students in a mentor-paced program be included in group activities such as classroom games. However, these students should not be required to sit through the regular mathematics class or complete the regular math assignments if they are already working with a mentor on more advanced mathematics.

For the students in a mentor-paced program, it is important to provide a quiet setting with adult supervision so they can work on mentor-assigned homework while other students are in the regular math class. These special arrangements should be structured so that students do not feel ostracized or punished. Parents, mentors, school personnel, and the students themselves should discuss this and ensure that all parties involved are fully aware of the reasons for the special arrangements (Lupkowski & Assouline, 1992).

### Many Teachers Worry That Removing Talented Students From Their Classes Will Remove an Important Role Model for Average Students

In light of the cooperative learning movement that was promoted in the 1990s and remains popular in many schools, this remains a common myth. This concern is also voiced in statements that question whether ability grouping is beneficial to students. Schunk (1987) has stated that effective role models must be somewhat close in ability to those who would benefit from exposure to the models. Social comparison theory tells us that average students would not look upon exceptionally talented students as academic role models. In other words, average students view exceptionally talented students as too different from themselves.

There are other related issues. For example, large differences in ability within a classroom may promote arrogance on the part of the high-ability student. Conversely, if a teacher teaches a mixed-ability group at a high level and fast pace (appropriate for the extremely mathematically talented student in the classroom), an average student may experience unnecessary pressure from a set-up for failure. Furthermore, having mixed-ability grouping in mathematics with extreme variation in aptitude increases the teacher's management problems. On the other hand, teachers of students who participate in a mentor-paced program can concentrate on tailoring their teaching to the majority of their students and can be satisfied that their highly able students' needs are also being met (Lupkowski & Assouline, 1992).

### How Are Student Evaluation Issues Determined?

For work that is completed, students should receive both a grade and credit. There are many different ways in which school personnel can address this issue. For example, a teacher might add special notes to a student's report card to indicate what grade-level mathematics the student studied that term. If the student works with a mentor outside of the school setting, the mentor might supply the student's grade to the regular classroom teacher to record on the report card. Sometimes, mentors give chapter tests to teachers to administer, and the grades on those chapter tests are used to determine the grade for that marking period. These careful records of a student's progress are essential; they are needed when the time comes to make placement decisions, especially if the student transitions from a mentor-paced program into the school-based curriculum (Lupkowski & Assouline, 1992).

### How Do Educators Respond to the Mentor-Paced Student's Need for Acceleration?

By definition, mathematically talented students who participate in a mentor-paced program will be accelerated in mathematics. These students are participating in a program that is designed to move them through the curriculum at a challenging pace. Some educators will be very pleased by this acceleration, while others will be extremely defensive. Research over the last 50 years has shown that acceleration for mathematically talented students is an appropriate and useful option (e.g., Southern & Jones, 1991; see also Chapter 6 for a detailed discussion of the merits of acceleration, along with supporting research).

Before having students begin participating in the DT→PI process, parents and school personnel should discuss the long-term plans for the students' mathematics education (Lupkowski & Assouline, 1992). To illustrate, if exceptionally mathematically talented students participate in a mentor-paced program for a period of time, they may be ready to take high school mathematics courses (e.g., algebra and geometry) several years before they are chronologically old enough to be high school students. If these students are to study mathematics in a regular mathematics class, special transportation arrangements may have to be made so they can move from one building to another in the middle of the day. Scheduling math class will also be an issue. For example, it would be most efficient if math classes were offered at the same time so that accelerated students wouldn't have to miss class in another subject in order to take the right level of mathematics. Also, as students move through the grades, they may complete all of the mathematics courses a school district has available before they graduate from high school. Those students might need to take more advanced math courses through a local college or university or through a distance-learning program. Then, their study of mathematics will not be interrupted.

### How Long Does a Mentor-Paced Program Last?

Mentor-paced programs can last for a few hours or for a few years. The DT→PI model is highly individualized, and the length of time in which the student participates in the program depends on his or her needs. We like to think of the mentor-paced program as a bridge that prepares students to take the next level of mathematics in their own schools. One precocious student who needed to use the DT→PI model for a short period of time was preparing to take Algebra II with older students. She spent the last several weeks of the summer meeting with a mentor to ensure that she had mastered the concepts taught in Algebra I, which she had never taken in a formal course. In other cases, students might need the program for one semester or for a complete school year. An extreme case is that of an exceptionally mathematically talented student who studied high school geometry when he was 10 years old. That young man needed to participate in a mentor-paced program for several years in order to receive the right level of mathematics, while still being able to take other subjects with his agemates.

Participation in a mentor-paced program is not an all-or-nothing activity. Students might participate in a program for a period of time, reenter the regular mathematics class (at a higher level) for a year or more, and then find that they are no longer being adequately challenged by the level of mathematics they are studying. These students might return to a mentor-paced program for another period of time.

In order to make the best use of resources, we suggest that students complete a mentor-paced program and reenter a classroom setting (most likely with older students) as soon as is practical. There are many considerations involved in deciding when to reenter the classroom setting. One consideration is the student's level of precocity and another is the level of cooperation from the school system. The more precocious the student and the less cooperative the system, the longer a mentor-paced program needs to last.

For example, we recognize that the instruction prescribed for a third grader included in the DT→PI process will be more prolonged and more individualized than the instruction prescribed for a sixth grader. We are not advocating having these young students rush into Algebra I. We want to be sure their formal reasoning skills are well developed so that they are indeed ready to study challenging mathematics. Students in this situation have the opportunity to participate in a great deal of challenging, enriching mathematics (see Chapter 7). For third graders and fourth graders in particular, the DT→PI process will probably require a longer term commitment and more resources.

### Is There a Cost to the Program?

Yes. The mentors are not expected to volunteer their time. In fact, volunteering is not considered a good idea because neither party feels the same sense of investment if they do not make a financial commitment, as well as an intellectual commitment.

If the mentoring occurs outside of school, parents are expected to pay the mentor an hourly fee that would be comparable to the fee parents usually pay tutors in that area. Parents may also need to pay for the cost of books and materials. Ideally, the local school district should pay for the program, especially if it is offered in school and mentors are school district employees. However, parents should not let the political realities, which may not match the ideal, interfere with implementation of the program.

## Who Coordinates the Mentor-Paced Program?

Successful mentor program coordinators have been university staff members, gifted education teachers, or other members of the school staff familiar with standardized testing procedures and the school's mathematics curriculum. The person who coordinates the program identifies students who would benefit from the program, assesses their mathematical abilities and achievements via above-level tests, and matches them with appropriate mentors. Coordinators regularly consult with mentors to get updates on the students' progress and to help them secure appropriate materials for their students to use. The coordinator frequently administers posttests and keeps school personnel informed of the student's progress. Many times, the coordinator becomes the student's advocate, especially in the case of a school district that resists having students participate in a mentor-paced program. In this situation, the coordinator needs to be aware of and present to school personnel the research demonstrating the success of these types of programs. One often-overlooked task of a program coordinator is program evaluation. Evaluation serves many purposes, including improving decision-making for future students and adjusting the program to serve current students' needs (Borland, 1997).

In the situation where only one student in a district participates in a mentor-paced program, the mentor takes on the coordinator's role. In this case, the mentor communicates directly with the parents, classroom teacher, and principal concerning the student's progress.

Mentor-paced programs such as the one described here are conducive to Clasen and Hanson's (1987) system of double mentoring. In double mentoring, two mentors attend to the student's needs. The first mentor, the classroom teacher, attends to the student's developmental needs, while the second mentor, the mathematics mentor, attends to the student's needs in mathematics. Thus, the two mentors work in tandem to foster both the student's intellectual and social/emotional development. Double mentoring is enhanced by a program coordinator.

## What Makes the DT→PI Process a Success?

Mentor-paced programs are most successful if:

1. Mentor, school personnel, parents, and student cooperate.
2. The mentor is involved in Steps 2 and 3, Diagnostic Testing and Readministering of Missed Items. These activities aid the mentor in developing a clear understanding of what the student is ready to learn.
3. The mentor sets goals and outlines a linear progression of topics as part of developing a systematic plan for the student.
4. The mentor has a good understanding of the scope and sequence of the K–12 mathematics curriculum.
5. The curriculum is challenging and enjoyable (but not necessarily entertaining!).
6. There is a coordinator.
7. The student is excused from doing the classroom math work assigned to his or her age peers.
8. The student receives credit for completing the mentor-assigned work.
9. There is a clear plan for the student's future placement in mathematics.
10. There is a clear plan for program evaluation (see Borland, 1997).

## What Types of Accommodations Might Be Established for Students Who Are Talented in Mathematics, But Would Not Benefit From a Mentor-Paced Approach?

We have found that the DT→PI model, as it is described in this chapter, is most effective for exceptionally talented youngsters who demonstrate significant motivation to move ahead in mathematics. For other students who may be mathematically talented, but not extremely so, it may be necessary to develop other accommodations. Various accommodations that might be appropriate for these students are discussed in Chapter 6, including ability grouping and enrichment within the regular classroom.

The section on Resources provides an extensive list of materials that parents and teachers might use to enrich the mathematics curriculum. These include books, mathematics contests, computer programs, and other activities. Additional suggestions for enriching the mathematics curriculum for talented students are included in Chapter 7.

### How Effective is the DT→PI Model?

Most of the research with the DT→PI model has been conducted with students in seventh grade taking the SAT and subsequently completing high school mathematics courses. Their stories are highly successful. For example, students scoring 600 or above on SAT-Mathematics completed two high school mathematics courses in just 50 hours of in-class instructional time (Bartkovich & Mezynski, 1981). Many students have mastered an entire year's worth of material with just 75 hours of instruction (Olszewski-Kubilius, Kulieke, Willis, & Krasney, 1989). Students participating in fast-paced classes do not suffer ill effects in their long-term retention of the subject matter (Benbow 1992b; Benbow, Perkins, & Stanley, 1983) and perform very well in the next course in the sequence offered in their schools. For example, most students completing Algebra I in a DT→PI program were placed in Algebra II or Geometry and earned As in that course (Mills, Ablard, & Lynch, 1992). Olszewski-Kubilius (1998) noted that, "Talent search summer programs have shown that some students can learn at a much faster rate and instruction can proceed at a much faster pace than heretofore believed without sacrificing the level of subject mastery or preparation for future courses, all with higher student satisfaction" (p. 111).

## Conclusion

The goal of the DT→PI model is to match the level and pace of mathematics instruction to the academic needs of the student. Because mathematics is presented at an individualized pace in the DT→PI model, each student covers the material at an appropriate rate. Students are not required to study topics they already know well, which gives them more time to study new and challenging topics in greater depth than would be possible in the regular classroom. Students cannot move on to the next topic before attaining mastery, and, in this way, the model is self-correcting. The DT→PI model also avoids the pitfalls of the gaps that may occur if a student skips a grade. The student is consistently challenged by the pace at which the advanced material is presented.

Another benefit of the DT→PI model, in addition to ensuring that the student is consistently challenged in mathematics, is that these students avoid developing bad habits such as not writing out or checking their work when solving problems or doing complicated computations. They have to develop good mathematical habits of mind because they are working on difficult topics at a rapid pace. Students also learn that testing is useful for reasons other than evaluation; in the DT→PI model, testing is diagnostic and is used to determine where instruction begins.

We would like to emphasize the importance of having parents, school personnel, and the student cooperate in making this process work. All individuals involved must consider the ramifications of participation in the DT→PI procedure. Important issues to consider before embarking on this procedure are earning school credit for advanced work completed, placing the student in advanced courses in the future, issues of credit and placement for the student, and how the mentoring experience will fit into the school's curriculum and grading procedure.

The DT→PI model allows students who are exceptionally able in mathematics to progress at an appropriately accelerated rate through a mathematics curriculum. These few students will move more rapidly through the school's curriculum than is typical. This can be an accelerative model, or what Elkind (1988) called "tailoring." According to Elkind,

Promotion [in grade placement or subject matter] of intellectually gifted children is simply another way of attempting to match the curriculum to the child's abilities, not to accelerate those abilities. Accordingly, the promotion of intellectually gifted children in no way contradicts the accepted view of the limits of training on development, nor the negative effects of hurrying. Indeed, the positive effects of promoting intellectually gifted children provide additional evidence for the benefits of developmentally appropriate curricula. (p. 2)

The DT→PI approach provides a nice alternative to whole-grade or subject skipping. This is just one option for talented students, their families, and teachers to consider. Many more options for talented youth are discussed in Chapter 6.

# 5 Talent Searches for Elementary Students

## Key Points

- The goal of an academic talent search is to discover, via above-level testing, students who are ready for advanced academic challenges that are not typically offered as part of the regular school curriculum.

- Academic talent searches have been in existence for over three decades. The first talent search was conducted in one community and served only a few hundred students in grades 7 and 8.

- The talent search model has grown to serve students in grades 2–9, is conducted throughout the United States and several other countries, and has expanded to include several types of above-level tests.

- Talent search participants, although much younger than the students for whom the tests were intended, typically earn higher scores on the tests than the students for whom the test was developed. Thus, initial concerns that students who participated in the talent search would be unnecessarily frustrated are unfounded.

- Advantages of participating in a talent search include educational diagnosis, tailoring recommendations to the abilities of the student, educational opportunities, educational information, and scholarships.

- The talent search model is more comprehensive than above-level testing. University-based talent searches also provide summer and academic-year programs for identified students, by-mail programs, and teacher training, and they conduct research on the effectiveness of the model.

IN THE LATE 1960s, JULIAN STANLEY PIONEERED the talent search concept by offering a college entrance exam, the Scholastic Aptitude Test (SAT, now called the Scholastic Assessment Test, SAT I) to two bright eighth graders. These two boys had already performed very well in school, and they were searching for ways to be challenged (Stanley, 1996). Stanley used Leta Hollingworth's (1942) concept of above-level testing when he selected the SAT. He knew that bright youngsters who took grade-level standardized tests often got all or almost all of the items correct. Instead of developing his own test to measure academic talent, Stanley used a test that was designed for older students. He chose the SAT because it was an excellent test of reasoning ability with sufficiently difficult questions that were not overly dependent upon exposure to a specific curriculum (Stanley, 1991). In addition, the SAT was carefully developed and normed, was secure, and the scores were easily understood and interpreted by school personnel. The two young students performed very well on the SAT, and Stanley realized it had the potential to identify talented youngsters who could reason extremely well.

Stanley and two of his graduate students then administered the SAT to seventh graders in a large testing in January 1972, and the talent search was born. Since that time, under the auspices of a university-based talent search, hundreds of thousands of students have taken the SAT (now the SAT I) or the ACT, developed by American College Testing, Inc. These talent searches are now available in every state and in a few countries outside of the United States. Students who participate in these university-based talent searches are then eligible for many educational services, including summer programs, newsletters, parent meetings, and by-mail programs (Assouline & Lupkowski-Shoplik, 1997; Cohn, 1991; Lupkowski-Shoplik, Benbow, Assouline, & Brody, 2003; Stanley & Benbow, 1986).

Researchers and program planners realized that the same concept that worked so well for seventh-grade students could be adapted for younger students. In 1981, Sanford J. Cohn pilot-tested a search for academically talented students younger than seventh grade at Arizona State University. As the first researcher to adapt the talent search process for younger students, Cohn (1991) used the Sequential Tests of Educational Progress (STEP) and the School and College Ability Test (SCAT) for students as young as age 7. In 1985, Cohn brought this concept to the Center for the Advancement of Academically Talented Youth (CTY) at Johns Hopkins University, where a Young Student's Program has grown steadily ever since.

Large-scale talent searches for students in sixth grade, or younger took off in the 1990s (Lupkowski & Assouline, 1993; Mills & Barnett, 1992). The foundation for our work with extending the talent search concept to students in sixth grade and younger began when we were postdoctoral fellows with Julian Stanley's Study of Mathematically Precocious Youth (SMPY) at Johns Hopkins University in the late 1980s. At SMPY, we frequently received calls from parents of mathematically talented fourth and fifth graders who were looking for more challenges. At the time, there were no large, systematic talent searches for students younger than seventh grade to refer the families to, so we realized there was a need for work in this area. Building on Stanley's talent search concept, we began by testing a few students individually. As we were initiating the Elementary Student Talent Search, the Center for Talented Youth (CTY) at Johns Hopkins University began using the Upper Level of the SSAT in a widespread talent search (Mills & Barnett, 1992). CTY worked with the Educational Testing Service (ETS) to develop the PLUS test as an above-level test for fifth and sixth graders in its Young Students Talent Search (Johns Hopkins University, 1999). CTY now offers programs to elementary-age students on an annual basis.

For our above-level test, we experimented with the Lower Level of the Secondary School Admission Test (SSAT-L), which was designed for students in grades 5–7. We administered this test to third, fourth, and fifth graders, and we found that the test effectively discriminated among mathematically talented students (Lupkowski & Assouline, 1993) and was useful for identifying students for special programs (Lupkowski, Assouline, & Vestal, 1992).

We were pleased with the results of our "talent searching" with third through fifth graders and broadened our use of the SSAT-L in several large talent searches in Texas, Iowa, and Pennsylvania. After using the SSAT-L for a few years, we decided to try another test that had just come on the scene— the EXPLORE, developed over a 3-year period by American College Testing (ACT). The EXPLORE met the same requirements that the SSAT-L had previously met: It was a carefully developed, standardized, nationally normed test of mathematical and verbal reasoning. The EXPLORE offered additional advantages:

1. EXPLORE contained a measure of Science Reasoning, which was not explicitly measured on the SSAT-L.
2. ACT was willing to work with us to establish local test sites that would be convenient for our students.
3. EXPLORE was less expensive to administer, resulting in lower costs for student participants.

The first Elementary Student Talent Search using the EXPLORE test was conducted by Susan Assouline at the University of Iowa and Ann Lupkowski-Shoplik at Carnegie Mellon University in January 1993. A total of 4,089 Pennsylvania and Iowa students took the EXPLORE at that time (a detailed presentation of the Iowa results is found in Colangelo, Assouline, & Lu, 1994). We have used the EXPLORE each year since then. The Center for Talent Development at Northwestern University and the Talent Identification Program at Duke University began using EXPLORE in 1994, and the Elementary Student Talent Search has continued to grow. Today, approximately 18,000 students per year take EXPLORE as part of a university-based Elementary Student Talent Search (ACT, 1999). Students in all 50 states in the U.S., as well as in parts of Canada and Australia, have access to above-level testing and subsequent advanced programming in a variety of subjects through one of the talent searches listed in Table 5.1. Students may choose from the EXPLORE test or the PLUS test. (For more information about PLUS, contact the Center for Talented Youth, Johns Hopkins University, 3400 N. Charles St., Baltimore, MD 21218). The remainder of this chapter will focus on the EXPLORE test.

## How Are Students Selected for the Talent Search?

Students first take a standardized, nationally normed achievement test such as the Iowa Tests of Basic Skills (ITBS), Stanford Achievement Test, or Metropolitan Achievement Test, usually done as part of the school's regular testing program (Colangelo, Assouline, & Lu, 1994). Criteria vary somewhat from program to program, but the university-based talent searches usually use the 95th or 97th percentile cutoff. Research has shown that the 95th percentile is an appropriate cutoff for talented third through sixth graders taking the EXPLORE test (Lupkowski-Shoplik & Swiatek, 1999). Students scoring at or above this cutoff on the Composite, Math Total, Language Total, Vocabulary, Reading, or Science subtests are recommended for further testing. These students have already demonstrated that they can do very well on tests designed for their age group. In fact, they have reached or are near the ceiling of the test. They have answered all or almost

**Table 5.1**
**University-Based Academic Talent Searches**

| Program | Address and Web Site | Type of Talent Search |
|---|---|---|
| Carnegie Mellon Institute for Talented Elementary Students | Carnegie Mellon Univ. 4902 Forbes Ave. #6261 Pittsburgh, PA 15213 (412) 268-1629 http://www.cmu.edu/ cmites | Elementary for grades 3–6 offered in Pennsylvania. |
| The Belin-Blank Center | The Univ. of Iowa Blank Honors Center Iowa City, IA 52242 (319) 335-6148 http://www.uiowa.edu/ ~belinctr | For third–ninth graders in many states, as well as Australia and parts of New Zealand and Canada. |
| Talent Identification Program | Duke Univ. Durham, NC 27708 (919) 684-3847 http://www.tip.duke.edu | Elementary and middle school talent searches offered in many states. |
| Center for Talented Youth | Johns Hopkins Univ. 3400 N. Charles St. Baltimore, MD 21218 (410) 516-0337 http://www.jhu.edu/~gifted/ index.html | For second–eighth graders in many states. |
| Center for Talent Development | Northwestern Univ. 617 Dartmouth Pl. Evanston, IL 60208 (847) 491-3782 http://ctdnet.acns.nwu.edu | For third–eighth graders offered in many states. |

| | | |
|---|---|---|
| Rocky Mountain Talent Search | The University of Denver Denver, CO 80208 (303) 871-2983 http://www.du.edu/ education/ces/rmts.html | For fifth–ninth graders offered in many states. |
| Academic Talent Search | California State Univ. (Sacramento) 6000 J St. Sacramento, CA 95819-6098 (916) 278-7032 http://edweb.csus.edu/ projects/ATS/ | For elementary and middle school students offered for northern California students. |
| Halbert Robinson Center for the Study of Capable Youth | The Univ. of Washington Box 351630 Seattle, WA 98195 (206) 543-4160 http://depts.washington. edu/cscy/ | For fifth–eighth graders in Washington State. |
| Gifted Education Research, Resource and Information Centre | Univ. of New South Wales GERRIC School of Education Sydney 2052, Australia +612 9385 1972 http://www.arts.unsw.edu. au/gerric | Elementary (Primary) student talent search. |
| Centre for Gifted Education | University of Calgary 170 Education Block 2500 University Dr. NW Calgary, AB, Canada T2N 1N4 (403) 220-7799 http://www.acs.ucalgary.ca/ ~gifteduc | Elementary student talent search. |

all of the items correctly, and the test does not contain enough difficult items to measure their abilities accurately. Therefore, taking a more difficult test that was designed for older students is appropriate.

Elementary Student Talent Search participants pay fees ranging from $40 to $60 to cover the costs of test administration, mailings, educational information, and newsletters and other program information. Students on the free or reduced-cost lunch program at school may receive a fee waiver.

## What Test Is Used?

To measure their abilities more accurately, students take an above-level test. In this case, third through sixth grade students take EXPLORE. An above-level test that contains more difficult items (and thus has a higher ceiling) allows students to demonstrate the full range of their abilities. Above-level tests spread out the scores of able students, helping us to differentiate talented students from exceptionally talented students. This information is useful for good educational planning. Elementary Student Talent Search participants take EXPLORE as part of a special test administration for young students.

EXPLORE was developed by American College Testing (ACT, 1997a) and first used as a test for eighth graders in 1992. It is a multiple-choice instrument and includes the following tests: English, Mathematics, Reading, and Science Reasoning. The tests are designed to measure eighth-grade students' "curriculum-related knowledge and the complex cognitive skills important for future education and careers" (ACT, 1997a, p. 4). Each of the four multiple-choice EXPLORE tests takes 30 minutes, and scale scores are reported on a range of 1–25. The Composite is an average of the four tests. Usually, when students take the EXPLORE, they take all four tests.

The EXPLORE–English test contains 40 items and is comprised of two subtests: (1) Usage/Mechanics, which measures a student's understanding of standard written English (punctuation, grammar, etc.), and (2) Rhetorical Skills, which measures a student's understanding of the use of strategy, organization, and style in writing.

EXPLORE–Mathematics is a 30-item test that measures mathematical reasoning, rather than the ability to do involved computations or memorize formulas. The Mathematics test emphasizes the ability to solve practical quantitative problems and covers three areas: basic skills, application, and analysis. Topics include prealgebra, elementary algebra, geometry, and statistics/probability. Students have calculators available when taking the test.

The 30 items on the EXPLORE–Reading test measure reading comprehension by focusing on skills needed when studying written materials from different subject areas. Students must derive meaning from three prose passages; determine implicit meanings; and draw conclusions, comparisons, and generalizations.

The EXPLORE–Science Reasoning test contains 28 items presenting sets of scientific information in one of three different formats: data representation (graphs, tables, and other schematic forms), research summaries (descriptions of several related experiments), or conflicting viewpoints (descriptions of several related hypotheses inconsistent with each other). The Science Reasoning test measures how well students understand scientific information and draw conclusions from it.

All four tests of EXPLORE are scored on a scale ranging from 1–25 and were normed on a national sample of eighth graders. Average scores of Elementary Student Talent Search participants from 1996–1999, as well as the eighth-grade normative sample, are reported in Table 5.2.

## Results of the Above-Level Testing

Research findings on the EXPLORE test have been consistent each year. The most important finding is illustrated in Figure 5.1. Namely, the scores of those students who were already in the top 5% of their age group (and, therefore, at or

| Grade | English | Reading | Math | Science Reasoning | Comp. |
|---|---|---|---|---|---|
| 3rd grade (n = 894) | 11.2 (3.8) | 10.1 (2.8) | 9.6 (4.0) | 11.5 (3.8) | 10.7 (3.0) |
| 4th grade (n = 8,970) | 13.5 (3.7) | 11.7 (2.7) | 12.3 (4.3) | 13.5 (3.6) | 12.9 (2.9) |
| 5th grade (n = 23,355) | 16.1 (3.5) | 14.0 (3.0) | 15.4 (4.5) | 16.0 (3.7) | 15.5 (3.0) |
| 6th grade (n = 21,445) | 18.0 (3.3) | 16.6 (3.4) | 18.0 (4.1) | 18.1 (3.7) | 17.8 (2.9) |
| 8th grade norm group (n = 14,000) | 14.0 (4.8) | 14.3 (4.2) | 13.6 (5.8) | 14.1 (4.6) | 14.1 (4.4) |

**Table 5.2
Average EXPLORE Scores**

*Note.* Standard deviations are in parentheses.
Third-, fourth-, fifth-, and sixth-grade scores are based on a national sample of students participating in the Elementary Student Talent Search in 1996–1999. Eighth-grade scores are based on the national sample of eighth graders reported in ACT, 1997.

near the ceiling of the grade-level test) were spread out when they took the EXPLORE as an above-level test (Colangelo, Assouline, & Lu, 1994; Lupkowski-Shoplik & Swiatek, 1999). Section A of Figure 5.1 shows the normal curve that illustrates the results from all students in a particular grade taking a grade-level achievement test. When the top 5% of those students take an above-level test such as EXPLORE, their test scores are spread out into a new normal curve (see Section B). Section B shows that most Elementary Student Talent Search students earned scores in the middle of the EXPLORE range, while a small number earned low scores and a small number

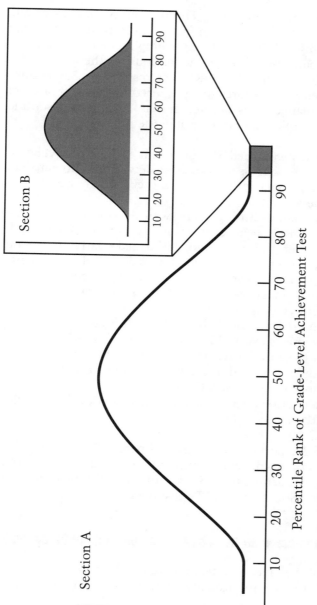

**Figure 5.1 Above-Level Test Score Distribution for Students Scroring High on Grade-Level Test**

*Note.* From "Talent searches: A model for the discovery and development of academic talent" (p. 171), by S. G. Assouline & A. Lupkowski-Shoplik, in *Handbook of Gifted Education* (2nd ed.), ed. N. Colangelo & G. A. Davis, 1997, Boston: Allyn and Bacon. Copyright © 1997 by Allyn and Bacon. Reprinted with permission.

of students earned high scores. Through our research, we have concluded that the EXPLORE effectively discriminates among students at high ability levels, thus helping us to make more appropriate educational recommendations for them.

In looking at the EXPLORE test results for Elementary Student Talent Search participants similar to those reported in Table 5.2, Colangelo, Assouline, and Lu (1994) and Assouline and Lupkowski-Shoplik (1997) noted the following:

1.  The scores earned by students at each grade level consistently increased (fourth graders scored higher than third graders, fifth graders scored higher than fourth graders, etc.).
2.  Not many third graders were encouraged to take EXPLORE because it is so far above grade level. However, those who did, performed relatively well on this challenging test, which was designed for students with 5 more years of educational experience.
3.  Fourth graders performed close to the average score for eighth graders.
4.  Fifth graders scored above the eighth-grade average on all subtests except Mathematics, and those scores were very close to the average score earned by eighth graders.
5.  Sixth graders performed better than eighth graders on all four tests of EXPLORE.
6.  Students seemed to have the most difficulty with the Mathematics subtest.

Table 5.3 reports frequencies and percentile rankings for third through sixth grade students participating in the Elementary Student Talent Search in 1996 through 1999 in the Midwest, Southeast, and Pennsylvania.

## How Can the Scores Be Used by Parents and School Personnel?

Results of above-level testing are much more useful than grade-level testing for exceptionally talented students. On

## Table 5.3
## Frequencies and Percentile Rankings on the EXPLORE–Mathematics Test for Elementary Student Talent Search Participants, Grades 3–6, 1996–99

| Score | Grade 3 Local Freq | PB | Nat'l PB | Grade 4 Local Freq | PB | Nat'l PB | Grade 5 Local Freq | PB | Nat'l PB | Grade 6 Local Freq | PB | Nat'l PB |
|---|---|---|---|---|---|---|---|---|---|---|---|---|
| 25 | 2 | 99 | 99 | 6 | 99 | 99 | 70 | 99 | 99 | 367 | 99 | 99 |
| 24 | 0 | 99 | 99 | 1 | 99 | 99 | 57 | 99 | 99 | 317 | 98 | 99 |
| 23 | 1 | 99 | 98 | 9 | 99 | 98 | 104 | 99 | 98 | 545 | 97 | 98 |
| 22 | 0 | 99 | 96 | 12 | 99 | 96 | 153 | 99 | 96 | 764 | 94 | 96 |
| 21 | 4 | 99 | 94 | 15 | 99 | 94 | 259 | 98 | 94 | 925 | 91 | 94 |
| 20 | 0 | 99 | 91 | 24 | 99 | 91 | 373 | 97 | 91 | 1138 | 86 | 91 |
| 19 | 1 | 99 | 87 | 37 | 99 | 87 | 512 | 96 | 87 | 1419 | 81 | 87 |
| 18 | 5 | 99 | 83 | 135 | 99 | 83 | 1430 | 93 | 83 | 2949 | 75 | 83 |
| 17 | 9 | 99 | 77 | 141 | 97 | 77 | 1225 | 87 | 77 | 1880 | 61 | 77 |
| 16 | 24 | 98 | 72 | 494 | 96 | 72 | 3283 | 82 | 72 | 3717 | 52 | 72 |
| 15 | 13 | 95 | 62 | 398 | 90 | 62 | 2076 | 68 | 62 | 1755 | 35 | 62 |
| 14 | 22 | 93 | 56 | 673 | 86 | 56 | 2687 | 59 | 56 | 1850 | 27 | 56 |
| 13 | 41 | 91 | 46 | 888 | 78 | 46 | 2936 | 48 | 46 | 1362 | 18 | 46 |
| 12 | 139 | 86 | 38 | 1956 | 68 | 38 | 4094 | 35 | 38 | 1522 | 12 | 38 |
| 11 | 106 | 71 | 26 | 1038 | 47 | 26 | 1508 | 18 | 26 | 415 | 5 | 26 |
| 10 | 104 | 59 | 20 | 1106 | 35 | 20 | 1248 | 11 | 20 | 297 | 3 | 20 |
| 9 | 175 | 47 | 13 | 1181 | 23 | 13 | 923 | 6 | 13 | 191 | 1 | 13 |
| 8 | 94 | 28 | 7 | 453 | 10 | 7 | 293 | 2 | 7 | 47 | 1 | 7 |
| 7 | 92 | 17 | 4 | 316 | 5 | 4 | 128 | 1 | 4 | 26 | 1 | 4 |
| 6 | 40 | 7 | 2 | 70 | 1 | 2 | 26 | 1 | 2 | 5 | 1 | 2 |
| 5 | 15 | 3 | 1 | 23 | 1 | 1 | 8 | 1 | 1 | 1 | 1 | 1 |
| 4 | 6 | 1 | 1 | 13 | 1 | 1 | 1 | 1 | 1 | 0 | 1 | 1 |
| 3 | 1 | 1 | 1 | 2 | 1 | 1 | 1 | 1 | 1 | 1 | 1 | 1 |
| 2 | 1 | 1 | 1 | 1 | 1 | 1 | 0 | 1 | 1 | 0 | 1 | 1 |
| 1 | 0 | 1 | 1 | 0 | 1 | 1 | 0 | 1 | 1 | 0 | 1 | 1 |
| N Talent Search | 895 | | | 8892 | | | 23395 | | | 21493 | | |
| Mean | 10.1 | | | 11.7 | | | 14.0 | | | 16.6 | | |
| SD | 2.8 | | | 2.7 | | | 3.0 | | | 3.4 | | |
| Nat'l Mean | 14.3 | | | 14.3 | | | 14.3 | | | 14.3 | | |
| SD | 4.2 | | | 4.2 | | | 4.2 | | | 4.2 | | |

*Note.* In 2001, ACT, Inc., rescaled the EXPLORE tests so that the EXPLORE scores were aligned with the two other tests in their assessment program, the PLAN (10th grade) and the ACT Assessment (11th and 12th grade). The changes were very minor. In rescaling the test, the "Standards for Transition" for the EXPLORE tests were also refined. Throughout this book, our discussion is based upon the most up-to-date data available during the writing (1996–1999 scores). In this book, all of the case students and reports to which EXPLORE are referenced are based upon the 1996–1999 scores. Parents and educators who used EXPLORE as an above-level test for their students should participate in one of the university-based talent searches to have the most up-to-date norming and programming recommendations. As with all testing companies, ACT, Inc., will continue to update their testing programs.

grade-level tests, students "bump" against the ceiling of the test and do not have an opportunity to show their abilities. To illustrate this, consider the example of two students: Chris and Terry. Both students took the California Achievement Test (CAT) in fourth grade. They both performed exceptionally well on the Mathematics sections of the test (see Table 5.4). Their CAT grade-level scores were identical, which might cause educators to believe that they would need similar curricular adjustments in mathematics. When they took the EXPLORE test, however, Terry's EXPLORE–Math scale score was 24 (out of a possible 25, placing him at the 99th percentile when compared to the eighth-grade norm group), while Chris scored 10 (placing him at the 20th percentile when compared to the eighth-grade norm group).

Although these two students appeared to have identical profiles on the grade-level standardized test (the California Achievement Test), they clearly have very different abilities and needs in mathematics, as demonstrated by their scores on the EXPLORE. Unfortunately, the two students are currently placed in the regular classroom for mathematics. Although they are in the gifted program at their respective schools, the programs stress enrichment, therefore they do not receive any differentiation for mathematics. Both students need additional challenges in mathematics, including participating in contests and competitions, being grouped with other talented students for mathematics instruction, and perhaps compacting a course sequence by taking 2 years of mathematics in 1 year. Terry's needs in mathematics are even more pronounced. He would benefit from all of the options previously suggested, plus individually paced instruction during the school year or summer, as well as course skipping or grade skipping, if all academic areas are advanced.

## Standards for Transition for the EXPLORE Mathematics Test

Parents and school personnel can use information developed by the American College Testing Program (ACT) to help

| Test | Chris | Terry |
|---|---|---|
| **Table 5.4**<br>**Grade-Level Test Scores**<br>**and Above-Level Test Scores of Two Students** | | |
| Grade-Level Test, Fourth Grade: California Achievement Test, Math Concepts | 99th percentile | 99th percentile |
| California Achievement Test, Math Problems | 99th percentile | 99th percentile |
| California Achievement Test, Math Total | 99th percentile | 99th percentile |
| Above-Level Test, Fifth Grade: EXPLORE–Mathematics (percentile compared to eighth graders) | Scale score = 10 (20th percentile) | Scale score = 24 (99th percentile) |

them interpret students' EXPLORE scores and make appropriate recommendations for them. ACT has developed the "Standards for Transition" (ACT, 1997b), which are statements describing what students who score in various score ranges are likely to know and to be able to do.

[The Standards for Transition] reflect the progression and complexity of skills in the four academic areas measured in EXPLORE—English, mathematics, reading, and science reasoning—and are provided for five score ranges (9–11, 12–15, 16–19, 20–23, and 24–25) along the EXPLORE score scale. Students who score between 1 and 8 are most likely beginning to develop the skills and knowledge described in the 9–11 score range. EXPLORE is designed to measure students' progressive development of skills and knowledge in the same four academic areas as PLAN and the ACT Assessment. (ACT, 1997b)

The statements below describe what students who score in the specified score ranges on the EXPLORE–Mathematics test are likely to know and be able to do. All information regarding the Standards for Transition, as well as the statements describing what students who score in the specified score range are likely to know and be able to do, were developed by ACT and copyrighted by ACT in 1997. Used with permission.

### Score Range 9–11

Students can order whole numbers and perform one-operation computation with whole numbers and decimals. In probability, statistics, and data analysis, they can identify the relative size of entries in a table or chart. Their algebra skills include demonstrating some intuitive knowledge of expressions and equations (e.g., identify an expression for a total as b + g).

### Score Range 12–15

Students can solve problems in one or two steps using whole numbers, recognize one-digit factors, perform common conversions (e.g., inches to feet or hours to minutes), and find equivalent values of coins. In probability, statistics, and data analysis, they can use information provided in a table or chart that meets a given criterion to compute another value, and they can compute the average of a list of whole numbers. Their algebra skills include the ability to solve equations in the form $x + a = b$, where $a$ and $b$ are whole numbers or decimals. Their geometry skills include the ability to identify the location of a point with a positive coordinate on the number line and to estimate or calculate the length of a line segment based on other lengths given on a geometric figure.

### Score Range 16–19

Students can solve one-step and two-step arithmetic problems that have decimal numbers, and they exhibit knowledge of place value and rounding. In probability, statistics, and data analysis, they are able to use data from a table or chart combined with additional information to solve a mathematics problem, to solve routine average problems, and to exhibit some knowledge of the definition of probability. Their algebra skills include the ability to compute the value of expression by substituting whole numbers and to solve simple equations that involve whole numbers (e.g., $2x - 6 = 24$). They exhibit some knowledge of squaring numbers and inequalities (e.g., list values of $x$ such that $x < 5$ and $x > 1 + 2$). Their coordinate geometry skills include the ability to locate points on a number line and to exhibit elementary knowledge of concepts related to the coordinate plane (e.g., how to find an entry in a chart arranged in rows and columns). Their geometry skills include computing or identifying the perimeter of polygons when all side lengths are provided.

### Score Range 20–23

Students can solve straightforward problems involving rates, proportions, percentages, and fractions, and they can solve multistep problems in the context of money. In probability, statistics, and data analysis, they can translate data from one representation to another, find the average of numbers when given various settings, and comprehend the definition of probability. Their algebra skills include the ability to find the value of an expression by substituting decimals for unknown quantities, to solve simple equations when using decimal numbers, and to identify expressions of equations that model some settings. Their coordinate geometry skills include the ability to locate points using coordinates and properties of vertical and horizontal lines. Their geometry skills include exhibiting knowledge of right angles, straight angles, and 180 degrees as the sum of the angles in a triangle; computing the area and perimeter of some rectangles and triangles; and computing using formulas when all necessary information is provided.

## Score Range 24–25

Students can solve multistep arithmetic problems that involve planning or drawing conclusions based on given information, and they can solve problems involving proportional reasoning. In probability, statistics, and data analysis, they can manipulate data to solve problems, apply the concept of average to find an unknown value, and use the definition of probability to solve problems in various settings. Their algebra skills include the ability to interpret the meaning of a variable within the context of the problem and to identify an expression or equation that models the context of the problem. Their geometry skills include the ability to identify angles in relationship to transversal and parallel lines, compute the area and circumference of circles given only the necessary information, to compute the volume of rectangular prisms (boxes), and compute the perimeter of simple composite geometric figures with unknown side lengths.

## Programmatic Guidelines for Students Who Have Taken the Above-Level EXPLORE Test

After determining what students know and are able to do in mathematics, the next step is to devise an appropriate program for them. We used the 1996–1999 EXPLORE data collected on over 55,000 students who participated in the Elementary Student Talent Search to help us relate scores on the EXPLORE assessment to various program options. The program options we considered were based on over a decade of experience in creating programs for the range of talents demonstrated by the gifted students who take EXPLORE.

First, we divided EXPLORE scores into three ranges: Range A, Range B, and Range C (listed in Table 5.5). We deliberately made the ranges overlap (for example, for fourth graders, Mathematics Range A contains scores from 1 to 9, while Mathematics Range B contains scores from 9 to 12). This is done to emphasize that the skills associated with these scores are on a continuum. The score guidelines in Table 5.5 were not designed to be strict cutoffs. Rather, they were developed to give parents and educators an idea of how to interpret EXPLORE scores and help students to be challenged appropriately in school.

In Range A, each of the cells begins with 1 (for example, 1–8), and they constitute the bottom range of the EXPLORE scale. The astute reader will notice that, in the frequency distribution tables provided in Table 5.3, no students earned a score of 1 on the Mathematics test. In fact, very few students earned a score lower than 7.

Although Range B, the middle range, is rather narrow (only three or four points on the EXPLORE scale), this band represents the largest group of students taking the EXPLORE test. The students in this group have performed in approximately the top half of their age group when compared to other gifted students in the Elementary Student Talent Search.

Range C represents the highest scoring group of students in the Elementary Student Talent Search. Students in this group have scored well above other gifted students in their age group (approximately the top quarter of their age group when compared to other gifted students). This is the most talented group of students with the greatest need for a differentiated mathematics program. The reader will note that, for Range C, the third-grade scores appear to cover quite a broad range; however, most of the scores clustered around 12–16, with very few students earning scores above 16.

It is very important to note that students earning scores within Range C may still have different needs. For example, in the 1996–1999 sample, there were 894 third graders tested. Of

### Table 5.5
### EXPLORE—Mathematics Scores Ranges A, B, and C

| Range | Grade | | | |
|---|---|---|---|---|
| | 3 | 4 | 5 | 6 |
| A | 1–8 | 1–9 | 1–11 | 1–14 |
| B | 8–11 | 9–12 | 11–15 | 12–19 |
| C | 11–25 | 12–25 | 15–25 | 19–25 |

*Note.* Each of the ranges in a grade overlap to emphasize that the skills associated with these scores are on a continuum.

those, 2 students earned a score of 25, which means they have very different needs in mathematics compared to the 139 third graders who earned a score of 12, even though we have placed all of them in Range C.

Figure 5.2 illustrates the Pyramid of Educational Options for Elementary Student Talent Search participants (Assouline & Lupkowski-Shoplik, 1997). We related the options depicted on the pyramid to the Score Ranges A, B, and C. Again, we would like to emphasize that the scores we recommend for certain options are meant to be guidelines. These are not hard and fast cutoff scores. The options on the Pyramid are in ascending order, with enrichment-based options at the bottom and accelerative options at the top. All students participating in the Elementary Student Talent Search would benefit from the options listed at the bottom of the Pyramid, while the more accelerative options would be recommended for those students earning higher scores on the EXPLORE test. Acceleration and enrichment as programming options are thoroughly discussed in the next chapter.

Our goal in developing Ranges A, B, and C and relating scores to the options listed on the Pyramid of Educational

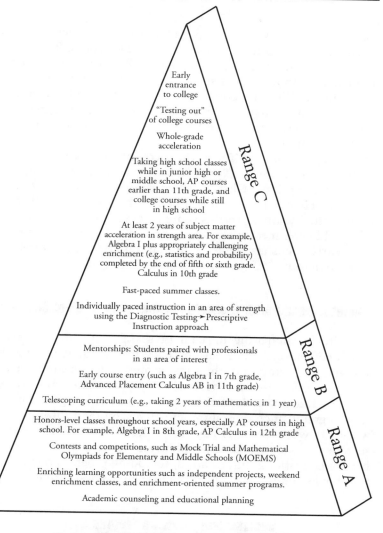

Early
entrance
to college

"Testing out"
of college courses

Whole-grade
acceleration

Taking high school classes
while in junior high or
middle school, AP courses
earlier than 11th grade, and
college courses while still
in high school

At least 2 years of subject matter
acceleration in strength area. For example,
Algebra I plus appropriately challenging
enrichment (e.g., statistics and probability)
completed by the end of fifth or sixth grade.
Calculus in 10th grade

Fast-paced summer classes.

Individually paced instruction in an area of strength
using the Diagnostic Testing → Prescriptive
Instruction approach

Mentorships: Students paired with professionals
in an area of interest

Early course entry (such as Algebra I in 7th grade,
Advanced Placement Calculus AB in 11th grade)

Telescoping curriculum (e.g., taking 2 years of mathematics in 1 year)

Honors-level classes throughout school years, especially AP courses in high
school. For example, Algebra I in 8th grade, AP Calculus in 12th grade

Contests and competitions, such as Mock Trial and Mathematical
Olympiads for Elementary and Middle Schools (MOEMS)

Enriching learning opportunities such as independent projects, weekend
enrichment classes, and enrichment-oriented summer programs.

Academic counseling and educational planning

Range C

Range B

Range A

# Figure 5.2 Pyramid of Educational Options

*Note.* Students who participate in above-level testing while in grade 3 and who earn a Mathematics score of 10 or lower should consider retaking the EXPLORE test in grades 4, 5, or both. Because students experience so much cognitive growth during those 2 years, recommendations regarding advanced coursework from testing subsequent to the testing in grade 3 are more valid.

Options was to give educators and families guidance in selecting appropriate options for their talented students. It is important to keep in mind that the score is not the only piece of information to use when selecting program options for a student. In addition to consideration of the locally available resources, one must also bear in mind the age and maturity level of the student, as well as the student's grade and individual learning style.

So, for Chris and Terry, the two students we mentioned earlier, we can use the Pyramid for guidance in selecting programmatic options. Chris's scaled score of 10 places him in Range A. He would benefit from all of the options listed at the base of the Pyramid. Terry's score places him in Range C, and he would benefit from all of the options listed in the Pyramid. He clearly needs acceleration in mathematics beyond the regular curriculum.

## What Happens After Students Participate in a Talent Search?

After participating in a talent search, students are given much educational information. They receive their test results and an interpretation of their test scores. Talent search personnel also offer them advice about appropriate educational options. Talent search participants also become eligible for special programs, including summer classes, by-mail tutorials, and weekend workshops. Finally, the elementary student talent searches provide resource booklets and newsletters containing lists of educational information, including program opportunities, books to read, and resources for parents and teachers.

## Summer and Weekend Programs Provided by the Talent Searches

Summer programs offer students the opportunity to study advanced topics in-depth with intellectual peers. The regional talent searches listed in Table 5.1 offer summer programs for talent search participants. These summer programs may be residential or nonresidential and may last from one to several weeks. Some programs are accelerative in nature, while others offer excellent academic enrichment courses. For example, ChESS (Challenges for Elementary School Students) is provided for participants in the Belin-Blank Exceptional Student Talent Search, offered by the University of Iowa. These classes are offered at various sites in Iowa, Florida, Illinois, and Nebraska. Classes for elementary students in this nonresidential program are typically 3 hours per day and last 1–2 weeks. Most of the classes are connected with the major subjects (English, math, and science), but may include computers and foreign languages. Another program, C-MITES (Carnegie Mellon Institute for Talented Elementary Students) offers summer programs at schools throughout Pennsylvania. These summer classes are similar to the ChESS classes, and courses include Robotics, Mathematical Problem Solving, Computer Math Mania, Probability and Statistics, Informal Geometry, Mathematical Experiments, and Electrons and Magnets. Numerous other summer programs for talented students are available. Although families must pay tuition for most of these programs, need-based financial aid is available.

Many of the regional talent searches offer students courses on weekends during the school year. These courses, frequently offered on college campuses, give students a chance to interact with instructors who are experts in their field and to join other like-minded students for a brief academic experience. For example, the C-MITES weekend workshops and the WINGS program offered by the Belin-Blank Center offer 3-hour classes in robotics, lasers, bugs, architecture, and chemistry. They also offer workshops for parents.

## Advantages of Participating in a Talent Search

Obviously, we are advocates of the talent search approach to identifying mathematically talented students. The benefits of the approach, as described by Rotigel and Lupkowski-Shoplik (1999), include:

Educational Diagnosis

Above-level tests, such as EXPLORE, measure talented students' abilities more accurately than grade-level achievement tests do. They spread out the scores of academically talented students, resulting in a bell-shaped distribution (Lupkowski-Shoplik & Swiatek, 1999). Chris and Terry's test results, described earlier, illustrate this point clearly. Only after we have an accurate measure of students' abilities are we able to offer specific recommendations for their educational programs.

Educational Recommendations Tailored to the Abilities of the Student

Researchers who have used the SAT with hundreds of thousands of seventh graders have developed guidelines for educational recommendations for students scoring at particular levels (Cohn, 1991). These recommendations represent a continuum of modifications that best match a child's demonstrated ability and achievement, ranging from enrichment options to accelerative options (Cohn; Olszewski-Kubilius, 1998). The goal is to match the level and pace of the curriculum to the child's needs by finding the "optimal match" (Robinson & Robinson, 1982). After testing thousands of third through sixth graders, we developed similar guidelines for the students taking the EXPLORE as depicted in Table 5.5 and Figure 5.2.

Educational Opportunities Provided by University-Based Talent Searches

University-based talent searches offer summer programs, weekend programs, correspondence courses, and online programs (Olszewski-Kubilius, 1998). These enrichment and accelerative programs offer students the opportunity to study topics that might not be offered at their local schools (Lupkowski-Shoplik & Kuhnel, 1995; Piskurich & Lupkowski-Shoplik, 1998). Residential summer programs offer talented students the opportunity to make gains in emotional and social development, as well as to take advanced classes (VanTassel-Baska, 1996). Through these programs, students are given the opportunity to meet and study with other talented youngsters.

## Appropriate Educational Information

By participating in a talent search, students obtain a more accurate measure of their academic abilities and, therefore, learn more about their abilities. When they participate in specially designed programs to explore topics of interest, they are better informed about the the their own achievements and abilities when the time comes to select a college or a career (Brody, 1998). Talent searches provide printed material on educational opportunities and encourage students to maximize their abilities. Students enter college better prepared and ready for even more challenges (Brody, 1998). The invitation to participate in a talent search also does much to enhance the individual student's academic self-concept (Swiatek & Lupkowski-Shoplik, 2000a). This is especially true for students who qualify for the talent searches, but have not qualified for their local school's gifted and talented program.

## Honors, Awards, and Scholarships

Students may earn a variety of awards due to their excellent performance on a talent search measure (Cohn, 1991). Demonstration of advanced reasoning may result in special opportunities at some of the university-based programs. For example, students may receive merit scholarships to attend university courses.

## The Success of the Talent Search Model

The evidence overwhelmingly supports the use of talent search to identify highly able reasoners who are eager to develop their abilities. Higher scoring participants tend to earn more honors and more advanced standing, enter college earlier, and complete college with greater success than those who score less well. . . . An important fact to remember is that the accomplishments of thousands of these academically able young people are dramatically large. They are accomplishments unheard of prior to the start of the talent searches. In research studies documenting the value of the SAT as a predictor of academic success the findings are not merely statistically significant. The programs are profound in their capacity to enable highly able and eager students to proceed educationally as fast and in as great a depth and breadth as they wish. (Cohn, 1991, pp. 169–170)

Due in large part to the success of the talent searches, there has been an exponential increase in the opportunities available to gifted students, especially with regard to opportunities for residential academic programs on college campuses. The foundation of the talent search model, above-level testing, is a simple, yet powerful, method of identifying talented students. Since the first talent search with seventh and eighth graders in 1972, Julian Stanley and his colleagues at numerous universities have identified millions of students who have benefited from the early identification and special programming options the talent searches offer (Lupkowski-Shoplik et al., 2003).

The Diagnostic Testing→Prescriptive Instruction model, advocated by the talent searches, allows identified students to move ahead in their areas of strength at an appropriate level and pace. It effectively challenges academically talented students and has demonstrated long-term positive outcomes (Stanley, 1996; Swiatek & Benbow, 1991b).

The talent search concept has deeply affected our ideas about appropriate programming for gifted and talented learners. Educational interventions need to be talent specific and responsive to individual needs. . . . The true beauty of aptitude testing, such as that done through the talent search, is that it provides administrators with important diagnostic information for curriculum planning. (VanTassel-Baska, 1996, p. 239)

As described by VanTassel-Baska (1996), the talent searches, with their strong research base and practical approach to educating talented youth, highlight the following concepts:

- Programs and curricula should be matched to the abilities of a student.
- The more academically talented the student, the greater the need for intensification and extension of services.
- Acceleration is a necessary aspect of gifted programming.
- Accelerated, advanced, and challenging work on an ongoing basis is a powerful incentive to achievement at later levels (e.g., Swiatek & Benbow, 1991a).
- The talent search concept has had an important impact on curriculum and instruction. For example, we have seen more interest in classic subjects such as Latin, Greek, philosophy, and rhetoric and greater interest in rigorous treatment of standard courses.
- Higher education institutions have become involved in educating academically talented precollege students. Many colleges and universities offer courses for precollege students, have developed an ongoing research agenda concerning talented youth, and have developed graduate programs to provide for the education of teachers and other professionals in gifted education.
- The staff at talent searches model a mentoring approach. They often work individually with students and their families to help the students realize their talents by helping them select appropriate educational options.
- Talent searches have provided a research and developmental base for content and other forms of acceleration.

## Research Findings on the Elementary Student Talent Search

Although the talent searches for elementary school students have only been in operation since the early 1990s, they have begun to establish a sound research base. The research that has already been conducted answers a variety of questions, from "Who should be tested?" to "How well do the students do?" Some of the research questions are addressed below.

### How Do We Know Which Level of a Test is Appropriate for Young Academically Able Students?

An important consideration with any test is whether or not the items are appropriately difficult. The test must meet the "Goldilocks Standard"—not too hard, not too easy, but just right! A talent search instrument must have a sufficient number of difficult items to be challenging for the extremely able students, but also must not be unnecessarily frustrating for the less-exceptional students. For academically talented students, above-level tests are generally more appropriate than grade-level tests, and EXPLORE is a highly effective talent search instrument for third through sixth graders (Colangelo, Assouline, & Lu, 1994; Lupkowski-Shoplik & Swiatek, 1999). EXPLORE has been used in the Elementary Student Talent Search with over 50,000 students. A review of the distribution of the scores earned by bright elementary students reveals a bell curve. In other words, EXPLORE has enough easy items and enough difficult items, which allows us to distinguish among an already bright group of students (ACT, 1996).

Additionally, EXPLORE has enough difficult items for the older, very bright students (i.e., talent search sixth graders). A study completed by ACT confirmed that the EXPLORE–Mathematics test was an appropriately challenging above-level instrument for bright elementary students, neither too easy nor too difficult. Of note, however, is the fact that, on many items, talent search fifth and sixth graders performed as well as, if not better than, the normative sample of eighth graders (ACT, 1996; Colangelo, Assouline, & Lu, 1994).

### Do Students Who Take EXPLORE Come From an Appropriately Selected Sample?

Students are invited to participate in the elementary student talent searches based upon scores they earned on grade-level tests. We recommend they earn a score at the 95th percentile or above on at least one section of a grade-level standardized test before taking EXPLORE. For students meeting this initial criterion, EXPLORE has been found to be appropriately challenging, without being a frustrating experience (Assouline, Colangelo, McNabb, Lupkowski-Shoplik, & Sayler, 1993; Lupkowski-Shoplik & Swiatek, 1999). Specifically, Lupkowski-Shoplik and Swiatek found that less than 10% of the third-grade Elementary Student Talent Search participants meeting the initial 95th percentile equivalent earned very low scores ("chance" scores) on the EXPLORE–Mathematics test. For fourth through sixth graders, less than 2% of the students earned those very low scores. Therefore, we concluded that the 95th percentile criterion is appropriate.

We do tend to be cautious, however, when we are helping families of third graders make the decision of whether or not to take the EXPLORE test. We remind them that EXPLORE was designed for eighth graders and may be quite difficult even for a bright third grader who has had little standardized testing experience. Although less than 10% of the third graders taking the test earn very low scores, we are still concerned that the third graders have a much higher potential for being frustrated by taking the EXPLORE. Therefore, we suggest to families that they think carefully about their child. Children who don't handle frustration well or tend to become very upset if they don't know all of the answers are not good candidates for taking EXPLORE in third grade; we recommend that they wait until fourth grade to take the test.

### Are There Differences in the Performances of Boys and Girls?

Researchers with the Study of Mathematically Precocious Youth at Johns Hopkins University have reported consistent gender differences in mathematics in gifted junior high school students: Boys score significantly higher than girls on the SAT–Mathematics, and there are more boys than girls who score at the highest levels of the test (Benbow, 1988; Benbow & Stanley, 1980). Researchers with the Elementary Student Talent Search are interested in investigating the question of gender differences in the population of younger mathematically talented students. Because the talent search with elementary students is still relatively young, researchers have just begun to investigate gender differences in this population.

Gender differences favoring boys in the elementary student talent searches have been found, but the magnitude of these differences has not been consistent. Colangelo, Assouline, and Lu (1994) and Assouline and Doellinger (2001) found that boys scored significantly higher on EXPLORE–Mathematics than girls did. These differences were statistically significant, although effect sizes were in the negligible range, indicating that the differences were not of practical significance. Swiatek, Lupkowski-Shoplik, and O'Donoghue (in press) found the same type of results in their sample: Boys scored an average of 13.22 on EXPLORE–Mathematics, while girls scored 12.62. This difference, although statistically significant, was not meaningful.[1]

In looking at the highest scoring students (those earning a score of 22 or higher on EXPLORE–Mathematics), however, the researchers found twice as many boys as girls earned such high scores. Therefore, they concluded that important gender differences are evident in mathematically gifted students, even as early as elementary school. This research coincides with our anecdotal evidence that many more boys than girls are exceptionally mathematically talented. The gender differences found in large research samples help us to realize how important it is to provide special programming for mathematically talented girls in elementary school.

---

1. The effect size was calculated to be .18. Effect size is a statistical indication of the importance of the magnitude of the difference between two means (averages). Cohen (1988) arbitrarily classifies effect sizes below .20 as "negligible."

## Are There Gender Differences in Attitude About Mathematics?

In their research sample of Elementary Student Talent Search participants, Swiatek and Lupkowski-Shoplik (2000) found a pattern similar to that found in older gifted students: Boys demonstrated more positive attitudes than girls toward science and computers, while girls showed more positive attitudes than boys toward English, writing, and reading. Findings reported by Colangelo, Assouline, and Lu (1994) were similar, although there was no significant difference found between boys and girls in attitude toward science. We need to note, too, that the difference between boys and girls in *liking* mathematics was "negligible" in the Swiatek and Lupkowski-Shoplik study, although Colangelo, Assouline, and Lu found that a significantly greater number of boys than girls indicated that they *loved* mathematics. Statistical analyses in the Colangelo, Assouline, and Lu study revealed that more boys than girls responded "I love it" to the question, "How do you feel about mathematics?"

These two studies of gifted elementary students may indicate the beginning of a trend that becomes more apparent as students grow older. Taken together, these observations are consistent with the suggestion of Benbow (1988) and Benbow and Stanley (1982) that the important issue may not be that academically talented girls like math and science less than boys do, but that they like verbal subjects more than boys do.

## What is Known About How the Talent Search Students Perform in the Areas Measured by EXPLORE–Mathematics?

Assouline and Doellinger (1999) conducted a study examining the individual items of the EXPLORE–Mathematics test. This test covers four areas of math: prealgebra, algebra, geometry, and statistics/probability. They found that the talent search sixth graders exceeded the performance of the normative sample of eighth graders on 23 of the 30 items, while fifth graders outperformed the normative sample on 8 of the 30 items. In general, their performance was very strong in prealgebra, geometry, and statistics/probability. The "weakest" area of performance by the talent search students was in algebra (which most of the students had not taken, of course). This means that academically able students in sixth grade and younger perform as well as, or better than, average eighth graders on a test of mathematical achievement. The evidence is clear that these students need something beyond that which the typical sixth-grade curriculum provides: they are indeed ready for more challenging material, such as that offered in Prealgebra and Algebra I.

Further analysis of the data revealed that talented elementary students performed well in the content areas of statistics and probability, geometry, and prealgebra. Such a strong performance suggests that, in general, these content areas should be introduced earlier than they are, and the treatment of these topics should be at a higher level of challenge for these talented youngsters.

## What Can Above-Level Testing Tell Us About the Curriculum?

The developers of the EXPLORE test have been able to tie score ranges for each test to specific skills and objectives. Therefore, used in combination with the Standards for Transition described earlier in this chapter, the results from EXPLORE provide an appropriate starting point when determining the programs and curricula for talented students.

# 6 Programming

- There are many educational options for mathematically talented students, ranging from enrichment within the regular classroom to radical acceleration. No one option is "right" for all students.

- The "optimal match" means obtaining objective information about the student's abilities and achievements and then matching those abilities and achievements to the appropriate level and pace of the mathematics curriculum.

- Acceleration is appropriate and necessary for many mathematically talented students. Acceleration as a successful program option has been strongly researched for several decades.

- Several exemplary programs offer illustrations of the variety of approaches for talented youth programs.

*If I tell you what to do on Monday, who will tell you what to do on Tuesday?*

IN THE PREVIOUS chapters, we have discussed both philosophical and practical issues concerning assessment and planning. In Chapter 5, "Talent Searches," we presented evidence concerning the range of mathematical talent, with an emphasis on the importance of using objective information from testing as a way to better understand the student's need for additional challenge. The present chapter will focus on specific programs that can be used to meet the academic needs of mathematically talented students.

Mathematically talented students have many different educational options from which to choose. Rather than giving educators and parents a list of clever activities to do with students in a random fashion, we present a smorgasbord of choices available to students and suggest how to match these choices to the students' needs in a systematic manner. Our goal is to help educators determine not only what to do on Monday morning, but also on every day of the week throughout a student's elementary, middle, and high school years.

The first section of the chapter describes our overall philosophy of programming: finding the optimal match between a student's learning needs and the program that will meet those needs. Teachers and parents will need to consider broad philosophical issues such as acceleration versus enrichment, as well as individual issues with respect to the student.

## Finding the Optimal Match

On a daily basis, we try to help parents who want to know how to challenge their children in school. Inquiries usually sound like "My child is gifted, but she doesn't seem to be challenged by the gifted program. What can I do to challenge her?," or "My son is very good in math, but he hasn't been identified as gifted, and he's bored with the regular math curriculum.

Step 1    Assess academic abilities and achievements.

Step 2    Choose the general grade level of curriculum for further assessment of specific knowledge.

Step 3    Offer curriculum-based assessment using chapter tests and pretests.

Step 4    Place the student in the appropriate level of the curriculum for instruction.

Step 5    Reassess—Is the student being challenged, but not overly frustrated?

### Figure 6.1. Finding the Optimal Match

What can we do?" The first step in helping these families and the school personnel who work with their children is to obtain objective information about the student's abilities and achievements. The next step is to match the ability and achievement of the student to the appropriate level and pace of the elementary and middle school mathematics curriculum. Robinson and Robinson (1982) called this finding the "optimal match" (see Figure 6.1). An optimal match between the curriculum and the student's abilities occurs when a student feels sufficiently challenged and engaged by the material. The student is "stretched," but not overly frustrated. Both the pace and the level of instruction need to be matched to the students' abilities and prior achievements. In this chapter, we discuss how this is accomplished.

*Step 1: Assess academic abilities and achievements.* Before selecting a program or curriculum for a student, we first need to obtain specific information about his or her academic abilities and achievements. A variety of measures can be used for this purpose. Some of these measures—such as teacher-developed tests, student products, and grade-level standardized tests from the school's regular testing program—are already available and are widely used. However, these measures may not give a complete picture of the student's level of ability or achievement because they are not as reliable or valid as standardized measures (see Chapter 3).

Other measures may also be administered. Above-level testing (such as EXPLORE testing for third through sixth graders) usually provides a more accurate indicator of talented students' abilities than grade-level standardized tests because the former raise the ceiling typically imposed by the latter (see Chapter 3 for more information). In other words, the information from above-level tests guides our thinking with respect to determining the level of challenge that is appropriate for gifted students. For example, fifth grader Joshua took the EXPLORE test, which was developed for eighth graders. He scored 12 out of a possible 25 on the Mathematics section of the test, placing him at the 38th percentile compared to eighth graders in the norm group. This indicates that he performed as well as or better than 38% of eighth graders taking the test. This performance has specific implications regarding his need for challenge throughout his academic years, indicating that he needs to be placed in a math class that is at a more challenging level and is taught at a more rapid pace than the typical fifth-grade math class. He will continue to need advanced programming throughout his middle school and high school years.

*Steps 2 and 3: Choose the general grade level of curriculum for further assessment of specific knowledge.* Then, offer curriculum-based assessment using chapter tests and pretests. It is not enough to test a student and then say that he or she is exceptionally talented in math, science, or reading. As explained in Chapter 3, testing is a necessary (but not sufficient) first step to prescribing an appropriate educational program developed to match the curriculum with the student's abilities. After determining the student's mathematical aptitude (often by using above-level testing), school personnel can choose the general grade-level of curriculum at which to begin further assessment of a student's specific knowledge. This is called a *curriculum-based assessment*. Curriculum-based assessment tests are developed from the actual curriculum used in the school or district and allow for the most valid programming by a school for a student. For example, chapter tests and pretests (from the appropriate grade level) can be used to measure mastery of specific content and topics. This step in the process is important because it helps determine what the student already knows and what the student has yet to learn.

Joshua's EXPLORE test results were obtained during the middle of his fifth-grade year. After his results came back (and because his mathematics score was at the 38th percentile when compared to eighth graders), it was appropriate to consider advanced programming in mathematics. His teacher administered the end-of-book test for fifth-grade mathematics. He correctly answered 91% of the items, indicating that he had mastered a good deal of the fifth-grade mathematics curriculum. He was also tested using the sixth-grade mathematics chapter tests for the first 6 months of the school year (Chapters 1–8). Joshua's scores ranged from 92 to 100 on each of the tests.

*Step 4: Place the student in the appropriate level of the curriculum for instruction.* When studying the curriculum, the student might be placed with age peers or with older students to study mathematics. The student might study mathematics in a classroom setting or individually with a teacher or mentor. More information about these various options is offered later in this chapter.

Joshua had performed so well on the sixth-grade chapter tests that he was placed in the sixth-grade mathematics class in the middle of his fifth-grade year. His teacher worked with him closely to ensure that there were no gaps. He completed the sixth-grade curriculum with an A average. Joshua also enjoyed participating in enrichment mathematics courses offered on weekends at a local university.

*Step 5: Reassess—Is the student being challenged, but not overly frustrated?* When matching the curriculum to the student's abilities, it is important to discern his or her optimal learning rate and precise academic strengths. Students should feel that they are making steady progress in mastering a subject, not moving too quickly, and not doing unnecessary review work. The goal is to match student ability with academic challenges (Center for Talented Youth, 1993). Good programs for gifted students (and for all students) have one primary goal: matching the abilities of the students to appropriately challenging coursework and programs. If the material is too difficult, students will become frustrated and will not learn; if it is too easy, they will become bored and "turned off."

In Joshua's case, the teacher asked him periodically if he understood the material and if he was having any difficulty. Joshua reported he was enjoying the challenges presented by the sixth-grade class. The following year, sixth grader Joshua was placed with seventh graders in Prealgebra. Again, he performed very well and responded positively to the challenge.

## Enrichment and Acceleration

### Enrichment

The debate about acceleration versus enrichment is decades old. Enrichment proponents are concerned that accelerating students means that they will learn information in a rapid, superficial manner, while advocates of acceleration are frustrated by the repetitive tasks students are asked to do even if they have already demonstrated mastery of a topic. George, Cohn, and Stanley (1979b) presented an excellent treatment of the issues.

The major issue is that acceleration as an educational strategy for challenging gifted children is clearly supported by research, but it has received only minimal support from educators in the field. Stanley (1979b) described four forms of enrichment and several issues associated with enrichment, all of which remain relevant today. Despite the fact that Stanley's descriptions were generated in the 1970s, there have been no new developments. The four forms of enrichment are:

1.  *Busywork*: More of the same, but in greater quantity than required of most students in the class.
2.  *Irrelevant academic enrichment*: A special subject or activity meant to challenge the academic experiences of the student; however, the subject has very little to do with the talent area (e.g., the mathematically talented student spends "enrichment time" working on a class newspaper).
3.  *Cultural enrichment*: While not relevant to the specific talent area, the activity has cultural merit (e.g., attending a theatrical or musical performance).
4.  *Relevant academic enrichment*: There is exposure to special topics in the specific talent area, such as a unit on tessellations, which may or may not be related to the topics being covered in the class.

Chapter 7 presents many resources for enrichment topics that can be used effectively by the regular classroom teacher and others. The remainder of this chapter presents programming ideas for systematically exposing students to the mathematics curriculum and moving them through it at a pace commensurate with their aptitudes.

### Acceleration

Starting in 1972, the Study of Mathematically Precocious Youth (SMPY) at Johns Hopkins University began offering fast-paced mathematics classes to academically talented students in grades 7 and 8, with the goal of allowing students to move through mathematics at a pace matched to their abilities. The outcomes of the program have been impressive. For example, junior high students who successfully completed SMPY's first series of fast-paced precalculus classes achieved much more in high school and college than matched-ability students who elected not to participate. They were also much more accelerated in their education than nonparticipants, and they reported that they were satisfied with their acceleration (Stanley & Benbow, 1986).

Extensive reviews of the literature have demonstrated that the evidence for acceleration is generally positive for students in prekindergarten through graduate school (e.g., Daurio, 1979; Janos & Robinson, 1985; Kulik & Kulik, 1984; 1987; Passow, 1996; Reis et al., 1993; Sosniak, 1997; Southern & Jones, 1991). Brody and Benbow (1987) reviewed data from a follow-up study of SMPY students and found no harmful effects of acceleration and a number of positive effects. Students who were more accelerated in school earned more awards, attended more selective colleges, and were more likely to plan to earn doctorates or other advanced degrees than the less-accelerated students. They found no differences in the accelerated and non-accelerated groups in terms of social and emotional adjustment. Kulik and Kulik's meta-analytic review of 26 studies on the effects of acceleration on gifted students revealed that gifted students' achievement was significantly higher in accelerated classes than nonaccelerated classes. Brody, Lupkowski, and Stanley (1988) found that college students who had previously accelerated were overall very happy that they had done so. They were pleased to be placed in a more challenging environment, and they reported that any inconveniences they suffered (e.g., not being able to drive at the same time as their older classmates) were temporary and relatively minor.

Among the educational options listed by Benbow (1986) are many ways for students to accelerate their educational program. The options range from entering kindergarten early or skipping a grade, to participating in an individually paced program (see Table 6.1).

*Two Examples of Accelerative Math Programs.* Mills, Ablard, and Gustin (1994) described an accelerative mathematics program for third through sixth graders that used a curriculum developed specifically for exceptionally mathematically talented students. In this program, developed by the Center for Talented Youth (CTY) at Johns Hopkins University, students attended 3-hour classes on weekends during the school year and worked on required homework an

---

**Table 6.1
Sample of Accelerative Options**

- Enter kindergarten early
- Skip a grade
- Participate in fast-paced classes
- Condense 4 years of school into 3
- Receive credit by examination
- Participate in subject-matter acceleration
- Participate in individually paced programs

---

additional 2–3 hours per week. Students worked individually, in small groups, and as a whole class. They worked through the mathematics curriculum in a systematic, linear fashion by studying a topic thoroughly, demonstrating mastery, and then moving on. The pace of the class was matched to the students' abilities. Students were placed in the class based on ability, and there were no restrictions on age or grade. For example, a class could have been composed of third, fourth, fifth, and sixth graders all completing the same course within 7 months.

Careful study of students' progress revealed that participants in this program showed remarkable gains. Their progress was evaluated by giving them above-level assessments (see Chapters 3 and 5). Their scores were compared to those of older students in the comparison group for that test. At each grade level, students improved their performance significantly. Third graders showed the greatest increase (moving from the 35th to the 81st percentile when compared to the sixth-grade norm group). In each grade level, at least 87% of the students exceeded normative gains. In other words, almost 9 out of 10 students achieved at higher levels than would have been expected.

When considering participation in a fast-paced, accelerative program, many people ask if students can retain the knowledge learned for any length of time. To address this important issue, students took a posttest 5 months after completion of the course, and scores remained relatively the same (Mills, Ablard, & Gustin, 1994).

The Academically Talented Youth Programs (ATYP) represent another example of content acceleration and fast-paced instruction designed for academically talented students. McCarthy (1998) described the nearly ideal application of the talent search model, upon which ATYP was established, to communities in Michigan. Mathematically talented middle school students in the Kalamazoo, Michigan, area were provided with 180 hours of instruction scheduled over 2 school years. This permitted the completion of 4 years of high school mathematics (i.e., 2 years of algebra, plane/solid geometry, and precalculus prior to 10th grade). The point of ATYP was not to rush the students through the mathematics curriculum, but rather to have a process that "matches students to the curriculum and instructional pace appropriate to their need" (p. 122).

McCarthy (1998) described in detail the identification, programming, and evaluation of ATYP, which has been in existence since 1982. Best of all is the fact that the model has been replicated in four other communities in Michigan. Although each community has added its local flavor to the model, the integrity of the talent search assessment process and the match of the assessment to the program are integral components to the program's success. McCarthy reported that more than 1,500 students have been a part of this talent search accelerative program. In 1998, the annual enrollment was approximately 200 students per year, which represents a tenfold increase from the modest beginning with the first group of 20 students.

*Comments Concerning Acceleration.* In our experience, many school officials are categorically opposed to students accelerating in school (Assouline, Colangelo, Lupkowski-Shoplik, & Lipscomb, 1998; Southern & Jones, 1991). This opposition seems to stem from either one bad experience with acceleration or a major concern with students' social development. School officials and parents are concerned that, if a student is placed with others who are one or more years older, the accelerated student will be at some type of disadvantage, develop poor social skills, be "behind" the other students, or stand out compared to other students.

In response to these concerns, Assouline, Colangelo, Lupkowski-Shoplik, and Lipscomb (1998) developed the Iowa Acceleration Scale (IAS). This scale was designed to help educators and parents systematically consider all aspects of a student's development while discussing the decision to accelerate or not. It includes a discussion of the issues relevant to acceleration, and it guides educators systematically through questions about academic ability, school factors, family considerations, motivation, attitude toward learning, academic self-concept, developmental factors (age, physical size, and motor coordination), emotional development, relationships with peers, attitude toward acceleration, and parental support.

Accelerated students may have fewer opportunities to interact with same-age peers. However, we do not feel that this is a sufficient reason to hold students back. Students can have many opportunities to interact with age peers through informal play with neighborhood children, participation in church groups, extracurricular activities at school, and so forth.

Lupkowski and Assouline (1992) listed five important points concerning acceleration:

1. Healthy social development means learning to get along with people of all ages and skills.
2. There are many opportunities outside of school to interact with age peers.
3. Having a large number of same-age friends isn't as critical to a child's healthy social development as having a few close friends with whom to share ideas.
4. An indicator of social readiness for acceleration is a preference for playing with more mature children.
5. Finally, long- and short-term planning is essential. Students, parents, and teachers need to remember that there may be a few years during adolescence when minor inconveniences become major ones. (p. 28)

We also noted:

> Acceleration accomplishes much that is useful. When implemented properly, it guarantees that an appropriate match between the talented student and curriculum has been found. Acceleration provides the opportunity for challenges that children might not otherwise experience.
>
> If a student is not permitted to accelerate, he or she may be locked into the traditional pace and sequence of study and denied the opportunity to study a more advanced subject later. For example, a student who waits until ninth grade to study algebra with the rest of his or her classmates may not be able to schedule more advanced mathematics courses such as calculus or differential equations, or advanced science courses requiring high-level mathematics. Although one might counter that these subjects can be studied in college, we disagree with that argument. . . . [W]aiting to study a subject eliminates the chance to take new, more challenging courses. The mathematically talented student who craves higher level mathematics and related subjects would be wise to pursue those interests. (Lupkowski & Assouline, 1992, p. 30)

### Linking Acceleration and Enrichment

In the face of so much evidence regarding the needs of academically gifted students, why has there been so little progress in educational programming for these students? What has changed in the decades since George, Cohn, and Stanley (1979) published their book?

We believe that much of the lack of educational progress is rooted in the acceleration versus enrichment debate. Politically, there is considerable concern about acceleration, and enrichment, no matter how irrelevant, seems to be the approach that is most widely preferred and used. One notable treatment of the acceleration versus enrichment issue merits mention. Schiever and Maker (1997) carefully explored the various forms of enrichment and acceleration and concluded, as did Stanley (1979b), that a combination of acceleration and enrichment makes the most sense. By definition, relevant enrichment in mathematics must have some acceleration and appropriate acceleration will have an enrichment component.

## What Are the Program Options for Mathematically Talented Students?

We recognize that students have a range of abilities, and we concentrate on trying to help them match their academic strengths to the appropriate curricular option. Since not all students are equally able in all academic areas, they need different programs and different approaches for various subjects. We recommend looking at each student individually and fitting the various programs the school offers to their needs.

We view the needs of mathematically talented students as being on a continuum. Students whose talents are somewhat above average need differentiation within the regular classroom, while students who are quite a bit above average need subject matter acceleration or curriculum compacting. Extraordinarily talented students need radical acceleration and individually paced programs. The Pyramid of Educational Options described in Chapter 5 shows the many educational choices available to mathematically talented students and relates those options to scores earned on the EXPLORE test.

### Appropriate Options Within the Regular Classroom

Bright students who love math and do well in class might be able to receive the challenges they need within a regular classroom. Perhaps they are the first ones done with their seatwork, and their teachers are always looking for ways to keep them challenged. Possible options within the regular classroom are listed in Table 6.2 and described on the following page.

---

## Table 6.2
## Instructional Options Within the Regular Classroom

### Appropriate Options

- *Breadth/Depth approach*: The same curriculum, greater depth
- *Enrichment topics*: Extend or enrich the regular curriculum
- *Math-related independent study projects*: Investigate a math topic
- *Curriculum compacting*: Eliminate some curriculum to allow more time for other activities
- *Telescoping*: Spend less time in a course of study (complete 3 years of high school in 2 years)
- *Subject-matter acceleration in mathematics*: Move up a grade for mathematics
- *Ability grouping*: Groups of advanced students study math together

### Less-Appropriate Options

- *Tutor other children*: Help others who are having difficulty in math. This is *not* a good substitute for learning new material.
- *Isolated, self-paced instruction*: Student works ahead in the textbook at his/her own pace. May result in feelings of isolation; student probably won't learn material well.

---

*Breadth/Depth Approach.* The goal of this approach is to refocus the objectives of an assignment from quantity to quality, in other words, to avoid giving students "more of the same." For example, if the class is working on computation skills and the assignment is to complete the even-numbered problems on a page, the gifted student is assigned *all* of the problems. On the other hand, an example of breadth/depth (i.e., quality) is to assign the gifted students the challenge of completing computations in bases other than base 10 (Pratscher, Jones, & Lamb, 1982).

The breadth/depth model is relatively simple for the regular classroom teacher to deliver because it does not require the development of a totally separate program for the gifted. Instead, the teacher matches in-depth activities with each level of the existing curriculum (Lupkowski & Assouline, 1992). However, there are two potential pitfalls of this option.

First, the student might see the additional activities as punishment for being talented in math. For example, if Sonja is required to do the same set of practice problems as the rest of the students and is also expected to complete another activity or problem set, she will probably resent the additional work. Sonja is more likely to remain engaged in the assignment if the teacher allows her to demonstrate mastery of the skill by permitting her to do fewer practice problems (i.e., one-half the amount assigned to the rest of the class). As soon as mastery is demonstrated, she should move on to the curriculum-related extension assignment.

The second pitfall is potentially more serious. It is highly probable that the student's teacher is not prepared to provide substantial horizontal or vertical enrichment that presents a broader range of mathematics concepts to these students or presents challenges to them that are typically reserved for older students. For example, elementary school teachers are not typically required to have a substantial background in mathematics in order to receive a teaching certificate. This is why it is so important to continue to upgrade teacher preparation programs and to offer additional training to experienced teachers. In the report, *Doing What Matters Most: Investing in Quality Teaching*, which was prepared by Linda Darling-Hammond, executive director of the National Commission on Teaching and America's Future, the following point is made:

> No other intervention can make the difference that a knowledgeable, skillful teacher can make in the learning process. At the same time, nothing can fully com-

pensate for weak teaching that, despite good intentions, can result from a teacher's lack of opportunity to acquire the knowledge and skill needed to help students master the curriculum. (Darling-Hammond, 1997, p. 8)

*Enrichment Topics in the Regular Classroom.* The variety and availability of enrichment activities has increased substantially in the past decade. The delivery of these activities is often through centers or stations that are set up by the teachers, but selected by the students. For example, most of the students in Mrs. King's fifth-grade regular classroom are expected to complete centers on metrics, estimation, and multiplication. In addition, there are centers on tessellations and the Fibanocci Sequence available to students who have the time, interest, and motivation to work on them. Examples of appropriate enrichment topics for these centers include probability and statistics, mental arithmetic, spatial visualization, algebra, geometry, and discrete mathematics (Wheatley, 1988). In the next chapter, we will discuss additional enrichment topics, as well as games, competitions, computer programs, and other activities for bright students in the regular classroom.

The disadvantages of this approach are the same as those mentioned previously: The enrichment topics might be seen as punishment for completing the other activities early, and the teacher may not be sufficiently comfortable with the activities. The resolution of these disadvantages is complex. At a minimum, to avoid the perception that the enrichment centers are a punishment, the students could be allowed to substitute a higher level, more challenging activity for one they have already mastered (Winebrenner, 2001).

*Math-Related Independent Study Projects.* The underlying assumption of this option is that gifted students will be given the same assignment as their classmates, but will be able to complete the assignment more quickly than the others. Therefore, they will have time to investigate a mathematical topic on their own with the teacher's guidance and perhaps the help of a community mentor.

Examples of independent study projects range from applied to theoretical. An example of an applied project is conducting a survey and reporting the results as part of an effort to resolve a community issue. An example of a theoretical project would be working with a university-level mathematician on an area of interest such as fractals. Working on math-related independent study projects is recommended as a supplement to the regular curriculum, but it is not meant to be a substitute for curriculum compacting and proper pacing (see the next section).

*Curriculum Compacting.* The goal of curriculum compacting is to determine which parts of the curriculum can be eliminated from a student's course of study and to use the time saved for other activities. Students' mastery of the subject is determined by pretesting. Curriculum compacting is designed to give the students additional time to study enrichment topics in the same subject, complete independent study projects, move more quickly through the curriculum, or pursue other worthwhile academic activities (see Winebrenner, 2001, for an extensive treatment of compacting).

Curriculum compacting is best accomplished by pretesting appropriately. We use the word *appropriate* because many educators use the pretests that are part of the textbook, but do not use the results to program for the students. For these teachers, the pretest is another activity, and the results have little impact on programming. Few teachers have training in the application of pretesting results. Since pretesting is the preliminary activity in compacting, teachers are often derailed from successfully implementing compacting at this stage (Chapter 4 offers more information about appropriately applying pretesting). This would be in contrast to the teacher who uses the time saved to have the student participate in an activity not related to mathematics, such as watching a movie.

Once the teacher determines what a student knows and doesn't know, the next step to compacting is documenting content still to be mastered and choosing appropriate replacement activities for the topics that have already been mastered. These may be enrichment-oriented activities that are related to the topics already mastered, accelerative activities that are more advanced, or unrelated activities. In a sequential subject such as mathematics, it may be difficult for regular classroom teachers to select appropriate enrichment activities that are not accelerative in nature. Also, teachers may not feel confident in choosing appropriate accelerative activities. Therefore, unfortunately, the replacement activities chosen are often unrelated to mathematics. They may keep the student occupied, but they do not move the student systematically through the curriculum or broaden the student's understanding of a topic. Chapter 7 offers some suggestions for appropriate activities.

*Telescoping.* In telescoping, students spend less time than normal in a course of study. For example, they may complete 3 years of high school in 2 years, or they may complete a 1-year mathematics course in a semester (Southern & Jones, 1991). Michigan's ATYP program, described earlier in this chapter, is a good example of telescoping. According to McCarthy (1998), the typical student in the ATYP program learns 2 years of high school math content in one-fourth the instructional time usually allotted in high school classrooms.

*Subject-Matter Acceleration.* Moving up a grade just for the mathematics class can be a good option for students who are exceptionally talented in only one content area, and this is a relatively easy way for schools to make accommodations for mathematically talented students. The major advantage to this approach is that the regular classroom teacher no longer has to search for additional enrichment materials because the talented student has been removed from the class during math period. The student is more likely to be grouped with intellectual peers, because he or she is cognitively ready for the more advanced material. Another advantage is that students will be given credit for work completed, which is not always possible when acceleration occurs within the regular classroom. One disadvantage of this acceleration is that the pace of the class a grade higher might still be too slow for these quick

---

**Table 6.3**
**Advantages and Disadvantages**
**of Subject-Matter Acceleration in Mathematics**

**Advantages**

- Regular classroom teacher does not have to search for materials for the advanced student, because that student is removed during math class.
- It is more likely that the student will be grouped with intellectual peers.
- Student is given credit for work completed.
- Student is appropriately challenged and therefore remains interested in mathematics.

**Disadvantages**

- The pace may still be too slow for the student.
- If only one year of acceleration is employed, there may be relatively little new content for the student.
- Long-term planning is essential, so the student does not "run out" of mathematics before graduating from high school.
- Student may not receive credit for high school math done previous to enrolling in high school.

---

learners and there may be very little content that is substantially new (Flanders, 1987; Plucker & McIntire, 1996). Table 6.3 presents the advantages and disadvantages of subject-matter acceleration in mathematics.

*Ability grouping.* When students of similar ability are grouped together, it is known as *homogeneous grouping.* This can occur when an entire classroom is composed of students of similar mathematical abilities or when a classroom of students with a wide range of abilities is divided into several groups based on ability. When implemented in the regular classroom, this grouping arrangement requires careful planning by the teacher. It can be an excellent way to meet an individual student's needs because the pace of the curriculum is matched to the pace of a small group of learners, rather than the whole class. Thus, talented students are given challenging activities, but are not forced to wait for everybody else to catch up.

Unfortunately for mathematically gifted students, homogeneous grouping became an unpopular option at about the same time that mixed-ability grouping became popular and was "sold" to administrators as a way to solve their scheduling problems induced by the inclusion and middle school movements. Also contributing to the wholesale application of mixed-ability grouping was the inaccurate association of the term *grouping* with *tracking*. The research by Oakes (1985), which described the deleterious effects of tracking on lower ability students, was interpreted by well-meaning educators as a signal to dispense with any type of grouping. The effects of the convergence of the antitracking movement with the inclusion, middle school, and back-to-basic text movements contributed negatively to the education of mathematically talented students.

Gifted educators have been steadily advocating for a return to ability grouping, especially for mathematically talented students (Rogers, 2002). In their advocacy efforts, gifted educators cite research demonstrating that ability grouping is one of the preferred options for academically talented students. For example, Kulik and Kulik (1997) reported that, when academically talented students were grouped for accelerated and enriched classes, they demonstrated academic gains. Grouping middle and lower aptitude learners, however, has little or no effect on their achievement test scores. Therefore, grouping students does not have the harmful effects that some fear, and it has large positive effects for academically talented students (Kulik & Kulik). When gifted students are grouped for enrichment or accelerative classes, they can interact with other students who have similar interests and abilities, they are given assignments at an appropriate level of difficulty, and they are allowed to work at a pace matched to their abilities.

With homogeneous groups, teachers can tailor instruction to a group of students, which is more effective and easier for the teacher than trying to teach a large group of diverse learners at once.

> [W]hen gifted students are in class with other students of similar ability, curriculum can be designed that goes well beyond the regular content in both depth and breadth. The syllabus for average learners can be compacted and the topics elaborated, but most importantly, the thinking can be on a higher plane with topics unified and synthesized. No other grouping model offers such potential. (Wheatley, 1988, p. 253)

### Less-Appropriate Options for Mathematically Talented Students

*Tutor Other Children.* It seems like a good use of resources to ask gifted students to tutor others in the class who have difficulty in math. After all, we all know that you learn something very well if you have to teach it to someone else. So, why isn't this a good idea?

First, we are asking students to do the teacher's job, for which a teacher has been trained for a number of years. Second, these students already know the material with which their classmates are struggling; they don't need additional time to master it. For example, they do not need more practice with two-digit addition because they mastered that concept long ago. Simply put, it is not a good use of talented students' time to tutor others instead of learning something new. Therefore, this option is not recommended as a means of challenging mathematically talented students.

*Isolated, Self-Paced Instruction.* Having a student work ahead in the textbook at his or her own pace while other students receive the regular mathematics instruction from the teacher is one of the easiest ways to fill a student's time, and it is a frequently chosen option. The student is permitted to approach the teacher with questions, but spends most of the time learning the material on his or her own. Although the student may study mathematics at a faster pace, he or she might experience feelings of isolation and probably will not learn the new material well or to any great depth. This option is also not recommended.

### Options Outside of the Regular Classroom

Although many mathematically talented students may be well served by their regular classroom teachers, they may also benefit from participating in options outside of the regular classroom. These options include competitions, summer programs, and weekend programs, all of which have the advantage of grouping talented students together, as well as individually paced programs, which have the advantage of tailoring the curriculum to the student's abilities and achievements (see Table 6.4).

*Mathematics Competitions and Clubs.* Competitions offer students the opportunity to practice higher level math skills than they might use in the regular classroom. They also give students the chance to interact with other mathematically talented students and adults who enjoy mathematics. Some competitions do not require students to travel away from their home schools in order to participate. This is an option that is relatively easy for even a small school to implement because students can participate on their own time or they can use their enrichment time within the regular classroom to prepare for the competition. Preparation for competitions often take place in school mathematics clubs. Some competitions may require a faculty sponsor, so a student might not be able to participate on his or her own. Through these competitions, students meet others with similar interests and abilities (Dauber, 1988). Usiskin (2000) has advocated for the role of mathematics clubs and school teams in pro-

---

## Table 6.4
## Instructional Options Outside of the Regular Classroom

- Mathematics competitions and clubs
- Summer programs for gifted students
- Weekend programs for gifted students
- Individually paced programs: The DT→PI model
- Magnet schools
- Distance-learning and correspondence sourses

---

moting a culture that makes it acceptable for students to express and develop their interest in mathematics. Recommended competitions include Mathematical Olympiads for Elementary and Middle Schools (MOEMS), MATHCOUNTS, the American Mathematics Competitions (AMC 8, AMC 10, and AMC 12), and the American Regions Mathematics League. More information about these competitions can be found in "Resources."

*Summer Programs for Gifted Students.* Residential and nonresidential summer programs offer an excellent option for students who need additional enrichment, acceleration, or both in mathematics over and above what their school provides. Summer classes for academically talented students in sixth grade and younger are offered by many universities, including Carnegie Mellon, Johns Hopkins, Northwestern, and the University of Iowa. The "Resources" section contains more information about summer programs for mathematically talented students, as well as several books listing additional opportunities for talented students. Several exemplary summer programs are described below.

The C-MITES Summer Program, offered by Carnegie Mellon Institute for Talented Elementary Students, is a 2-week commuter program offered at over 30 sites throughout Pennsylvania. Students are chosen on the basis of above-level test scores (such as EXPLORE), teacher recommendations, grades in school, and academic activities. During the program, students study one topic in depth. Courses include Probability and Statistics, Informal Geometry, Discrete Mathematics, Individually Paced Mathematics, Physics and More, Explorations in Science, and Robotics. Instructors are experts in the subject they teach, and most are certified teachers.

At the University of Iowa, the Belin-Blank Center for Gifted Students offers commuter programs for elementary students and residential programs for secondary students. The mission of the Belin-Blank Center programs is similar to that of the other talent search centers: to bring together bright students with similar interests so that they can enjoy intensely focused study in the company of their academic peers. The Belin-Blank Center courses are open to any talent search participant and include Math Problem Solving, Computer Applications, Science Investigations, Literature and Writing, and Language and Culture. The summer program faculty members are all experts in their area of instruction. Some members of the faculty are certified teachers, while others are university professors or clinicians.

The Center for Talented Youth at Johns Hopkins University also provides rigorous summer programs for gifted students who have completed grades 2–12. Most of the courses are available through the residential program, offered at several sites in the United States and abroad. Commuter options are available for second through sixth graders living in the Baltimore/Washington and Los Angeles metropolitan areas. Students in fifth grade and older may participate in the residential programs. Courses are offered in mathematics, science, and humanities. Students study one topic for 3 weeks, and they may be eligible for school credit upon successful completion of the course.

The advantages of participating in a summer program designed specifically for gifted students include:

1. Participants study a topic in depth for an extended period of time.

2.  Academically talented students are grouped together, giving them the opportunity to work together at a faster pace and in greater depth than they would in a typical class in school. They also enjoy interacting with other like-minded students.

3.  In an accelerative summer class, students may complete one or more years of mathematics and receive credit for one or more school courses. Therefore, they may be placed in a higher level, more challenging mathematics class when they return to their regular school in the fall.

4.  Research studies have demonstrated the effectiveness of participating in fast-paced, accelerative summer programs. For example, students completing a summer mathematics course at Johns Hopkins University took more advanced courses in high school and took more Advanced Placement exams at an earlier age than students who had scored similarly on above-level tests, but did not participate in summer programs (Barnett & Durden, 1993). Students participating in fast-paced mathematics classes were also more likely to attend a more selective undergraduate institution and to enter college earlier (Swiatek & Benbow, 1991b).

*Weekend Programs for Gifted Students.* Weekend programs may be offered by local schools or by universities, and they can include a series of sessions offered on successive Saturdays or 1-day courses. Many are enrichment courses, but some universities offer courses that carry high school or college credit for young students.

Students who do not live near a center offering programs designed for mathematically talented students can check with local museums, science centers, and universities concerning enrichment classes they offer. Mathematically talented students might take courses designed for older students in order to be challenged. The director or coordinator of the program can provide guidance in selecting challenging courses. Listed below are several examples of weekend programs designed specifically for academically talented youth.

Carnegie Mellon Institute for Talented Elementary Students (C-MITES) offers Weekend Workshops throughout the school year on the Carnegie Mellon University campus in Pittsburgh and in Abington, PA. These 3-hour experiences are offered on a first-come, first-served basis to academically talented students in kindergarten through seventh grade. Weekend Workshops for mathematically talented students include Fractals, Graphing Calculator, Math Olympiads, The Mathematics of Puzzles, Fun With Fractions, Tessellations, Mathematics Games, and Building a Geodesic Dome. Instructors are selected for the program on the basis of their expertise in mathematics and their experience in working with gifted youth. Students may attend one or more of the 3-hour workshops a semester. Scholarships are available, based on financial need.

The Saturday Enrichment Program, offered by the Center for Talent Development at Northwestern University, provides courses for students in preschool through ninth grade. These courses are available on the Evanston, IL, campus to students who meet the following criteria: (1) score at the 95th percentile or above on a nationally normed, standardized achievement test in the area that matches the class for which the student is applying and (2) a recommendation from a current teacher or gifted program coordinator. Students may attend one course for 8 weeks. Courses are offered in science, math, literature, drama, and other areas. Math courses include Problem Solving for kindergarten through first graders, Number Theory for grades 2–3, Mathematical Investigations for grades 4–5, Statistics and Probability for grades 5–6, and Problem Solving for grades 7–9.

The Weekend Institute for Gifted Students (WINGS), offered through the University of Iowa's Belin-Blank Center, offers Saturday classes for students in grades 4–9. The classes are 3 hours in length. The range of course topics is wide, as indicated by the titles, which include HyperStudio; Fossil-Mania; It's Force, of Course; Election 2000; Dentistry and

Forensic Science; Animal Medicine; Math Olympics; Brain Teasers and Head Scratchers; and Making Plays. A parent workshop is also offered during each WINGS session.

*Individually Paced Programs.* The Diagnostic Testing→Prescriptive Instruction (DT→PI) model is useful for students who are extremely talented in mathematics and who cannot typically receive adequate challenges in the regular classroom. Julian C. Stanley developed this model for use with mathematically talented youth in seventh grade and older (e.g., Stanley, 2001). We adapted Stanley's model for use with younger students (see Lupkowski & Assouline, 1992; Lupkowski, Assouline, & Stanley, 1990). Using this model helps us to know if a student would benefit from program options that are more accelerative in nature or more enrichment-oriented. Briefly, the DT→PI model includes five steps: aptitude testing, achievement pretesting, readministering missed items, prescribing instruction, and posttesting. The DT→PI model is discussed in depth in Chapter 4. It is an excellent option for students who can't be challenged by the regular school curriculum taught at the usual pace.

*Magnet Schools.* Many large communities have magnet schools, which bring gifted students together to learn as a group. These schools are able to offer special advanced coursework in specific content for their students. Bringing gifted students together in this way has several advantages: It is more efficient in terms of teacher time and district expense to have students grouped together in one building, and students benefit both academically and socially from being grouped with other talented peers. Grouping gifted students with their peers for instruction makes it easier for teachers to tailor instruction (Rogers, 2002).

One example of a secondary-level magnet school is Iowa's Des Moines Central Academy, created by the Des Moines Public School District in 1985. During its first year, 52 academically talented eighth graders from Des Moines Public School middle schools attended the magnet secondary school for part of their school day. The purpose of this "experimental" school was to prepare students for Advanced Placement (AP) courses and tests by the end of their sophomore year. As of 1985, no students in Des Moines had taken an AP test (although coursework had been offered). Three years later, in 1988, the first sophomore class took a total of 41 exams, and 85% of the class scored 3 or better on the tests. The participation of Des Moines Central Academy students in the AP program skyrocketed (up 400%) from 1988 to 1998, and it continues to propel forward.

*Distance Learning and Correspondence Courses.* Correspondence courses and computer-based distance learning courses are gaining popularity with academically talented students. These courses permit students to work at a level and pace commensurate with their abilities because they are computer-based. Most students work independently; however, the work of some students is monitored by a local teacher-mentor. Although students taking computer-based courses may have few interactions with other students studying the same material, they have the benefit of taking a course that might not be available in their home school due to low enrollments or lack of teacher expertise (Wilson, Litle, Coleman, & Gallagher, 1998).

Since 1991, the Education Program for Gifted Youth (EPGY) at Stanford University has offered computer-based courses in mathematics, physics, expository writing, and computer programming to high-ability students through the Stanford Continuing Studies Program. The courses are taught through multimedia CD-ROM presentations and online "virtual classroom" tutoring sessions. Students must have access to a computer and a modem or network connection. E-mail access is also required for communication with EPGY instructors and students. Over 1,400 students from 17 countries are enrolled in this program, and they range in age from 5 to 18 (see "Resources" for information about contacting EPGY).

EPGY courses are designed specifically for gifted students. EPGY accepts scores from many different tests for students to qualify for their programs. Students must show that they fall within the top 15% of students in mathematical ability on the basis of standardized testing. Courses are individualized so that fast learners can move quickly through the mathematics sequence with little repetition, while slower learners will receive additional instruction. EPGY mathematics courses use symbolic computation environments in which students construct proofs of their answers. Such exercises ensure that students know both how to solve problems and why their solutions are correct. Mathematics courses offered include K–2 Mathematics, 3–4 Mathematics, 5–6 Mathematics, 7–8 Mathematics, Beginning Algebra, Intermediate Algebra, Precalculus, Honors Geometry, Calculus A–C, Linear Algebra, and Differential Equations.

Because the EPGY courses are computer-based, students can take advanced courses without leaving their schools. They also eliminate the problem of being placed in a class with much older students. In EPGY, students progress through courses at their own pace, making it possible for them to move on to university-level courses in several subjects before leaving high school.

The University of Nebraska–Lincoln (UNL) Independent Study High School (ISHS) has provided distance-learning opportunities since 1929. As a high school, ISHS is fully accredited by the Nebraska Department of Education and the North Central Association Commission on Schools. Although originally developed as a way to offer subjects to rural Nebraska students that were comparable to those offered in urban areas, the student body has grown throughout the decades to include students from around the world. Students may enroll in ISHS independently, or a student's school may enroll for him or her.

Students may enroll via fax, the Internet, postal service, e-mail, or telephone, and those who live in or near Lincoln, NE, can walk in and register in person. All students are required to have a local supervisor who is responsible for maintaining test security, establishing testing conditions, proctoring tests, and submitting completed tests to ISHS. ISHS recognizes that many people, including parents, supervisors, and others (even siblings), play a supportive role in terms of helping students complete their assignments.

ISHS currently offers courses in all major curricular areas. Although course offerings may include basic courses for students with special needs, they also include advanced courses for accelerated students. For mathematically talented students, ISHS offers a full spectrum of classes, from the prealgebra, pregeometry level, to calculus.

Although the high school community of ISHS is virtual, it is clearly a high school and includes such traditional services as individual academic advising and a newsletter, the UNL's *High School World* (for more information, see http://dcs.unl.edu/ishs).

### Exemplary Mathematics Programs

Some school districts have made a conscious effort to identify their mathematically talented students and to provide a carefully planned program for them. Three exemplary programs for mathematically talented elementary students are described below. The first two, North Hills School District Math Mentor Program and the Des Moines, Iowa, Community School RadAcc, are accelerative in nature. In other words, they move students forward in the curriculum at a faster pace. The final program described here, C²Math, differentiates instruction according to students' abilities, but its orientation is to enrich the curriculum, rather than to accelerate.

*North Hills School District Math Mentor Program.* The North Hills School District in Pittsburgh offers a unique program for its mathematically talented students. Students are systematically identified for mathematics enrichment and accelerative programs using a two-step testing process. Starting in the spring of fourth and fifth grade, students' testing records are reviewed. Those who have scored at the 97th percentile or above (local norms) on the Mathematics Total of the Metropolitan Achievement Test as part of the regular dis-

trict standardized achievement testing are invited to participate in Level 2 Mathematics Screening, which includes
administration of the Quantitative Ability, Mathematics Part
I, and Mathematics Part II sections of the Comprehensive
Testing Program series (Level E, which was normed on sixth
through eighth graders).

The top-scoring 2–3% of fifth- and sixth-grade students in
the Level 2 screening are invited to participate in a mentor-
paced mathematics program. During the fifth-grade year,
these accelerated students meet with their mentor alone or in
small groups twice a week during the school day. These 45-
minute  sessions occur in the students' home schools, and the
mentor travels from one school to another each day. The sixth
graders participate in three 45-minute sessions per week.

Participation in the North Hills mentor-paced program
results in the students being accelerated at least 1 year in
mathematics. These students complete fifth- and sixth-grade
mathematics in the same year, and they take Integrated Math
I (a seventh-grade course) in sixth grade.

In the mentor program, students study mathematics
intended to replace the regular mathematics requirements.
Their report cards and permanent records reflect their participation in this special program. The district chose to offer this
accelerative program in response to needs they had seen in
their students. As a way of being conservative, they decided
to offer the option to accelerate in mathematics by only 1
year. Students do not typically advance 2 or more years in
this program.

Those students who are invited to take the Level 2 screening test, but do not meet the criteria for participation in the
Math Mentor Program, are automatically considered for
enrichment in the regular classroom. They participate in
planned enrichment activities on an as-needed basis. Students
are pretested on each chapter. If they demonstrate mastery
level learning (defined as 90% correct), they receive enrichment. The enrichment activities are frequently developed by
the elementary math mentor, and they are delivered by the
regular classroom teacher.

The Math Mentor Program began as a pilot in 1993 and was implemented districtwide in 1995. Since that time, the first group of students has moved to high school and beyond. To ensure that continuous challenges in mathematics will be offered, the district hired a secondary math mentor to continue working with them as they progress through the secondary grades. When students have completed all of the math courses offered on the North Hills School District campus, they may take classes at the University of Pittsburgh (just a few miles away) or take Internet Calculus using computers in the school district.

*Des Moines Public School RadAcc.* In Iowa, the Des Moines Public School System implemented RadAcc, a specially designed program for their upper elementary students who are exceptionally talented in mathematics. There are four steps to entry into RadAcc. Step 1 is the establishment of a pool of potentially qualified fifth-grade students based upon either their third- or fourth-grade ITBS scores. Students qualify on the basis of an ITBS Math Composite percentile of 98 or 99 or Math Problem Solving or Math Concepts at the 99th percentile. There must also be evidence that the learner is self-directed. Students who do not qualify based upon their scores may be nominated based upon teacher recommendation.

Step 2 is the distribution of a letter to parents of students identified for the talent pool. Parents must then give permission for their fifth-grade child to take a sixth-grade district objective-based test. Students who demonstrate mastery (more than 80%) of the items on the test qualify for RadAcc. Parents are then invited to a meeting in which options, curricula, and restrictions are explained so that they may make a fully informed decision regarding their child's participation.

Step 3 is the participation of students in an intensive 3-week summer program. During this program, students review concepts missed on the district objective-based test and also cover seventh- and eighth-grade math concepts and problem-solving strategies.

From the results obtained in Step 3, there are six different recommendations for grade 6:

- Level A: Prealgebra (a significant percentage of the students from the pool);
- Level B: Seventh-grade honors math program (a significant percentage of students from the pool);
- Level C: Algebra I (some students);
- Level D: Traditional seventh-grade math (some students);
- Level E: Traditional sixth-grade math (very few students);
- Level F: Options above and beyond algebra (limited to a very few special cases).

Students who successfully complete Prealgebra in sixth grade take Algebra in seventh grade and, beginning in eighth grade, use the secondary magnet school, Des Moines Central Academy, to progress through Geometry, Algebra II, Trigonometry, Precalculus, Advanced Placement Calculus AB, and Advanced Placement Calculus BC. Since these students typically finish the available high school curriculum prior to graduation, they take college-level mathematics during their senior year.

*The Houston County Schools.** Personnel at the Houston County Schools in central Georgia realized they needed to develop a comprehensive plan for identifying and providing services to their mathematically gifted students (Culpepper, Finley, Gilreath, Powell, Cooper, & Gentry, 2000). The director of gifted education, gifted education teachers, mathematics coordinator, math facilitators, and the middle school and high school "Mathematics Vertical Team" leaders worked together to plan and implement a new program for all students in the school district (K–12) called the C²Math (Curriculum Compacting in Mathematics) program. These individuals

---

* We would like to thank R. Culpepper, S. Gilreath, and S. Powell for their helpful comments on an earlier draft of this section.

were interested in making sure mathematics was appropriately challenging "vertically," that is, from one grade level to the next, kindergarten through 12th grade.

Personnel recognized that students in their schools learned mathematics at different rates, had different backgrounds in mathematics, and were ready for different material at different times. They also recognized that many textbooks available today offer a weak treatment of mathematics to students in the elementary and middle school grades. They decided to develop their own comprehensive mathematics program using the compacting model of differentiated instruction.

The goals of the C²Math program were to improve mathematics instruction for all students in the district, offer gifted services to every student in his or her home school on a daily basis, provide talented mathematics students with instruction by gifted-certified teachers, and provide these services to mathematically talented students who might not have qualified for the district's gifted program under state criteria.

C²Math is an assessment-driven program. This means that students are tested to determine what they know and curricula are tailored to their needs, rather than using a set curriculum that is delivered to all students, regardless of ability. First, school personnel developed pretests based on the Georgia state curriculum standards. Students take these pretests before beginning each unit. Based on the results of the pretest, students are assigned to one of three flexible groups: Concept Development, Skills, or Extension. Scores are ranked in ascending order and students are grouped for instruction accordingly. Students in the Concept Development group have limited prior content knowledge and require the most basic instruction on the concept. Students in the Skills group have some knowledge of the topic. They have splintered skills on content knowledge and need instruction to fill in the missing pieces. Students in the Extension group have correctly answered most pretest items, thus demonstrating that they have a good knowledge of the topic and that they are ready for extended content. These students then receive mathematics instruction at the enrichment level.

The Concept, Skills, and Extension groups are flexible. Students are placed in different groups during the year depending on their prior knowledge of each unit's topic. For example, fourth-grade students studied six units during the year. At the beginning of the year, they were tested on the topic Number Sense and they were placed in one of the three groups for the first 6 weeks of the program so they could study that topic at the right level and pace for them. After those 6 weeks, students were pretested on the second topic, Multiplication. Students were then assigned groups for mathematics based on their Multiplication pretest results. Many students switched groups. In fact, during the year, 90% of the fourth graders changed groups at least once (Culpepper, Finley, Gilreath, Powell, Cooper, & Gentry, 2000).

$C^2$Math is not textbook dependent. Carefully tied to the Georgia state curriculum, it is a collaboration among the gifted education staff, the mathematics staff, the classroom teachers, and the teacher leaders (called the $C^2$ Facilitators). For the students in the Extension group, the planning team made sure that the mathematics was taught by a teacher who had earned the Georgia certification in gifted education. When the Extension group finishes working on the topic-related activities the planning team developed, they often have time for additional enrichment in mathematics. For example, the fourth graders completed the Number Sense topic in 4 weeks, instead of the 6 weeks allocated. In the 2 weeks they had left before beginning the next topic, the teacher provided enrichment on prealgebra topics.

After the Extension group of fourth graders completed work in the Data/Probability unit, they explored graphs of linear functions using graphing calculators. In every unit, extension teachers integrate more problem-solving and higher order thinking skills than in the Skills or Concept Development groups. Because this district's goal did not include acceleration but focused on enrichment, the teachers wanted to integrate as much challenge into their units as possible without accelerating the students. Instead of having the students move on to a new concept or new topic, they had them look at the same topic in a different way.

Houston County's middle and high school component of the "seamless curriculum" was developed using the Math Vertical Team approach developed by the College Entrance Examination Board (2001). The goal of this program is to align the curriculum vertically and to prepare more students to take advantage of the most challenging math courses in high school and college.

Vertical teaming eliminates repetition of previously learned material and provides students with meaningful instruction. Like C²Math personnel, these middle and high school math teachers found that the mathematics curriculum they were planning was richer and more challenging for all students. For example, they introduced graphing calculators in sixth grade and used them extensively as the students learned about functions, rates of change, and accumulation. Using graphing calculators allowed students to see the visual connections among abstract concepts. Teachers found that they were teaching mathematics concepts in greater depth than ever before.

The members of the planning group have worked hard to overcome challenges. For example, it was an adjustment for the C²Math teachers to be restricted to teaching one unit during a prescribed period of time and to teach all of the agreed-upon units in the same order. However, this restriction has allowed the program as a whole to be much more flexible and responsive to the abilities and needs of the students. One additional important limitation of this enrichment-based program as it is currently implemented is readily recognized by members of the planning team: It does not include a specific plan for acceleration for mathematically talented students. As the team noted, this is the next step in their program planning.

### Challenges in Developing Special Programs

When a school or school district devises a special program to recognize the needs of their exceptionally talented students, there may still be some difficulties. For example, if students are pulled out of the regular classroom and grouped to study mathematics for part of their school day, scheduling might be a challenge. If the school does not have block scheduling, for example, students will be pulled out of mathematics class at different times. This can make life very challenging for the teacher or mentor, as well, as he or she might end up traveling between several buildings several times a day, so that much time is wasted going from one site to another. For example, we know of one teacher whose Tuesday schedule dictated that she should be in each building no longer than one period; in effect, she had to be in seven different buildings in a seven-period day.

When students participate in a special program that pulls them out of the regular mathematics class, the math mentors need to be very sensitive to the needs and feelings of the regular classroom teachers. They need to be aware that some teachers might resent the fact that someone else provides the curriculum for their mathematically talented students, which might imply that the regular classroom teacher cannot provide it appropriately him- or herself. In some cases, the mentors are also expected to provide the regular classroom teacher with activities for the enrichment students, and again this must be handled with sensitivity.

## Issues in Planning Programs
## for Mathematically Talented Students

To this point, we have discussed many of the different program options for mathematically talented children. Each of these program types has advantages and disadvantages. As school personnel design programs and parents make decisions about appropriate options for their talented children, they need to think about many issues, which are discussed below and are summarized in Table 6.5.

### A "One-Size-Fits-All" Program Doesn't Fit All

Mathematically talented students have varying abilities in mathematics. Some students identified as mathemati-

---

## Table 6.5
## Issues in Planning Programs
## for Mathematically Talented Students

- A "one-size-fits-all" program doesn't fit all.
- Students may be gifted in math, but not in other subjects.
- The gifted program might not address the needs of the mathematically talented students.
- "Acceleration vs. enrichment" is a false dichotomy.
- Acceleration doesn't necessarily produce gaps.
- Students extremely talented in mathematics may make computation mistakes.
- Special programs need to be integrated into district-wide objectives so they can survive changes in personnel.

---

cally talented may be somewhat advanced compared to other students in their grade, while others may be exceptionally advanced. To challenge these students appropriately, we encourage educators to match the program and the curriculum to the students' abilities. Some talented students might be ready to skip ahead two grades in mathematics and work with a mentor; others might need enrichment within the regular classroom. What is important is that the curriculum be matched to the abilities of the student by adjusting the pace and the depth at which the material is presented.

### Students May be Gifted in Math, But Not in Other Subjects

Many mathematically gifted students with whom we work are exceptionally mathematically talented, yet they are not equally talented in other academic areas. For this reason, they might not be placed in their school district's gifted program or have opportunities to advance their mathematical skills. It is important not to deny mathematically talented students opportunities because they have not been labeled "gifted." For example, one school district did not permit a mathematically precocious student the opportunity to participate in a Mathematical Olympiads for Elementary and Middle Schools competition because that student had not been identified as gifted.

### The Gifted Program Might Not Address the Needs of the Mathematically Talented Student

Unfortunately, in some cases, even though a mathematically precocious student might be identified for a special program for gifted students, the program itself might be inadequate to meet his or her needs. In many school districts, the gifted program is a pull-out program, meaning that students are pulled out of the regular classroom for a specified period each week to work on challenging assignments. In many cases, the gifted program is enrichment-oriented. Time might be devoted to field trips, writing plays, or learning music history. While all of these may be worthwhile pursuits, they do not address the everyday needs of the mathematically talented student to learn new, challenging mathematics. "The gifted program will meet mathematically talented students' needs only if the students are permitted to move ahead in the mathematics curriculum at an appropriate pace and depth, not if they are given random enrichment activities" (Lupkowski-Shoplik, 1996, p. 7).

### "Acceleration vs. Enrichment" Is a False Dichotomy

Enrichment and acceleration are not mutually exclusive concepts. Good enrichment in mathematics is accelerative, while good acceleration practices include adding enriching activities and concepts. Allowing students to move along at an appropriately rapid pace and encouraging them to study mathematics in great depth are both needed for the curriculum to be correctly matched to the students' abilities.

## Acceleration Doesn't Necessarily Produce Gaps

One major concern that is often mentioned when considering accelerating a student is that they will have gaps in their backgrounds if they skip ahead in mathematics. An effective way to alleviate these concerns is to test the student to determine what he or she does and doesn't know (see Chapters 3 and 4). What concepts does the student still need to master before being ready to advance? A teacher or mentor can work with the students on the concepts they have not mastered. Within a fairly short period of time, the accelerated students will have filled in the gaps and will be ready for the new challenges of the more advanced class.

## Students Extremely Talented in Mathematics May Make Computation Mistakes

Students who have advanced understanding of mathematical concepts may not demonstrate the same high level when it comes to computation tasks (Lupkowski-Shoplik, Sayler, & Assouline, 1994). For example, a student who understands the concept of multiplying 2 two-digit numbers might make an addition error while solving a problem. In a study of 1,667 students, Rotigel (2000) found that mathematically talented youth consistently scored higher on measures of mathematical concepts than on measures of mathematical computation. She listed several explanations, including:

1. Talented students might perform better on conceptual tasks than on computation tasks because conceptual tasks seem to be easier for them to solve using their reasoning abilities, while solving computation problems may be more dependent on direct instruction (Lupkowski-Shoplik, Sayler, & Assouline, 1994).
2. These mistakes may be a result of carelessness if talented students have become bored and have developed the bad habit of doing mathematical calculations too quickly, without writing down their thought process.
3. Because mathematically able students may have impressed others with their logical reasoning abilities,

they may have been able to avoid the memorization and drilling needed to be more accurate when working computation problems.

## Special Programs Need to Be Integrated Into Districtwide Objectives So They Can Survive Changes in Personnel

Frequently, special programs for mathematically talented students are established because of the commitment and hard work on the part of one or two individuals. These programs might thrive as long as the key individual is still in the same position. If that key person leaves, however, is there a guarantee that the program will still continue? We have developed a "To Do" list to help institutionalize the program so that it becomes a part of the school and not dependent upon one or two individuals:

1.  Create ownership for the constituents (parents, students, principals, gifted coordinators, and regular classroom teachers). People feel the program is "theirs" if they are involved from the beginning. They begin by taking a role in the planning phase of the program. Through a group approach, they come to an agreement on how to provide services for the mathematically talented students they have identified. They are involved in the design of the program and in decision making as the program begins. In the case of a program using a mentor approach, for example, regular classroom teachers and mathematics specialists can be included so they have input into making the program work smoothly.
2.  Document what has happened. Gather a copy of all of the letters sent to parents. Keep careful records of test results and placement decisions. Track students' progress through the program. Make a handbook for the new people who will be joining the team. This handbook might include a yearly calendar that indicates what needs to happen when. For example, when should assessment occur? When are placement deci-

sions made? The handbook should also include a statement of purpose, an explanation of how students are identified for the program, summaries of program evaluations, and so forth.

3.  Devise a written plan. Develop a written schedule of goals for the program for the next several years. Develop a plan for growth of the program. Provide information that addresses the question, "What happens to the students after the program ends?"

4.  Gather data and conduct evaluations that demonstrate the program works. Concrete data, such as test scores showing the students in the program have made greater gains in achievement test scores than students of equal ability who are not in the program, are important.

5.  Listen for the success stories. Students who have completed the program can return to tell teachers, school board members, and others how the program had an impact on their education. Written testimonials about what a difference this special program made can be powerful. Copies of newspaper articles and other public relations materials are also useful.

6.  Make sure there is articulation within the curriculum. People who will be involved at the high school level need to be aware of this program so they can begin planning for these students when they get to higher grade levels.

## Long-Term Planning

The following is a list of eight points for students, families, and teachers of mathematically talented youth to consider as they plan a student's educational program.

1.  "Elementary students who are extremely talented in mathematics need time to develop the necessary cognitive structures that characterize mathematical maturity" (Lupkowski & Assouline, 1992, p. 129).

"How do I know when my child is ready to study algebra?" asks the parent of a mathematically talented second grader. Although we are strong advocates of acceleration for mathematically talented youth, we also realize that few students are ready to study algebra at this young age. The goal for elementary students is "mathematical maturity" before moving on to algebra, geometry, and so forth. This maturity is characterized by a thorough background in general mathematics (arithmetic), the structure of the number system, arithmetical problem solving, and Piagetian formal operational thinking (Piaget & Inhelder, 1969).

2. "In order to start at the right point and ensure that students develop strong mathematical underpinnings, it is extremely important to assess carefully what skills and content have been mastered" (Lupkowski & Assouline, 1992, p. 130).

This point follows directly from the point listed above. For the parent of the precocious second grader, the answer is not to rush the student into algebra. Instead, we recommend carefully assessing his or her background and mathematical abilities and moving ahead at a pace appropriate for the student (see Chapter 4). This might result in the student accelerating 1 or more years in mathematics. At the same time, the precocious second grader might demonstrate mastery of skills that have not been formally taught to him or her; instruction should begin at the point where students have mastered the content and are ready for new material.

3. "Mathematically brilliant youths should study mathematics at their appropriate level of mental functioning and at a steady rate" (Lupkowski & Assouline, 1992, p. 130).

Students do not benefit from racing ahead in mathematics only to find themselves so far ahead of the mathematics delivery systems at their schools that they go for months (or even years) at a time without studying new topics. Students do not need to study mathematics intensively for hours every day.

Instead, the goal is to offer students opportunities to study mathematics at a steady rate throughout their schooling. This might mean weekly meetings for 2 hours with a mentor, rather than five 45-minute periods of mathematics every week. Students might need to participate in after-school or summer programs to be challenged adequately. Other students who are in a challenging mathematics program during the school year won't need an accelerative summer program. They would benefit from other pursuits.

4. "Mathematically talented students need to balance their accelerated study of mathematics with the study of other academic subjects and participation in extracurricular activities" (Lupkowski & Assouline, 1992, p. 131).

Parents and teachers need to see to it that students do not become too focused on their study of mathematics. Accelerated students have the luxury of time; if they have moved ahead of their agemates by one or more years, they can take the time to do an in-depth math or science fair project. They have the time to explore nonacademic areas and study academic subjects in depth. Although our goal is not to guarantee that mathematically talented students are "well-rounded," students do benefit from exposure to different subjects, trying out different hobbies, playing with friends, having time alone, and having unstructured time. Many enrichment programs on diverse topics are available at local museums, summer camps, and so forth.

5. "Teachers, mentors, clubs, and competitions can enrich an accelerated mathematics curriculum for talented youths" (Lupkowski & Assouline, 1992, p. 131).

Just as students benefit from studying mathematics in a formal setting, they can also benefit from learning mathematics in an informal setting. Teachers and mentors can give students interesting problems to try, and students can participate in math clubs or competitions (see "Resources"). Thus, students are moving ahead in mathematics, but they are also taking advantage of the range of mathematics enrichment opportunities that are available to them.

6. "Moving ahead extremely fast in the mathematics sequence is likely to catapult the elementary student beyond the offerings of the school system before high school graduation" (Lupkowski & Assouline, 1992, p. 132).

It is extremely important to consider carefully the impact a grade skip or subject-matter acceleration will have on a student's educational program. The problem is not that the student will "run out" of mathematics to study. It is simply that the school district might not have any more formal mathematics courses for the student to take! There is always more mathematics for students to study (ask any mathematics professor who is conducting mathematical research and trying to invent new mathematics daily). The question is, how does the student get to the class? There might be problems with transportation, timing of courses, not taking mathematics with agemates, and so forth. All of these things are important to think about. Plan for the eventuality that the student will move beyond the course offerings of the school system. He or she might take more advanced courses by attending college part-time, working one-on-one with a math teacher, or taking a distance-learning course.

7. "Academic programs offer varied opportunities for able students to forge ahead in mathematics" (Lupkowski & Assouline, 1992, p. 132).

School is not the only place where students have the opportunity to study mathematics. They may participate in accelerative mathematics opportunities through Johns Hopkins University's Center for Talented Youth (CTY) or enrichment opportunities through the Belin-Blank Center at the University of Iowa or the C-MITES office at Carnegie Mellon University. Today, there are hundreds of interesting opportunities for motivated students, ranging from accelerative classes, to competitions, to science projects, to mentorships. These talented students should be made ready by age 12 or 13 to study algebra and subsequent courses quickly and well. The use of the DT→PI model ensures that students do not skip important concepts. A variety of challenging programs are listed in the "Resources" section and academic talent searches are discussed in Chapter 5.

8. "Before moving on to college coursework, students should take the most challenging coursework available at the high school level" (Lupkowski & Assouline, 1992, p. 133).

It does not make sense to rush through high school and move on to college just to be faced with needing to take remedial courses. Taking the most challenging courses available in high school ensures that the student is well prepared for college. Advanced Placement (AP) courses provide college-level work to students before they graduate from high school. Students may earn credit for one or many courses, leading to early graduation from college or the opportunity to take more advanced or varied courses in the undergraduate curriculum. Students may also benefit from online courses, such as those offered by Stanford University's Education Program for Gifted Youth, which was mentioned earlier in this chapter.

## Evaluating Programs for Mathematically Talented Youth

Belcastro (1987) outlined a set of principles that gifted programs for mathematically talented elementary students should meet and proposed a series of excellent questions that program personnel should ask in reviewing their program:

1. Is the program for mathematically talented elementary students part of the regular curriculum? It is recommended that delivery of services occur through the subject area (mathematics), not through a general

gifted program where mathematics would be only a part of the activities. This program should be guided by a teacher assigned to the regular elementary curriculum and who also has a mathematics specialty. The program offered by the North Hills School District, mentioned earlier in this chapter, is a good example of a program that addresses this principle.

2. Is there a rigorous identification procedure? Students selected for advanced programming in mathematics should be identified by assessing their mathematics abilities (e.g., through a mathematics achievement test).

3. Is the program in effect every day? Students in the regular classroom study mathematics every day, and mathematically talented students should have that same opportunity. The advantages of having the program in effect every day include constant interaction with and attachment to a teacher of the mathematically gifted, the enthusiasm for mathematics that can be achieved only through continuous time, and the joy of moving ahead rapidly in mathematics or delving deeply into it.

4. Does the program provide placement and interaction with peers who are mathematically talented? Research shows that ability grouping is an extremely effective method for educating gifted students. The advantage of ability grouping for mathematics is that students study mathematics with others who have similar abilities, feelings, interests, problems, and goals.

5. Is faster pacing of the mathematics group facilitated? Mathematically talented students need less time than others to learn information, and they don't require constant repetition. The pace of the program should be matched to the student's learning rate.

6. Are students challenged at their own level using advanced strategies? Belcastro (1987) responded to his question,

The mathematics curriculum designed for mathematically gifted elementary students should be different from the mathematics curriculum offered other students. It should pay greater attention to advanced skills and techniques and advanced conceptualizations that by definition cannot be easily understood by students of similar age but of average or below-average ability in mathematics. Further, the teachers of the mathematically gifted must present mathematical content on higher levels of abstraction and in more complex form than is done for students average in mathematics. The program for the mathematically gifted should challenge them at their own levels in mathematics. (pp. 8–9)

7. Are teachers selected who are trained in the education of the mathematically gifted? Teachers in a program designed for mathematically gifted students should be excellent teachers who have a content specialization in high-level mathematics and therefore can answer students' high-level questions. These teachers will also be familiar with the scope and sequence of the K–12 mathematics curriculum. It is imperative that they understand the unique characteristics of mathematically talented youth and that they be aware of challenging opportunities where these students can interact with their mathematically talented peers.

We would like to add another question to Belcastro's list: Was a needs assessment conducted when the program was designed? It is important to discern why a program is being developed, for whom it is developed, what will happen, and who the key players will be because they all have an important role in the planning process. This creates a sense of ownership and helps ensure that the program will exist even if one or two key players leave.

## Conclusions

After mathematically talented students are identified, it is important to recognize the kinds of programs that will be beneficial to them. A wide range of programmatic options is available to mathematically talented students, from enrichment within the regular classroom, to fast-paced, individualized instruction. We have tried to emphasize in this chapter and throughout this book that the important idea is achieving the "optimal match," that is, matching the right level and pace of curriculum to the abilities of the talented student.

Learning occurs only when there is an appropriate match between the child's ability and the circumstances he or she encounters (Hunt, 1961). We recommend carefully assessing students' levels of general ability, specific aptitudes, and achievement and matching the curriculum to them. For some students, enrichment programs provide enough stimulation. Other students need a program that is radically accelerated.

# 7 Curricula and Materials

- It is important to develop differentiated curricula for mathematically talented students.

- Mathematically talented students should study a variety of topics, including problem solving, geometry, algebra, arithmetic, number systems, probability and statistics, spatial visualization, and ratio and proportion.

- The core curriculum presented to mathematically talented students needs to be enriched in a systematic manner.

- Teachers of mathematically talented students should go beyond the textbook to differentiate the curriculum by using manipulatives, math games, and computer programs.

- The National Council of Mathematics Teachers standards should be adapted to accommodate the academic needs of mathematically talented students.

*My child, then in second grade, had tested at the eighth-grade level on [a standardized math] test. I tried advocating for him with the math teacher, who considered this for a moment and thoughtfully replied, "I can't teach your child. I have to teach the curriculum."*
—*Zelda, quoted on The Stupid Things I Heard Today, http://www.hoagiesgifted.org/stupid_things.htm*

WHEN WE BEGAN to write this chapter on curricula, our desks were covered with stacks of math enrichment books, algebra books, and elementary math curricular materials. How should we guide teachers and parents in selecting the appropriate curriculum? We quickly realized that we couldn't single out one curriculum or book to recommend for all mathematically talented students or we would be like the second-grade teacher in the quote above. The point we had to make is that the everyday curriculum offered in most schools is not challenging enough, and our job is to provide guidance on how to supplement and differentiate it for the individual student.

At the same time as we are making suggestions about how to modify the core curriculum for gifted students, we concur with Dana Johnson (1994), who wrote,

> Appropriate curriculum and instruction for mathematically gifted learners cannot be delivered only through a supplemental program or enrichment materials. The core curriculum for those students must be modified so that the daily exposure to mathematics is closely aligned with their abilities. (p. 233)

Johnson is absolutely right in stating that mathematically talented students need something different from what is offered in the typical elementary classroom. Not only do they need a modified program, but they also need a predetermined scope and sequence that allows them to progress systematically through a challenging mathematics curriculum. This predetermined scope and sequence will most likely be developed according to the resources available within a district because this is not a prepackaged curriculum that you can go out and buy. However, we recognize that few schools have developed the predetermined scope and sequence for their mathematically talented youth. They are not able to offer a truly differentiated curriculum for mathematically talented students. Therefore, our goal in this chapter is to offer the classroom teacher the tools needed to differentiate the "regular" curriculum for highly able students.

## Acceleration and Enrichment

The typical elementary and middle school curriculum is simply not challenging enough for mathematically talented students. Assouline and Doellinger (2001) documented this statement in a study of over 6,000 academically talented third through sixth graders. As a group, these students performed well on items measuring concepts in geometry, prealgebra, and probability and statistics. "This is a strong indication that these content areas should be introduced earlier and at higher challenge levels than typically provided by a traditional elementary curriculum" (Assouline & Doellinger, p. 132; see also Lupkowski-Shoplik, Assouline, Benbow, & Brody, 2003).

The choices for the delivery system for this advanced content include acceleration, enrichment, or both (see Chapter 6). When enrichment is relevant and appropriate, students benefit from studying a topic in more depth or learning about a topic that is not covered in the regular mathematics curriculum. The advantages of this enrichment include giving the students more challenging work, exposing them to different topics in mathematics, or helping them to learn a topic in greater depth. Enrichment requires that the teacher offer something different to the student, which requires extra work on the part of the teacher. It also assumes that the teacher has the adequate mathematics background to give the student relevant horizontal or vertical enrichment.

Acceleration is easy to implement; in its simplest form, a student merely leaves the regular classroom to go to a higher grade level for mathematics and returns to the regular classroom after the mathematics period ends. This student is treated like all of the other students in the math class, and no "extra" work needs to be done by either of the teachers. For this reason, acceleration has a distinct advantage over enrichment. However, one of the problems with acceleration is that, even though a student moves up to a higher grade for mathematics, the curriculum for the older grade might still not be advanced enough or offered at a fast enough pace. Therefore, differentiation would still be needed.

As we stated in Chapter 6, a combination of acceleration and enrichment makes the most sense. For mathematics, relevant enrichment has some accelerative components, and appropriate acceleration includes some enrichment (Schiever & Maker, 1997; Stanley, 1979b). Sheffield (1999b) has taken this a step further. Since the typical U.S. curriculum lacks depth—it has been called a mile wide and an inch deep (Schmidt, McKnight, & Raizen, 1996)—Sheffield suggested developing offerings for mathematically talented students that combine depth or complexity, breadth, and rate. Programs for mathematically talented students should not only increase the pace of the curriculum offered, but they should also offer greater depth and help students to see the mathematical connections among concepts.

## Key Elements of a Curriculum for Mathematically Talented Students

Johnson (1994) has recommended six key elements of a curriculum for mathematically gifted students:

1. The *scope* of content must be as broad as possible.
2. The content must be presented at a *greater depth* and with a higher level of complexity, combined with abstraction of concepts.
3. The curriculum must be presented with a *discovery orientation* that allows for exploration of concepts.

4. Instruction should continue to focus on *problem solving*.

5. Teachers should use a *metacognitive approach* to solving problems, that is, teachers should take advantage of systems such as Polya's, in which students actively think about their problem-solving process as they (a) understand the problem, (b) make a plan to solve it, (c) carry out the plan, and (d) look back to evaluate the process and the solution.

6. Mathematics should be *connected to other disciplines*. For example, there is an obvious connection between math and science, but there is also a documented connection between math and music. Two examples of curricula that make math/science connections are Great Explorations in Math and Science (GEMS) and Activities in Math and Science (AIMS).

No one curriculum will meet the needs of all mathematically talented youth. As discussed in the previous chapter, the instructional goals and the program options will vary, depending upon the needs of the student.

## What Should Mathematically Talented Students Study?

With all of these important elements in mind, let us now turn to more specific information about the topics mathematically talented students should study in elementary and middle school. Mathematically talented students need to have a thorough understanding of elementary school mathematics before moving on to the formal study of algebra. Listed in Table 7.1 are the topics students are recommended to study. This list is drawn from topics provided by Wheatley (1983; 1988), Johnson (1994), and Sheffield (1994). Not only should students study all of these areas, but the curriculum for them should also be enriched in these areas. And, as we have described in Chapter 4, once students have mastered topics in a given area, they are ready to move on to the next level.

---

### Table 7.1
### Essential Topics
### for Mathematically Gifted Elementary Students

- Problem Solving
- Geometry and Measurement
- Math Facts and Computation Skills
- Arithmetic and Algebraic Concepts
- Computer Programming
- Estimation and Mental Math
- Structure and Properties of the Real Number System
- Probability and Statistics
- Spatial Visualization
- Ratio, Proportion, and Percent

---

## Problem Solving

Problem solving provides opportunities for higher order thinking skills in the context of real-world, interdisciplinary applications (Johnson, 1994). Children do not develop the ability to solve problems automatically as they master computational skills; they need to be taught problem-solving skills (Lenchner, 1983). Solving problems differs from simply doing an exercise in mathematics. Mathematics exercises are used to practice a known procedure; the means to arriving at the solution of an exercise is evident. Typically, teachers teach a concept, give practice exercises, and check the exercises to be sure students have learned the procedure. In contrast to an exercise, when students are presented with a math problem, the solution or the means to solving that problem is not always apparent. Correctly solving the problem generally requires some degree of originality or creativity on the part of the problem solver (Lenchner). Thus, problem solving is a skill requiring more sophisticated cognitive skills than those required for basic computation.

George Lenchner's *Creative Problem Solving in School Mathematics* (1983) provides an excellent resource for teaching problem-solving skills. Lenchner includes classic problem-solving methods, such as drawing diagrams, making lists, finding patterns, working backward from the solution, and testing and verifying. Other helpful problem-solving books include *Reasoning and Problem Solving: A Handbook for Elementary School Teachers* by Stephen Krulik and Jesse A. Rudnick (Allyn and Bacon, 1992), *Problem Solving Strategies: Crossing the River With Dogs* by Ted Herr and Ken Johnson (Key Curriculum Press, 1994), and problem sets from the Mathematical Olympiads for Elementary and Middle Schools (see Appendix). Helpful problem-solving books include sample problems, activities, games, and methods for teaching problem-solving skills.

We are pleased that problem-solving activities have become more and more a part of the regular curriculum because all students benefit from them. However, we have noticed a disturbing trend: Some schools have turned to the abundant materials available on problem solving and are using the activities as their "gifted program" in mathematics or to enrich the regular mathematics program, thus avoiding having to do any other programming. Although problem-solving activities are challenging and fun for talented students, they do not provide all the mental stimulation they need. In other words, problem solving is not the one answer to gifted students' needs in mathematics. In fact, no single area can provide the challenge that talented students need. Rather, they need a complete and balanced program in mathematics.

### Geometry and Measurement

Mathematically talented students benefit from an exposure to geometry long before the time of the typical 9th- or 10th-grade geometry class. Rather than studying formal theorems or proofs, as in a formal geometry class, elementary and middle school students benefit from a study of geometry that emphasizes concepts and principles. This approach goes beyond the focus on simply defining terms and shapes that previously characterized elementary students' study of geometry. One text that might be helpful to young students who are not yet ready for a formal high school geometry course is

*Experiencing Geometry* by James V. Bruni (1977, Wadsworth), which is an informal, intuitive introduction to geometry. It contains numerous concrete models and illustrations and encourages readers to investigate fundamental geometric concepts through observation and experimentation.

The Carnegie Mellon Institute for Talented Elementary Students (C-MITES) summer program offers third through sixth graders a 2-week course called "Informal Geometry." Students in this class use tangrams and pattern blocks to investigate geometric concepts and vocabulary and dot-paper to make congruent and similar figures. These activities provide concrete, hands-on experiences with fractions. Students also learn about transformations and the four types of isometries (translations, rotations, reflections, and glide reflections). In addition, in the spatial visualization component of the class, students use concrete manipulatives to help them visualize and represent three-dimensional objects from two- and three-dimensional pictures. Then, they use cubes to construct buildings from plans. Students learn to distinguish different orientations, recognizing left and right views as reflections. The casual classroom visitor might perceive that students are merely playing with blocks, when actually they are struggling with mentally rotating objects and interpreting two-dimensional plans using three-dimensional objects. This is the most challenging aspect of the course for some students. While students in this class never complete a formal proof, they learn many challenging concepts that are typically reserved for 10th-grade geometry classes. One of the resources that "Informal Geometry" teachers use is Michael Serra's *Discovering Geometry: An Inductive Approach* (1997, Key Curriculum Press), which investigates topics including inductive reasoning, using tools of geometry, transformations and tessellations, and deductive reasoning.

As the description of the C-MITES Informal Geometry course indicates, it is essential that elementary students use manipulatives to study geometry. Obviously, using manipulatives makes abstract topics more concrete and understandable. For example, students can calculate the area of a rectangle using unifix cubes. Students should also learn how to use a protractor. More information about manipulatives and useful geometry books can be found in the "Materials" section starting on page 245.

## Math Facts and Computation Skills

Good computational skills with fractions, decimals, and integers are essential for work with many higher level concepts (Johnson, 1994). Elementary and middle school students need to master the basic facts of arithmetic because further study in mathematics requires accurate calculations. We advocate the use of calculators, but we also recognize that children need to learn their basic facts. Students still need to be able to estimate and verify their answers.

Even exceptionally mathematically talented students need drill and practice. Some talented students become very good at convincing their parents and teachers that they don't need to do *any* drill or repeated practice. In one case, a mathematically talented girl complained of headaches when asked to practice the multiplication tables or if she didn't know the answer to a multiplication problem. Mastery tests showed that she did not have a good knowledge of basic multiplication facts, and we assumed that she was using her headaches as an excuse not to do something she did not feel confident in doing. Therefore, she needed opportunities to practice computation skills. Since school personnel recognized her level of mathematical talent, however, she was not held back in other areas because of her lack of knowledge of multiplication facts. Instead, she was given plenty of opportunities to practice computational skills while still working with more advanced concepts (Lupkowski & Assouline, 1992).

## Arithmetic and Algebraic Concepts

Some of the important arithmetic concepts that elementary students need to learn include prime, composite, factor, divisibility, ratio, and proportion (Johnson, 1994; Wheatley, 1983). Elementary students also need to study the concepts of variable, signed numbers, equations of curves in a plane, and intuitive solutions of number sentences (Wheatley, 1988). Students might find using manipulatives especially helpful when studying these topics. The standards for school mathematics set forth by the National Council of Teachers of Mathematics (NCTM, 2000a) encourages teachers to present algebraic concepts starting in kindergarten.

## Computer Programming

Computers have become a standard piece of educational equipment. Rather than using computers in math class strictly for drill and practice, mathematically talented students benefit from using them for developing their computer programming skills. Computer programming is valuable for its own sake, and it is beneficial in helping children to practice logic. Writing and debugging programs require reasoning and discipline (Wheatley, 1983). Students can begin studying simple programming such as Logo in the primary grades. Logo is useful for developing logic skills, solving geometry problems, and exploring concepts.

LEGO/Logo links LEGO building toys with the Logo programming language. Students begin by building machines out of traditional LEGO pieces, as well as gears, motors, and sensors. Students then connect their creations to a computer and, using a modified version of Logo, they can write simple programs to control their own machines. Students have built model houses that have lights that turn on and off at predetermined times, cars that follow a path, and model garages whose doors open when a car approaches. The LEGO company now sells a commercial version of LEGO/Logo. Experimental versions have been used in programs for gifted students at Carnegie Mellon University and at the Massachusetts Institute of Technology (MIT).

Johnson (1994) has recommended that, by fourth grade, a unit on BASIC programming should be taught with extended topics in the following years. BASIC is a computer language with many uses; students who study and experiment with it will be able to transfer their knowledge when learning more advanced languages later. For all of these computer programming languages, rather than spending a lot of time teaching it in depth, students might benefit from learning only a few programming statements and then being presented with problems to solve on the computer (Wheatley, 1988).

The C-MITES program has used the FUNdaMENTAL programming software extensively in a computer programming course during the summer, and gifted fourth through sixth graders have been very successful with it. Designed for sixth through ninth graders, FUNdaMENTAL is a complex, object-oriented programming language (i.e., rather than typing in lines and lines of computer code, students can simply look at the screen and move graphic representations around) developed specifically for educational purposes. FUNdaMENTAL allows students to develop sophisticated programs, but the drag-and-drop format makes it ideal for youngsters who may have the understanding, but not the typing skills or precision that an adult programmer would have. This allows students to be creative without getting hung up on typing in line after line of computer code. Students can build programs that make simple animations, all the way through elaborate interactive games that respond to keystrokes and mouse clicks. For more information about the FUNdaMENTAL language and programming environment, see http://www.kartoffelsoft.com. The FUNdaMENTAL software can be shipped within the continental U.S. and Canada. Since development on this software stopped in 1997, the inventory is somewhat limited, and it has not been tested on recent versions of Macintosh or PC platforms. We contacted the FUNdaMENTAL staff in April 2002, and they told us there were many copies in stock and they would be happy to move them from the warehouse into the hands of kids. This software is available for home or school use.

### Estimation and Mental Math

Mental arithmetic requires an understanding of relationships among numbers, not just remembering mechanical algorithms. Mental math skills should be encouraged continuously, beginning in the preschool years. Johnson (1994) recommends one unit each year on estimation, while encouraging estimation in all computational work throughout the year (see also Wheatley, 1988).

Even though calculators and computers are commonplace in elementary classrooms, elementary students still need to learn to estimate their answers. When students are able to estimate their answers, they can evaluate the results they get from calculators and computers and develop a sense of the "reasonableness" of an answer (Wheatley, 1983). See the books *Mental Math in the Middle Grades* by Jack A. Hope, Barbara Reys, and Robert Reys (1997, Dale Seymour) and *Estimation and Mental Computation: 1986 Yearbook of the National Council of Teachers of Mathematics* by Harold L. Schoen and Marilyn Zweng (1986, NCTM).

Specialists at the Center for Talented Youth at Johns Hopkins University, which offers the Young Students Classes for mathematically talented elementary students, recommend that children develop the habit of always checking out a problem before beginning any computation to determine approximately what their answers will be and, after working out the answer, asking themselves if it makes sense (Mills & Wood, 1988).

### Structure and Properties of the Real Number System

In the early grades, mathematically talented students need to learn some elements of the real number system, including whole numbers, fractions, and decimals. In upper elementary school, they need to be exposed to a unit emphasizing the concept of a system along with the teaching of irrational numbers before they begin the formal study of algebra (Johnson, 1994).

An interesting way to enrich the study of numeration and number systems is to study the history of mathematics. For example, students can study the number systems used by ancient cultures and can even make up their own number systems. By studying other numeration systems, students will better understand the base-10 system (Wheatley, 1983).

## Probability and Statistics

Before students take Algebra I, they should study probability and statistics (Johnson, 1994). At a young age, students can experience these topics by gathering data and making tables and graphs. Students in preschool and kindergarten enjoy collecting data using survey questions such as "What is your favorite kind of pet?," tabulating the responses, and graphing the results. Older students might enjoy more complex problems, such as surveying a sample of adults and predicting the results of a local election (Pratscher, Jones, & Lamb, 1982).

Nancy Pfenning used her expertise as a statistics professor to present sophisticated concepts to groups of mathematically talented fourth through sixth graders. Her book, *Chances Are* (1998, Prufrock Press), includes the curriculum she wrote for a two-week summer course in probability and statistics for gifted students at Carnegie Mellon University. In her book, Pfenning teaches the students proper notation, vocabulary, and advanced concepts, but does it in a manner that is very accessible to elementary and middle school students. Students in her class learn concepts that go well beyond mean, median, and mode; the book covers concepts as sophisticated as standard deviation, the normal curve, and sampling theory.

## Spatial Visualization

Spatial visualization means the ability to visualize spatial transformations (e.g., mentally rotating a cube). Wheatley (1988) cited a number of research studies that document the importance of recognizing spatial visualization as an ability in mathematics. Wheatley claimed that "of all intellectual factors, spatial visualization is the most highly correlated with mathematics achievement and least addressed in the mathematics curriculum" (p. 255). This skill is important for doing mathematics, science, and engineering. Manipulating real objects helps students to develop an understanding of spatial relationships, which helps prepare them to manipulate objects mentally. Many commercially available computer games can help students practice this skill. Also, making three-dimensional models using tangrams, tessellations, and graphing help children learn to think visually (Wheatley, 1983). Johnson (1994) recommended including a short unit on spatial visualization each year throughout elementary and middle school. In our university-based programs for mathematically talented students, we have noticed that some mathematically talented students who were outstanding in number sense, computations, and problem solving had a relatively difficult time with spatial visualization activities, but they benefited from exposure to and practice with such activities, including the ones found in the *Spatial Visualization: Middle Grades Mathematics Project* by Mary Jane Winter, Glenda Lappan, Elizabeth Phillips, and W. Fitzgerald (1986, Addison-Wesley).

### Ratio, Proportion, and Percent

Wheatley (1983) recommended studying ratio, proportion, and percent, and it is relatively simple to show students applications of these topics because proportional thought is the basis for much work in the sciences. Johnson (1994) specified that mathematically gifted students should be introduced to percents by third grade, and they should continue practicing and applying concepts of percent so that they are proficient by seventh grade.

### Other Topics

Sheffield (1994) listed many other topics that mathematically gifted students would find challenging. These are included in Table 7.2.

## Adapting and Enriching the Mathematics Curriculum in Your School

Challenging mathematically talented students is a major challenge for classroom teachers. Some teachers find it so

---

## Table 7.2
## Interesting Enrichment Topics
## for Mathematically Gifted Students

- Fractals and chaos
- The Pythagorean Theorem and Pythagorean Triples
- Fibonacci Numbers
- Finite differences
- Pascal's Triangle
- Golden Rectangle
- Magic Squares
- Other numeration systems (Babylonian, Egyptian, Chinese, Mayan, Roman, etc.)
- Figurate numbers (triangular, square, pentagonal numbers, etc.)
- Pi
- Topology
- Pendulums and other applied physics problems
- Transformational geometry
- Combinatorics
- Graph theory
- Computer programming and robotics, including Logo and LEGO-Logo

*Note.* Adapted from Sheffield (1994).

---

challenging that they totally ignore the situation and do nothing. Teachers and parents who are reading this book recognize that doing nothing is a disservice to the students and to their teaching and that they are able to rise to the occasion by adapting and enriching the curriculum. We value the contributions that Johnson (1994) and Sheffield (1999b) have made about programming and curriculum.

Johnson (1994) recommended the following:

1.  Mathematically talented students should be accelerated at least one grade level in the textbook series being used.

2. Teachers should give a preassessment to students to determine what they already know. If the teacher can eliminate some review material at the beginning of the year, it is more likely that they will reach the chapters at the end of the book, which presumably contain more new and challenging material.
3. Teachers should assign the harder problems at the end of a problem set, rather than those at the beginning of a problem set. Teachers should also assign the extension or "challenge" problems from the textbook.
4. The textbook should serve as a resource or support, rather than the only source of curriculum. Teachers should use additional materials to enrich and extend the textbook topics.

Sheffield (1999b) added another point:

5. "A program that helps students develop their mathematical abilities to the fullest may allow them to move faster in the class to avoid deadly repetition of material that they have already mastered" (p. 46).

Therefore, both the level and the pace of the mathematics curriculum need to be adjusted. These adjustments can occur in several ways: (1) through the Diagnostic Testing→ Prescriptive Instruction model, (2) by compacting the curriculum within the regular classroom, or (3) by adjusting the curriculum and grouping talented students together for math instruction.

### DT→PI Model

The Diagnostic Testing→Prescriptive Instruction (DT→PI) model was discussed thoroughly in Chapter 4. It involves pretesting students and then tailoring instruction to their needs. Thus, it is a highly individualized program that allows students to study mathematics at the appropriate pace and level.

## Adjusting the Curriculum
## and Grouping Students Together

Winebrenner (1992) suggested developing a "compactor" for each student individually; assessing his or her strengths, weaknesses, and interests; and designing alternative activities for the individual student. Pretesting is an important component of this process. Once mastery is attained, the time saved can be used in a variety of ways. The most important step in this process is selecting appropriate alternate activities. These activities should be closely tied to the mathematics curriculum, yet they should not be merely busy work. We prefer that students be allowed to move on in the curriculum (an accelerative model), yet we recognize that sometimes this is not possible. If the student does not simply move on to the next chapter or topic, it is important to choose carefully the right kinds of enrichment activities that will be meaningful and challenging. If the time saved is used for the student to go to the library, do an independent project, or play on the computer, is the student really advancing in mathematics or just doing busywork?

Another alternative to differentiating the curriculum for the individual student is to make a conscious, preplanned effort to devise a curriculum that is readily responsive to students' individual needs. This might include selecting a number of students for accelerated programming, as in the school district that selects four or five students each year to take Algebra I as sixth graders or modifying the curriculum in other ways. The program offered by the Houston County Schools in Georgia (see Chapter 6) for example, pretests students before each unit to determine what they know and don't know. Based on the results of each pretest, students are assigned to one of three flexible groups: Concept Development, Skills, or Extension. Students in the Concept group are given introductory material, students in the Skills group are given somewhat more challenging work, and children in the Extension group are given enrichment. The goal of this program is to develop a curriculum that is more responsive to the students' needs. The drawback of this particular approach is that there is no specific plan for accelerating the students through the curriculum; for example, if students in the Extension group finish their unit before the 6-week time period is up, the teacher is expected to do additional enrichment activities with the students, rather than simply allowing them to move on. The planning team for this program recognizes that they need to include an accelerative component.

## NCTM Standards and Their Impact on Mathematically Talented Students

The National Council of Teachers of Mathematics (NCTM) has developed a series of standards for assessing, teaching, and learning mathematics to assist school personnel in devising mathematics curricula for students in kindergarten through grade 12 (see NCTM, 1989, 1991, 1995, 2000a).

NCTM (1989) identified five goals for school mathematics that apply to all students:

1. Become a mathematical problem solver.
2. Learn to communicate mathematically.
3. Learn to reason mathematically.
4. Learn to value mathematics.
5. Become confident in one's mathematical ability.

The curricula developed and published in the 1990s reflect the 1989 standards. There is a new emphasis on group problem solving, hands-on experiences, and real-world problems, rather than on rote memorization of math facts (Johnson & Sher, 1997). The standards have had a positive influence on the teaching of mathematics for all students, but we feel that they did not do enough to address the needs of mathematically talented students. The standards simply state that the core curriculum should be enriched to meet the needs of mathematically talented students, and NCTM essentially dismisses acceleration as a method for matching the curriculum to the student before grade 9.

The standards have been useful in providing a common vocabulary for curriculum developers and educators as they establish the scope and sequence for the mathematics curriculum. Unfortunately, the standards are stated in very general terms and do not provide specific curriculum recommendations. Furthermore, the standards provide what would be considered an acceptable minimum level of requirements curriculum should include. What is needed though, are objectives that set specific recommendations and goals for mathematics curriculum. These curriculum objectives should not only be set at a minimum level, but should also include those set at an optimal level. (Assouline & Doellinger, 2001, pp. 123–124)

Sheffield (1994) carefully examined the 1989 NCTM Standards as they relate to mathematically talented students. She recommended that all students, including mathematically gifted students, should follow the core curriculum set forth in the standards. "Top students should explore topics in more depth, draw more generalizations, and create new problems and solutions related to each topic" (Sheffield, p. 21). Although all students should have access to technology and manipulatives, top students should use those materials to explore the topics even further. She added that,

Examples of superior student work should be available to students so they have something to strive for. Olympic athletes would not have progressed as far as they have, if they did not have superior examples of earlier athletes to emulate. The same is needed for student work in mathematics at all levels. (p. 9)

Johnson and Sher (1997) demonstrated how the 1989 NCTM standards needed to be adjusted for mathematically talented students (see Table 7.3).

| Table 7.3 Selected Mathematics Standards and Necessary Adaptations for High-Ability Learners | |
|---|---|
| **Standard** | **Adaptations for High-Ability Learners** |
| Grade K–4 Standard 8: Whole Number Computation | Accelerate students who have mastered computation. Include more open-ended problems and projects that challenge able students and keep their interest in the subject. |
| Grade K–4 Standard 9: Geometry and Spatial Sense | Identify challenging geometric problem solving tasks and advanced spatial tasks. |
| Grade 5–8 Standard 8: Patterns and Functions | Identify sources of high level pattern investigation problems. |
| Grade 5–8 Standard 9: Algebra | Offer more abstract problems and ideas than textbooks offer. |
| Grade 5–8 Standard 10: Statistics | Provide more in-depth study of statistics than texts provide. Develop challenging project ideas. |

Note. From *Resource Guide to Mathematics Curriculum Materials for High-Ability Learners in Grades K–8*, 1997, by Dana T. Johnson & Beverly Taylor Sher. Williamsburg, VA: Center for Gifted Education, College of William and Mary. Copyright © 1997 by the Center for Gifted Education.

VanTassel-Baska and Johnson (1994, cited in VanTassel-Baska, 1998) suggested specific approaches for modifying the NCTM content standards for gifted students. These include:

1. Conduct a careful diagnosis of the instructional level of students in each mathematics strand.
2. Select resources in each strand that allow students to move to the next level at a self-paced rate.
3. Ensure that problem sets are challenging.
4. Cluster gifted students together for math instruction.
5. Assess students at frequent intervals for mastery of key standards within and across strands. (p. 421)

Although it is inherent in point #2, we would like to highlight a sixth point: Permit and encourage students to accelerate in mathematics. Research has demonstrated that acceleration is a powerful, effective programming tool for mathematically talented students (see Lupkowski-Shoplik et al., 2003).

## How Do We Know When They're Ready to Study Algebra?

In the late 1980s, Wheatley (1988) addressed this question as an issue of curricular implementation. He acknowledged that the popular approach is to offer algebra at the eighth-grade level for gifted students and to open the course up to younger, exceptionally precocious students. But, that begs the question of when are the exceptionally precocious youngsters ready to study algebra? Students are ready to study algebra when they have formal reasoning skills; for example, when they can think abstractly and use symbols as part of their problem-solving strategy (Baldwin, 1980). This may happen for mathematically gifted student much sooner than the age of 13 or 14, when the average adolescent has developed these skills and algebra is typically introduced. The key is not the age or the grade, but the reasoning skills of the youngster (Keating, 1973).

The work by the Study of Mathematically Precocious Youth (SMPY) at Johns Hopkins University has been useful in helping school personnel determine when students have the formal reasoning skills needed to take a rigorous Algebra I course. SMPY defined *readiness* as having earned a score of 500 or above on the mathematics section of the SAT I before age 13 (see Lupkowski-Shoplik et al., 2003). In addition, the Raven's Progressive Matrices (Raven, Raven, & Styles, 1998) have been very useful in measuring abstract reasoning ability and the student's readiness for studying more advanced mathematics (see Chapter 3).

Algebra has been seen as the "gateway" to higher level mathematics and challenging science courses. The typical progression is Algebra I, Geometry, Algebra II, Precalculus, and Calculus. If a student waits until ninth grade to take Algebra I, he or she will be unable to study calculus until entering college unless he or she takes two mathematics courses during the same year in high school (Lupkowski & Assouline, 1992).

Usiskin (1999) offered an interesting discussion about developing mathematically promising students. He noted that, 20 years ago, eighth graders taking Algebra I were seen as gifted because only 13% of the eighth-grade population took that course. In more recent years, Algebra I has been offered more routinely to eighth graders; in fact, in some schools, as many as 50% of eighth graders take Algebra I, and, "in those schools, no one sees eighth-grade algebra as a sign of giftedness any longer" (p. 62).

This trend will, therefore, impact the curriculum of the lower grades and may require that teachers expose elementary students to a more challenging prealgebra curriculum. It may also mean that, finally, mathematically gifted students may be presented with more appropriately challenging curricula while in the upper elementary grades so that they can take Algebra I when they are ready for it, perhaps as early as sixth grade and, in some unique cases, as early as fifth grade.

## Concepts vs. Computation

As discussed in Chapter 6, mathematically talented students may not demonstrate equal strengths in mathematics concepts and mathematics computation tasks. In fact, Rotigel

(2000) documented our observation that mathematically talented students tend to perform better on measures of mathematical concepts than on measures of mathematical computations for a variety of reasons. The programming and curricular implication for this is not to hold students back from studying high-level concepts if their computational abilities are somewhat less developed. As Sheffield (1999b) stated so eloquently,

> Students who are challenged to find the answer in as many ways as possible, to pose related questions, to investigate interesting patterns, to make and evaluate hypotheses about their observations, and to communicate their findings to their peers, teachers and others will get plenty of practice adding two-digit numbers, but they will also have the chance to do some real mathematics. (p. 47)

## Materials

### Textbooks

Traditionally, textbooks have been the main teaching materials for mathematics. Although they use supplemental materials, teachers prefer to use a textbook as their "roadmap" for the school year. Most of the textbooks in the United States today are based upon the spiral curriculum, in which students are exposed to a topic one year, and then they return to it again in future years, presumably at a higher level. This means that first graders learn one-digit addition, second graders learn two-digit addition, and third graders learn three-digit addition. This approach is not the optimal one for mathematically talented students because they do not require this type of repetition and review in order to master a concept. Since the standard curriculum is so repetitive, students do not study much new material, especially in the middle school years. For example, in a classic study, Flanders (1987) examined three popular textbook series used in many schools and found the average number of pages offering new material for each year was quite low. He found that, for grade 4, only 45% of the material was new, while for grades 5 and 6, the percentages were 50 and 38, respectively.

When selecting materials for mathematically talented students, educators should choose those that emphasize higher order thinking skills, including analysis, synthesis, and evaluation, rather than rote learning and memory-recall questions. Topics should be presented in depth, and possibilities for extensions should be included. Textbooks will not provide all of the desired features, so teachers will need to seek out other materials or prepare their own (Johnson, 1994).

When selecting textbooks, we recommend texts that stress concepts, not computation. We also recommend using pretesting extensively, especially in the early chapters of the book, which tend to be review chapters. Students who demonstrate mastery of those review topics should be allowed to move on (Lupkowski & Assouline, 1992).

Textbooks that are concise, contain clear explanations, provide examples of completely solved problems, and contain large numbers of practice problems that could be assigned for homework are ideal for a student who participates in the DT→PI process (described in Chapter 4). If the answers to about half of those practice problems are provided in the text, students can check their own work (Bartkovich & George, 1980).

An important point that teachers should remember is that they do not have to start on page 1 and go through each and every page. They can selectively use portions of the textbooks. Pretesting students will allow teachers to determine what they already know, and they will be able to save valuable time by not spending excessive time reviewing "old" material.

## A Few of Our Favorite Math Books

Earlier in this chapter, we mentioned one of our favorite math books, *Creative Problem Solving in School Mathematics* by George Lenchner (1983, Houghton Mifflin, available from Mathematical Olympiads for Elementary and Middle Schools, http://www.moems.org). C-MITES and the Belin-Blank Center have used this book for over 10 years with great success. Written by the founder of the Mathematical Olympiads for Elementary and Middle Schools, it is an excellent problem-solving book. It doesn't require algebra, but the problems are high level and challenging, even for gifted sixth graders. We have successfully used it with gifted third through sixth graders. Related to that is another book by George Lenchner, *Math Olympiad Contest Problems for Elementary and Middle Schools* (1997, Glenwood Publications, also available from Mathematical Olympiads for Elementary and Middle Schools).

Another favorite is Edward Zaccaro's *Challenge Math* (2000, Hickory Grove Press). This book is packed with lots of fun, tough problems for teachers and students who love challenging math. An experienced teacher, Zaccaro wrote this book for mathematically talented fourth through eighth graders. The book contains more than 1,000 problems in 19 chapters/units. The emphasis of the book is on problem solving, and solutions are available in the back of the book. There are three levels in each chapter, the most challenging level being the Einstein Level. The purpose of the book is to understand the meaning of math in the world. Zaccaro suggests that teachers use Chapter 18 as a test chapter to see if students are ready for it. The Belin-Blank Center at the University of Iowa has used this book in its Challenge Math program. It might also be useful for homeschoolers.

Finally, for both teachers and students, we really like *Mathematics: A Human Endeavor* (3rd ed.) by Harold Jacobs (1994, Freeman), which is appropriate for mathematically gifted students in middle school. Chapters include Mathematical Ways of Thinking, Number Sequences, Symmetry and Regular Figures, Methods of Counting, and Topics in Topology. We have also used this book in our teacher-training programs at C-MITES as a way of enriching teachers' own understanding of mathematics and giving them confidence in teaching mathematics.

Other Resource Books

Below we have listed a number of resource books that parents and educators of mathematically talented students will find useful.

Bloomer, A. M. (1995). *Getting into area: Hands-on problem-solving activities for grades 4–6.* Palo Alto, CA: Seymour.

Cash, T. (1991). *101 physics tricks.* New York: Sterling.

Erickson, T. (1996). *United we solve.* Oakland, CA: eeps media.

Fitzgerald, W., Winter, M. J., Lappan, G., & Phillips, E. (1986). *Middle grades mathematics project: Factors and multiples.* Menlo Park, CA: Addison-Wesley. (This book is one in an excellent series of hands-on math books. We highly recommend the *Middle Grades Mathematics Project* series. We have used these books extensively in C-MITES classes.)

Johnson, C. V. (1994). *Packaging and the environment: Real-world mathematics through science.* Menlo Park, CA: Addison-Wesley.

Kleiman, A., Washington, D., & Washington, M. F. (1996). *It's alive!* Waco, TX: Prufrock Press. (This is a fun book of real-life math problems, such as "Have you ever wondered how many earthworms are in a football field?")

Kleiman, A., & Washington, D., & Washington, M. F. (1996). *It's alive . . . and kicking.* Waco, TX: Prufrock Press. (More fun, real-life math problems.)

Kremer, R. (1995). *From crystals to kites: Exploring three dimensions.* Palo Alto, CA: Seymour.

Kremer, R. (1989). *Exploring with squares and cubes.* Palo Alto, CA: Seymour.

Kroner, L. R. (1994). *Slides, flips and turns.* Palo Alto, CA: Seymour.

Lappan, G., Fitzgerald, W., Winter, M. J., & Phillips, E. (1986). *Middle grades mathematics project: Similarity and equivalent fractions.* Menlo Park, CA: Addison-Wesley.

O'Connor, V. F., & Hynes, M. C. (1997). *Mission mathematics: Linking aerospace and the NCTM standards.* Reston, VA: National Council of Teachers of Mathematics.

Pentagram. (1989). *Puzzlegrams*. New York: Simon & Schuster. (This is a hard-to-find book available in used book stores, but it's worth the trouble to find it. Pentagram has also developed *More Puzzlegrams*, which, like its predecessor, is packed with interesting math puzzles and gorgeous graphics.)

Pfenning, N. (1998). *Chances are: Making probability and statistics fun to learn and easy to teach*. Waco, TX: Prufrock Press. (This book was written by a C-MITES teacher, and it contains the curriculum she has used in her extremely successful and hands-on Probability and Statistics summer class, taught to gifted fifth through seventh graders.)

Phillips, E., Lappan, G., Winter, M. J., & Fitzgerald, W. (1986). *Middle grades mathematics project: Probability*. Menlo Park, CA: Addison-Wesley.

Poamentier, A. S., & Salkind, C. T. (1988). *Challenging problems in geometry*. Palo Alto, CA: Seymour.

Roper, A. (1991). *Cooperative problem solving with tangrams*. Sunnyvale, CA: Creative Publications.

Serra, M. (1997). *Discovering geometry: An inductive approach* (2nd ed.). Emeryville, CA: Key Curriculum Press.

Seymour, D. (1971). *Tangramath*. Sunnyvale, CA: Creative Publications.

Seymour, D., & Britton, J. (1989). *Introduction to tessellations*. Palo Alto, CA: Seymour.

Sherard, W. H. III (1995). *Cooperative informal geometry*. Palo Alto, CA: Seymour.

Shroyer, J., & Fitzgerald, W. (1986). *Middle grades mathematics project: Mouse and elephant: Measuring growth*. Menlo Park, CA: Addison-Wesley.

Shulte, A. P., & Choate, S. A. (1977). *What are my chances? Book B*. Mountain View, CA: Creative Publications.

Stenmark, J. K., Thompson, V., & Cossey, R. (1986). *Family math*. Berkeley, CA: Lawrence Hall of Science, University of California. (This book contains activities for parents to use at home with their children. It is also an excellent resource for school personnel who want to organize a "family math night.")

Thompson, F. M. (1994). *Hands-on math: Ready-to-use games and activities for grades 4–8*. West Nyack, NY: Center for Applied Research in Education.

Washington, M. F. (1995). *Real life math mysteries*. Waco, TX: Prufrock Press.

Winter, M. J., Lappan, G., Phillips, E., & Fitzgerald, W. (1986). *Middle grades mathematics project: Spatial visualization*. Menlo Park, CA: Addison-Wesley.

Willoughby, S. S. (1991). *Mathematics for a changing world*. Alexandria, VA: Association for Supervision and Curriculum Development.

## Web Sites

*Math Forum (http://mathforum.org.)*. This is an excellent resource for math students and teachers. Students can find answers to their burning math questions in the Ask Dr. Math section. The Internet Mathematics Library offers lesson plans, resources, and games. The Problems of the Week are designed to provide creative, nonroutine challenges for students in grades 3–12. Other sections on this site include mathematics appropriate for kindergarten through graduate school.

*Education Place (http://eduplace.com/main.html)*. This Web site contains sections for teachers, parents, and students. For example, the kids' section contains weekly brainteasers (see http://eduplace.com/math/brain).

*Hoagies' Gifted Education Page (http://www.hoagiesgifted.org)*. This is a classic resource for gifted education. One of the pages is specifically for mathematically talented students (http://www.hoagiesgifted.org/math.htm). It contains links to many other math-related Web sites that students will enjoy.

## Computer Software

We try to use certain rules of thumb when selecting software for mathematically talented elementary and middle school students. First, we like software that has a variety of components so that the level of challenge can be varied. Second, we look closely at the level of challenge. Often, if a piece of software is rated as appropriate for students in grades 6–8, for example, mathematically gifted students in fourth and fifth grade might be challenged by it. When selecting software that has been designed for older students, though, it is important to look at the language level, violence, and appropriateness of content for a younger student.

We prefer software that is intuitive and user-friendly, where students can just jump in and get started without having to read a lot of directions. It should be easy to access the help mode and to get answers to questions as students work through the software. It should also be varied enough so that students remain interested in working on it. We also try to find software that doesn't require a lot of reading, especially for the younger students, because their reading skills may be relatively less developed than their mathematics skills. Other important aspects of the software include quality of graphics, what types of teacher materials are provided, and the overall presentation.

We have chosen only a few pieces of software to present here. The Math Forum Web site offers a page of links to other Web sites that offer software reviews (http://mathforum.org/mathed/math.software.reviews.html) so readers can obtain information about the latest software. Below are listed some of our favorite pieces of software.

*Zoombinis Logical Journey (Broderbund; [800] 395-0277; http://www.broderbund.com; appropriate for gifted fourth graders and older).* Students in the C-MITES program have used this award-winning, fun piece of software for a number of years, and it is a favorite. The Zoombinis are imaginary creatures who must escape from the evil Bloats, who have taken over their island. The Zoombinis face obstacles they must overcome using the player's logical reasoning skills. They go through 12 puzzles, with four levels of difficulty each. For example, in the "Pizza Path" section of the game, the Zoombinis must arrange combinations of pizza toppings and ice cream toppings that are acceptable to one, two, or three evil characters. The first character might like plain pizza with ice cream topped with a cherry, while the second one prefers pizza with everything and plain ice cream. Players must figure this out by first using trial and error and then logical reasoning. Our students found this very challenging, and they used paper and pencil to make tables and charts to keep track of what was accepted and rejected. Solving Zoombinis puzzles requires good mathematical thinking. Students practice algebraic thinking , data analysis, graphing and mapping , logical reasoning, pattern finding, problem solving, statistical thinking , and theory formulation and testing.

We have used this software in a classroom situation, but it is also marketed for home use. A Parent's Guide explains the educational approach behind each puzzle.

*TesselMania (MECC; available through http://www. worldofescher.com; appropriate for gifted third graders and older).* Mathematics is connected to the world of art through this creative tool. Students create tessellations electronically by modifying outlines and adding interior details. The software offers animated sequences to show how tessellations are created. "Magic Buttons" demonstrate how tiles are moved to tessellate a plane. Students' creations can be saved and printed. A teacher resource binder is provided, and it offers lesson plans for developing connections between math and art.

This software is fun and easy to use. Young students will learn about the building blocks of higher level geometry as they learn about symmetry, patterns, and isometrics. Older students will benefit from examining the transformational principles of translation, rotation, and glide reflection in action. Students will also enjoy the artistic aspects of this software.

*Mathville Jr. and Mathville VIP (Courseware Solutions; http://www.mathville.com; appropriate for gifted students in grades 2–4).* Students use their math skills as they travel through "Mathville" completing tasks; the harder the task, the greater the rewards. The "money" students earn can be spent in a bakery, a food store, or an art store. Skills include numbers and operations, data management, geometry/measurement, and problem solving.

*Hot Dog Stand: The Works (Sunburst; [800] 321-7511; http://www.sunburst.com; appropriate for grades 5 and up).* Players manage a hot dog stand at a sports arena. They keep records, determine prices, and plan marketing strategies. Players practice mathematical problem-solving skills and communication skills, including arithmetic operations, estimation, data gathering, data analysis, interpreting graphs, recognizing patterns, working backward, writing, choosing appropriate tools, and translating information into different forms. Players analyze data to make informed purchasing and pricing decisions. They may use the estimator, electronic checkbook, franchise report, and word processing tools as they work. They must also handle unexpected events as they operate their hot dog stand.

*Math Munchers Deluxe (MECC; appropriate for grades 3–6).* This program gives students a chance to practice basic math skills as it simulates a TV game show of math problems. Players are presented with questions on the board and they must direct a "Muncher " to the correct answer. Examples of questions include "Find the factors of 3," "Find the proper fractions," or "Select the prime numbers." Players can change the game to allow bad critters to interfere with the Muncher's work. At the beginning of the game, the player is given four Munchers. If the player selects the wrong answer or allows the Muncher to run into a Troggle (the bad critter), the player loses a Muncher. *Math Munchers Deluxe* is highly entertaining, so children will want to play it. It is best-suited for individual or small-group use.

### Calculators

Students should be given ample experiences with mental math and opportunities to demonstrate facility with basic skills using paper and pencil. However, calculators can and should be used in working with problems that emphasize higher order thinking. As described by Johnson (1994), calculators should be used as follows:

1. when the numbers are cumbersome and the goal of the activity is not to practice arithmetic skills;
2. in discovery lessons when students are observing a pattern (in this situation, it is helpful to have a calculator to do computations quickly and accurately);
3. to check students' accuracy when estimating answers to arithmetic problems; and
4. to obtain information such as square roots, logarithms, and values of trigonometric functions (formerly found by using a table!).

## Manipulatives

Manipulatives are tools for problem-solving and a means to represent and embody mathematical thinking. . . . Sometimes children, particularly math-talented children, are heard to say they dislike manipulatives and find that they hinder or slow down their mathematical thinking. However, when manipulatives can be used flexibly and creatively to solve problems and to embody and communicate meanings, resistance to their use melts away and even very bright children become enamored with their possibilities. (Waxman, Robinson, & Mukhopadhayay, 1996b, p. 32)

Teachers shouldn't be discouraged by the vast array of manipulatives from which to choose. Admittedly, they are overwhelming (and expensive). At the same time, it's relatively easy to make your own math manipulatives from everyday materials. These simple materials can be just as challenging (or even more so) than expensive manipulatives kits. One book that might help teachers sort out the information about manipulatives is *Activity Math: Using Manipulatives in the Classroom, Grades 4–6* by Anne Bloomer and Phyllis Carlson (1992, Dale Seymour). Some of our favorite manipulatives include:

- cubes and blocks for studying classification, place value, area, volume, and operation on whole numbers;
- tangrams, which are geometric shapes that can be put together to form a rectangle, a square, and to make designs; tangrams reinforce copying, matching, problem solving, and logical thinking skills;
- counters and items that can be sorted and grouped (such as small plastic toys, buttons, and Bingo chips) and used for studying sets, bases, and statistics;
- dice and cards for probability experiments;
- cuisenaire rods, a classic manipulative used for counting, studying fractions, and studying different bases;
- weights;
- protractors, rulers, and compasses;
- fraction bars;
- geoboards;
- base-10 blocks; and
- dominoes.

### Mathematics Games and Puzzles

The Soma Cube, first discovered by Piet Kien, is composed of 27 cubes that can be glued together to form various shapes. These shapes can then be arranged to make a cube with side length 3. This is a fascinating puzzle, and it can be solved 240 different ways. For more information, see the two Web sites: http://www.geocities.com/dnehen/soma/soma.html or http://users.ids.net/~salberg/soma/Soma. html.

Other games use logic: Battleship, checkers, chess, Connect-Four, dominoes, GO, MasterMind, Othello, and Pente. These games require players to think in a logical, organized fashion and to use their reasoning skills.

## Essential Features of Curricula for Mathematically Talented Students

The type of curriculum selected depends, in part, on the type of program or delivery system in place for educating mathematically talented students. The curriculum would be very different in a supplemental pull-out program that meets once a week compared to a homogeneously grouped class for mathematically talented students that meets on a daily basis. The following is a list of questions to ask when evaluating curricula and programs for mathematically talented elementary and middle school students.

- Are expectations high (Sheffield, 1994)?
- Is the mathematics program a part of the regular math curriculum (Belcastro, 1987)?
- Is there a specific scope and sequence for mathematically talented students (Lupkowski & Assouline, 1992; VanTassel-Baska, 1998)?
- Do the students have early access to high-level math concepts (VanTassel-Baska, 1998)?
- Are students given daily instruction in mathematics (Belcastro, 1987)?
- Are students given the opportunity to work with other mathematically talented students (Belcastro, 1987; Sheffield, 1994)?
- Do the materials contain a high level of sophistication of ideas (Johnson, 1994)?
- Do the materials contain extensions that challenge the most able learners (Johnson, 1994)?
- Is the material presented at a faster pace than in the typical classroom (Belcastro, 1987)?
- Can the content be tailored to students' individual needs, for example, are problems coded by difficulty level (Johnson, 1994)?
- Are higher order thinking skills (analysis, synthesis, and evaluation) essential to the lesson (Johnson, 1994)?
- Once mastery level has been demonstrated, do the materials de-emphasize basic skills (Johnson, 1994)?
- Are students asked to go beyond the concrete, and is abstraction encouraged (Johnson, 1994)?
- Do the materials contain opportunities for exploration

and extension activities based on students' interests (Johnson, 1994)?

- Do students have the opportunity for independent research and investigations (Sheffield, 1994)?
- Are there opportunities to create products that are open-ended and use advanced strategies (Belcastro, 1987; Johnson, 1994)?
- Have the teachers received specialized training in differentiating curricula for talented students (Belcastro, 1987)?
- Do the curricular materials encourage students to ask questions and make generalizations that go beyond the original problem (Sheffield, 1994)?
- Is achievement measured in a variety of ways, including observations, interviews, demonstrations, portfolios, and open-ended questions (Sheffield, 1994)?
- Do students have in-depth opportunities for real-world applications (VanTassel-Baska, 1998)?
- Do the students have the opportunity to use math concepts in other subject areas and as a tool for conducting research (VanTassel-Baska, 1998)?
- Do major themes frame the curriculum, or are they integrated into the materials (e.g., problem solving, change, models) (Johnson, 1994)?

## Conclusion

The goal when selecting a curriculum for mathematically talented students is to provide a challenging, content-filled program that allows them to move steadily through mathematics. This includes opportunities to reason, relate ideas, formulate and solve problems, become competent with computers and calculators, and learn when and how to estimate. At the same time, students establish a firm foundation of mathematics concepts, principles, and rules. This chapter presented a rationale for developing a differentiated curriculum and resources for developing that curriculum, as well as guidance in selecting curricula from the already-existing materials for mathematically talented students.

Regular classroom teachers in elementary and middle school may not have the necessary background for developing and delivering a curriculum for mathematically talented students. Also, the fields of mathematics and mathematics education are changing, and we need teachers who can respond to those changes. All of these ideas speak to the specific point: More professional development is needed for in-service and preservice teachers. That is the topic of the next chapter.

# 8 Teaching Mathematically Talented Students

- Along with parents, teachers play a critical role in the academic and social/emotional development of students.

- The role of today's teachers has expanded to include mentor, counselor, content expert, and advisor.

- Despite this expanded role, or perhaps because of it, many teachers today do not feel prepared to work with mathematically talented children.

- Whereas teachers from yesteryear had the simpler task of teaching the three Rs, today's teachers are faced with many significant philosophical and pedagogical issues, including acceleration, cooperative learning, grouping, and testing. Other issues relate to curricular standards, grade level at which math topics should be introduced, and which specific techniques for teaching mathematical concepts are best.

259

*The whole art of teaching is only the art of awakening the natural curiosity of young minds for the purpose of satisfying it afterwards.*
*—Anatole France*

AS THIS CHAPTER was being developed, we struggled with our fundamental rationale for writing about teachers and the teaching profession. We know that teachers influence their students, and we believe that teachers agree with the ideal expressed in the introductory quote (i.e., that "awakening the natural curiosity of young minds" is a laudable goal). However, the ideal is tempered by the reality that, in many of today's classrooms, curiosity is diminished, rather than satisfied. Because so many bright students express dissatisfaction with the current state of education, parents and other community members often malign teachers and are pessimistic about the education of their children.

Nevertheless, there have been some significant developments in the broad field of education that may help educators attain the ideal goal of teaching: satisfying the learner's curiosity. We are optimistic about the potentially positive impact of these developments and, in our view, optimism trumps pessimism! Therefore, we will concentrate on reporting and discussing the advances that have been made in education and the ways in which these advances can influence specifically the instruction of the mathematically gifted child.

The field of teacher training is complex, and the psychological and physical demands on teachers are exacting. We present our views about teachers and their professional development from the multiple perspectives of parent, teacher, administrator, learner, and teacher trainer. As parents, we have first-hand experience with the fact that parents are a child's first teachers and remain teachers throughout their children's lives. As former classroom teachers, we are very cognizant of an educator's responsibility for addressing the individual needs of students while optimizing the learning experiences of an entire class. In our present capacity as administrators for specialized university-based classes, we are responsible for finding the best teachers to teach in our programs. We also aspire to be lifelong learners, with some of our most favorable learning opportunities emanating from our interactions with talented students and their parents and teachers. It is through our work as teacher trainers (i.e., the preservice training of undergraduate students in teacher preparation programs), as well as in-service work with class-room teachers who attend classes, workshops, and seminars in order to improve their knowledge and skills, that we are able to view most optimistically the developing landscape of teacher-student relationships.

This chapter begins with a discussion of the philosophical and pedagogical concerns for mathematically talented students from preschool through middle school. The philosophical concerns relate to the issues created when a student is accelerated beyond his or her agemates, and the pedagogical concerns relate to teaching issues (i.e., ability grouping, tutoring, and activities related to curricular implementation). We continue with a review of recent and contemporary educational trends and comment on the effects of these trends or movements on the instructional goals for mathematically talented students, including the current standards, reform, and middle-school movements.

## The Preschool Years and the Impact of Parents and Teachers on the Mathematically Gifted

The years before a child enters kindergarten are magical years, during which time parents rediscover the joy of learning something new through their children's first experiences. Parents of mathematically precocious children are astounded with their child's fascination with numbers. This fascination typically precedes any interest in numbers displayed by a child's agemates, and often will exceed that of the child's peers throughout the school years. In Chapter 9, we describe Zach's propensity to count and arrange things by groups well before kindergarten. Zach also preferred books that involved numbers and counting. Many parents respond to their child's curiosity similarly to

Zach's parents: They encourage and provide for individualized learning opportunities. For example, Sarah was first introduced to division on a napkin in a donut shop when she was 3 because, as her mother said, "That's where it came up!"

Preschool teachers, like parents, are so attuned to the developmental needs of their students that they also individualize and personalize the curriculum, and the mathematically precocious preschool student will typically experience much satisfaction with the preschool setting. Combined, our work with mathematically talented students spans nearly 30 years and, to date, we find that preschool teachers are more sensitive than their elementary and middle school colleagues to their students' needs for individualized and developmentally appropriate curricula. The calls—mostly from parents, but some from teachers—begin with the first day of kindergarten, when the child (and parent) are first introduced to the standardized, grade-level curriculum. If the kindergarten curriculum requires that students learn to count from 1 to 100, then that is what they will do, even if they are already doing addition, subtraction, and multiplication. It is almost as if a child enters an elementary school, and *bam!*, the door to curiosity, exploration, and individualization slams shut.

An extensive discussion concerning curricula for mathematically talented students was presented in Chapter 7. Our major point here is that teachers have been trained to follow a set curriculum developed for implementation as a lock-step sequence by grade level (rather than ability or aptitude level). When efficiency (i.e., teaching large numbers of students) is the goal, the standardized curriculum meets the purpose. However an effective standardized curriculum for large numbers of students comes at a cost to both the individual students and the teacher. Csikszentmihalyi, Rathunde, and Whalen (1993) highlighted the cost:

> the role of the teacher has largely evolved from a practitioner in a domain into that of a transmitter of information . . . modern curricula . . . tend to depersonalize even the transmission of information. In the name of

diversity and efficiency, relations between teachers and students are kept highly specialized, programmatic, and brief. The rapid transfer of facts to masses of learners is stressed, not the slow cultivation of a unique individual's diverse gifts. The roles and goals available to teachers within these standardized curricula are in turn impersonal. They emphasize external mass performance standards, the delivery of uniform services, and the insulation of the curriculum from the interests of the particular person conveying it. (p. 178)

This observation captures the transition from the free-spirited, curiosity-oriented years of the preschooler, where the teacher's role is as much guided by the child's interests as it is to guide the child's interests, to the lock-step, standardized years of elementary and middle school, where the child's interest is superseded by a predetermined curriculum. In the elementary years, the student's exposure to curricula is not guided by his or her needs; rather, it is predetermined by a curriculum committee.

## The Elementary Years and the Impact of the Teacher on the Mathematically Gifted Child

In a landmark, now-classic study of the development of talent, Benjamin Bloom (1985) provided a retrospective look at the influence of the elementary classroom teacher on the future of individuals who became prestigious mathematicians: "In general, the mathematicians were not at all enthusiastic about their elementary school experiences" (p. 289). Bloom explained this finding as a symptom of the condition that the average elementary school teacher is not trained in methods for identifying or instructing students with exceptional abilities. Therefore, the special abilities of these mathematicians remained undiscovered and, therefore, underdeveloped during their elementary years. The mathematicians in Bloom's study considered that the "best [elementary] teachers were seen as the ones who would supply books or materials so that the mathematicians could work on their own" (p. 293). We do not interpret these results to mean that independent work in lieu of an appropriately challenging curriculum is the optimal situation; rather, the students were so far advanced compared to their classmates (and their teachers) that the independent work was better than sitting through a curriculum that was not challenging.

Since the publication of Bloom's study, several generations of students have gone through the U.S. educational system. How much has changed for these subsequent generations? One important change has been the vocalization of an awareness of the need for rigor in coursework; this need is often expressed with the call for a standards-based curriculum. For some educators and parents, rigorous content is connected with increasing class time, which represents an additional concern. A study by McRel (Mid-continent Research for Education and Learning) reported results suggesting that an average of 1,100 hours of instructional time are needed at each grade level to address the standards in language arts, civics, mathematics, and science (Florian, 1999). However, it is estimated that there are 1,000 hours of classroom time in U.S. schools, and elementary teachers estimate that they only spend 68% of that time, or 680 hours, on instruction. The main finding of the McRel study was that standards-based instruction requires more than the available classroom time.

That "time is of the essence" was also a finding in *Prisoners of Time*, a report by the National Education Commission on Time and Learning (1994). This fascinating report is filled with interesting facts and recommendations that revolve around five design flaws with respect to the ways in which schools use time. These time-oriented design flaws present significant challenges for today's schools:

- The fixed clock and calendar is a fundamental design flaw that must be changed.
- Academic time has been stolen to make room for a host of nonacademic activities.

- Today's school schedule must be modified to respond to the great changes that have reshaped American life outside school.
- Educators do not have the time they need to do their job properly.
- Mastering world-class standards will require more time for almost all students. ("Dimensions of the Time Challenge," ¶ 5)

A discussion about time may imply that quantity of instruction is more important than quality of instruction; however, we concur with the basic premise of *Prisoners of Time* that quality and quantity of instruction are intertwined.

Quality of instruction is a dominant concern of the public, parents, educators, and national leaders in organizations such as the National Council of Teachers of Mathematics (NCTM), who are eager to increase the mathematical content expertise and quality of classroom teacher preparation of today's math educators (NCTM, 2000b). The aim of enhancing teacher expertise in mathematics has waxed and waned for the latter half of the 20th century. When the former Soviet Union launched Sputnik in 1957, the U.S. government expanded programming and funded numerous grants that resulted in improved math, science, and foreign language curricula. Funding was also available to encourage a generation of individuals in science and math professions to become teachers. However, for a number of political and sociological reasons, the level and energy associated with post-Sputnik funding for professional development all but disappeared during the late 1960s and 1970s.

Federal funding to address the professional development needs of teachers in mathematics and science was implemented through the Eisenhower Professional Development Program, which was established in 1984 and reauthorized in 1988 and 1994 (Garet, Birman, Proter, Desimone, & Herman, 1999). This comprehensive report provides much substance for our discussion. In particular, there are many recommendations concerning the need for, as well as the impact of, professional development for teachers so that teacher and student can work toward the goal of enhanced student learning through improved classroom instruction. The bottom line is that,

> Overall, effective instruction can be characterized by content that is aligned with high standards and pedagogy focused on active learning. Content includes both topics of instruction, such as fractions, and the teacher's expectations for student performance, such as memorizing or understanding concepts. Pedagogy refers to the types of activities used in instruction and typically includes dimensions such as whole class versus individual instruction or project versus text-based instruction . . . Content coverage matters for student learning. (pp. 2–4)

We strongly agree that content matters. However, content is not the entire story when it comes to effective pedagogy. Also, focusing on the type of instruction (e.g., small group or individualized) is not the entire story when it comes to pedagogy. In the next section, we describe a study in which students teach educators some important lessons about teaching and the relevance of a teacher's attitude.

## The Middle School Years: How the Teacher and the Classroom Culture Make or Break the Student

Csikszentmihalyi, Rathunde, and Whalen (1993) wrote a powerful book, *Talented Teenagers: The Roots of Success and Failure.* This book is the report of a quasi-replication of Bloom's (1985) study of talented individuals. The focus of the Csikszentmihalyi et al. study was a group of bright adolescents who were talented in one of five areas: math, science, art, music, or athletics. Even though the subjects of the Csikszentmihalyi et al. study represent a narrower age range than the focus of our book and the talent domains represent a broader picture than our specific focus on mathematics, we have read this book many times and found it to be a tremendous resource, both practically and philosophically, for individuals interested in developing the mathematical talent of elementary and middle school students.

This book is potent because it answers the following question: *Why do some gifted teenagers cultivate their talent while others, who are equally talented give up?* To answer the question, data were analyzed from 200 talented teenagers to identify major factors involved in engagement and disengagement with the teens' talent areas. Because understanding the factors connected with involvement or dropping out is relevant for teachers who participate in the academic lives of talented teens and talented preteens, we shall briefly describe some of the results from the chapter in *Talented Teenagers* devoted to the complex relationship among talent development, schools, and teachers.

Csikszentmihalyi et al. (1993) make many poignant points regarding the role of teachers in the lives of their students and introduce the relationship between the student's talent and the role of the teacher as follows:

> Natural ability is a great advantage in learning to enjoy a field of talent. It is the key that unlocks the potential for *flow* [italics added] in activities that others experience as difficult, tedious, or boring . . . a time comes when the exercise of pure ability must give way to the guidance of adults. (p.177)

Flow, as described in Csikszentmihalyi's (1990) opus on the psychology of optimal experience, is the interaction between ability and passion. Flow happens when an individual is so totally engrossed in an activity that time seems to be suspended. Csikszentmihalyi et al.'s (1993) discussion about the role of the teacher in the academic lives of students continues with the paradoxical observation that math teachers are often "industrious and even inventive purveyors of knowledge across diverse domains [however] they are rarely practicing mathematicians" (p. 177). This finding is commensurate with Bloom's (1985) findings from the previous generation of talented mathematicians, and, in our opinion, this gap between the practice of teaching mathematics and the practicing mathematician may partially explain why so many teachers are neither interested in discovering mathematically talented students nor in developing the mathematical talent of students whose learning needs are clearly outside of the parameters of the regular standardized curriculum.

Thus, the fact that today' mathematics teachers are rarely mathematicians is important to understanding how to improve the skills of the teachers of talented students (i.e., increase their content expertise). However, even that observation, according to Csikszentmihalyi et al., is not the main reason that talented students remain unmotivated in the typical classroom setting. The main reason, which will be described below, is due to a concept that is less tangible than curricular content: teacher attitude regarding the role of the teacher in his or her students' lives.

Rather than concentrate on what it is about schools that disengage students, Csikszentmihalyi et al. (1993) focused on what it is about teachers who are able to engage their students. The critical concept is that teachers who are able to motivate their students have a great deal of content expertise, but equally—or perhaps more importantly—they have the ability to transcend the traditional attitude about the teacher's role of competent information giver to that of an individual who serves as "a daily model of the deeply interested life, a life of full participation in the world of challenges afforded by the domain [mathematics]" (Csikszentmihalyi et al., p. 178). Thus, while we support a teacher's pursuit of additional expertise in a subject area as a means to more effective teaching, we maintain that adding more knowledge about math will only superficially improve the learning environment for the mathematically talented students. In fact, expertise that is translated into a strict, rigid, authoritarian teaching style will do little to enhance the motivational culture of a learning environment.

The key to motivating students is being an effective role model who demonstrates a passion for learning that is translated into action. An effective role model is comfortable with a shift in power from the traditional role of teacher as an impersonal provider of information to the personal approach that ultimately empowers the learner to a lifelong love of learning within the talent area. An effective role model establishes a positive classroom culture that motivates students.

The culture of the classroom also impacts the motivation of students. With such a simple statement, it may seem as if we are overstating the obvious, but that is not our intent. It is important to understand the more subtle psychology that underlies a motivating environment. Skill, challenge, and ability are closely intertwined in the psychology of the student, and unmotivating learning environments occur when there is an absence of both challenge and the "sense of exercising skill." So, why not insist that all classrooms have extremely rigorous content and be done with the discussion? Csikszentmihalyi et al. (1993) found that it takes more than rigorous content to motivate students. This is not to say that the talented teens were not focused when the content was rigorous; compared to average teens, they were very focused. However, focus, or attention, is but one component of motivation that needs to be considered when discussing the talented teen. The companion to focus is volition.

Volition, or desire, is also necessary for the positive energy associated with motivation. In other words, students have to concentrate on the curriculum *and* they have to desire to concentrate on the curriculum. In many traditional classrooms, especially when the content is rigorous, attention and volition are viewed as mutually exclusive. Students are expected to focus on rigorous content because of its rigor and challenge. Why they desire to focus on this content is not often considered. A rigorous curriculum is important for getting the student's attention, but the way in which the teacher presents the curriculum is critical to the student's volition. Interestingly, extracurricular activities represent the one learning situation in which volition and attention are equally and consistently high among talented teenagers. The moral of the story is not to schedule regular classes as extracurricular activities! Rather, structure the environment of the classroom similarly to that of extracurricular activities where volition and attention are companions.

Is there a formula for a good middle school teacher? At this point, we ask the reader to stop for a moment and try to recollect your feelings about school during your adolescent years. We suspect that many recollections will parallel the findings of the *Talented Teenagers* study: Teens are rarely in a focused and positive frame of mind when they are in class. There are many factors that contribute to this condition, most of which are beyond the control of an individual teacher. However, teachers do have control over their teaching style and the content and pace of the curriculum.

Now, pause again and recall your favorite teacher during your teen years. Why was that person your favorite teacher? Because of the rigor of the content? Because of the teacher's passion for the content? What did that teacher do to make you recollect him or her now? The teens in *Talented Teenagers* (Csikszentmihalyi et al., 1993) were uniquely sensitive to the style and quality of teaching. They were very dynamic when referring to their most and least favored teacher, and they offered specific criticism: "Math and science students in our study complained most often of the standardization and rigidity of the curriculum and of their teachers' reluctance to deviate from highly structured programs" (p. 194). They also had specific examples of their preferences:

> [T]eenagers—talented and average—are captivated by examples of adults, such as star athletes and entertainers, who enjoy what they do and achieve fame and riches in the process. More surprising is the ability of some exceptional teachers to find a permanent place in their students' memories. What most intrigues students about these teachers is their enthusiasm for subjects that seemed boring and purposeless in other teachers' classes. Memorable teachers challenge stu-

dents to expect more than just recognition or a paycheck from the work they choose . . . memorable teachers might be thought of as alchemists of consciousness whose art lies chiefly in transmuting abstract symbol systems into problems that matter to students . . . teachers who enjoy their subject have a distinct advantage in being able to focus the attention of their student. (Csikszentmihalyi et al., 1993, pp. 184–185)

Memorable teachers present a complex curriculum that is matched to their middle school students' abilities while stretching their students' skills beyond their current grasp of content. Contrary to popular opinion that students want to take easy courses so that they are not too stressed, Csikszentmihalyi et al. (1993) found that students had

an avid willingness to accept challenges and overcome obstacles when the problems were interesting and the necessary skills were within the individual's reach. Becoming engaged in such challenges yielded useful feedback about ability, and permitted deep and sustained immersion in activities that began to become rewarding in their own right. (p. 186)

Students expressed such sentiment as, "I like math most when there is a hard problem and I can figure it out. When it's really hard at first and then I look at it and see the light—that's when I like it" (p. 187). This student was expressing what Robert Browning so aptly phrased: "A [person's] reach should exceed his [or her] grasp or what's a heaven for?"

In sum, effective classrooms are free from extraneous distractions, students are exposed to challenging curricula; and teachers provide informed and timely feedback concerning student performance. But, that is not the entire formula for effective teaching,

[W]e assume that if the material is well organized and logically presented, students will learn it. Nothing is farther from the fact. Students will learn only if they are motivated . . . Unless a person enjoys the pursuit of knowledge, learning will remain a tool to be set aside as soon as it is no longer needed. Therefore we cannot expect our children to become truly educated until we ensure that teachers know not only how to provide information, but also how to spark the joy of learning. (Csikszentmihalyi et al., 1993, p. 195)

## Sparking the Joy of Learning Within the Current Culture of Schools

Teachers play a critical role in satisfying the natural curiosity of young minds by sparking the joy of learning. In the following pages, we address the effects on teachers of current educational movements that emerged during the last quarter of the 20th century. These educational trends include (a) standards-based curricula and international comparisons and (b) reform movements, including middle school movements, as well as various pedagogical "innovations" to the traditional setting of students in rows with a teacher in front of blackboard instruction (e.g., the infamous cooperative learning and the ubiquitous impact of technology). We briefly address each movement or innovation as it relates to mathematically talented students and their teachers.

### Standards-Based Curriculum: A National or an International Curriculum?

Since 1989, when the National Council of Teachers of Mathematics (NCTM) published the Curriculum and Evaluation Standards for School Mathematics, teachers of mathematics have had a "map" to guide them in establishing standards for their students, as well as for their profession. The map became even more detailed with the 1991 publication of Professional Standards for Teaching Mathematics and the 1994 publication of the Assessment Standards for School Mathematics. These three documents were developed for all students so the lack of specific standards for mathematically talented students was understandable, but unfortunate. Many teachers of mathematically gifted students were disappointed with the omission of a clear statement that mathematically talented students need to progress systematically through the curriculum at an accelerated rate. In fact, the 1989 standards, upon which many current K–12 curricula are based, actually caution educators that, "students with exceptional mathematical talent who advance through the material more quickly than others may continue to college-level work in the mathematical sciences. However, we strongly recommend against acceleration that either omits content identified in these standards or advances through it superficially" (NCTM, 1989,p. 124).

What teacher would disagree with the concern about mastering a curriculum that is superficial? However, that concern is misplaced because mathematically talented students need challenging curricula from the beginning, not just at the secondary level. Eventually, NCTM generated a position statement regarding mathematically gifted students. As reported in Sheffield (1994):

> It is the position of NCTM that all students can benefit from an opportunity to study the core curriculum specified in the Standards. This can be accomplished by expanding and enriching the curriculum to meet the needs of each individual student, including the gifted. (p. 2)

This position essentially pits enrichment against acceleration and implies that any acceleration will be superficial. However, when gifted students are forced to suffer through an underchallenging elementary and middle school curricula, then in high school they will be forced to double up on more challenging curriculum and, by necessity, may have only superficial exposure. In other words, the 1989 standards may have helped educators elevate the general mathematics curriculum for all students, but they were detrimental for the mathematically talented students who needed more systematic, progressive challenge provided by a more advanced curriculum. Because the standards sanction enrichment of a core curriculum, they discourage teachers from planning a differentiated, accelerated curriculum for their mathematically gifted students.

Fast-forward to the beginning of the 21st century and the promotion of the "new" NCTM standards (NCTM, 2002), which were generated under the shadow of a looming concern for the performance of U.S. students in math and science as compared to international students. The results of the Third International Mathematics and Science Study (TIMSS; U.S. Department of Education, 1998) yielded a wealth of important results. As suggested by the title of this study, it is an international comparison of teachers, students, and curricula in mathematics and science. If you are not a parent or educator of a student in the U.S., then you might consider these results to be good news (especially if you live in Germany, Japan, or Korea); if you are a parent or educator in the U.S., then you will find these results to be very disconcerting. We have elected to mention only two of the findings that seem most salient for this chapter:

1. The mathematics curriculum for grades 5–8 seems to be a weak link in the U.S. educational system. Whereas the performance of U.S. fourth graders was above the international average in mathematics, the performance of U.S. eighth graders dropped below the international average.

2. A possible reason for the results reported in the first point is that the U.S. middle school mathematics curriculum is far less challenging than curricula in other countries. All countries—except the United States—include algebra and geometry in the curriculum for all of their students in grades 5–8. In the United States, only students in honors and college-prep classes are "allowed" exposure to a formal course in algebra before ninth grade.

As put forward in the *Policy Brief: What TIMSS Means for Systematic School Improvement* (U.S. Department of

Education, 1998), "Holding teachers accountable to curriculum and performance standards is not enough; we must also change the processes that lead to classroom learning" (¶ 1). The TIMSS data resulted in extensive introspection for U.S. educators. As suggested, the data and reports themselves are valuable instructional material for professional development. The bottom line is that TIMSS supports what many have been saying all along:

> Many teachers at all grades need more content knowledge in math and science. And in secondary school, many more teachers must be prepared to teach advanced math and science subjects. . . . TIMSS researchers note that our lack of serious attention to teacher development is closely linked to the issue of teacher professionalism . . . In many other countries, teachers enjoy higher professional status and see themselves as having expertise they can contribute to improving their profession. (U.S. Department of Education, 1998, ¶ 8)

In 1991, the Mathematical Association of America (MAA) established standards for the preparation of teachers. For teachers in grades 5–8, there is a recommended emphasis on algebra, probability and statistics, and concepts and calculus. Sheffield (1994) also recommended that teachers of gifted and talented mathematics students have the following traits:

- an enthusiasm for mathematics and for teaching. Teachers need to be able to convey a sense of the beauty and wonder of mathematics.
- a confidence about their own mathematical abilities. Teachers may not know all the answers to the students' questions, but they should be unafraid to admit a lack of knowledge and to model for their students ways in which to reach an answer on their own.

- a strong mathematical background. In order to challenge students with appropriate problems, teachers must have knowledge of a variety of mathematical topics and should be actively involved in professional development in the field.
- a flexibility and a willingness to be coinvestigators with the students. Students will frequently ask questions that lead the class in directions not foreseen by the teacher. Teachers should be ready and willing to follow the lead of the students as they investigate unplanned areas.
- a willingness to give up the lectern and the chalk. Gifted students need to take over the direction and responsibility of their own learning of mathematics with teachers acting as the "guide on the side." (pp. 27–28)

## Impact of Reform Movements on Mathematics Curricula and Classroom Organization

The emergence of the national curriculum standards movement combined with international comparisons of student performance in math and science has impacted teachers and their classrooms. Complementing this combination was the publication of end-of-century, start-of-millennium goals such as, "By the year 2000, U.S. students will be first in the world in science and mathematics achievement" (U.S. Department of Education, 1991). The influence of the goals, standards, and comparisons all seemed to manifest themselves via the reforms and innovations that infiltrated many general education and gifted education programs.

### Middle School

Sometime during the 1970s, junior high schools were no longer in vogue and, by the late 1980s, two-thirds of public schools were educating their sixth through eighth graders in middle schools (Sicola, 1990). As described in Sicola's article, the differences between middle schools and junior high schools extend beyond the name and include a strong philosophical distinction that is apparent via major schoolwide changes. Principally, middle schools are known for their focus on social and emotional development. Often, middle schools are designed so that a team of teachers implements an interdisciplinary curriculum to a heterogeneous (i.e., mixed-ability) class with an emphasis on teachers as teams to work with consistent groups of students.

The early emphasis of the middle school philosophy seemed to pit academics against self-concept, and the "winner" was the latter. General educators overlooked, however, the important fact that, for many gifted students (especially those who are academically talented), further development of their academic strengths contributes to the development of a positive self-concept. Gallagher, Coleman, and Nelson (1995) investigated the differences in perception between regular educators and gifted educators and determined that, with respect to the middle school agenda, the major differences are in the perceived value of ability grouping and the social consequences of labeling. The gifted educators were strong proponents of both ability grouping and labeling as being beneficial to gifted students.

## Cooperative Learning

The middle school movement and cooperative learning are related in that both trends emphasize "equity goals" and social behavior over academic excellence (Gallagher, Coleman, & Nelson, 1995). However, the middle school movement represents a schoolwide effort at educational reform, while cooperative learning is a classroom approach. Cooperative learning occurs when teams of students work together to accomplish a common goal. Typically, cooperative learning groups are composed of students having a range of academic abilities. The objective of the cooperative learning approach is to promote peer interaction and cooperation while learning academic subjects.

Cooperative learning gained momentum as educators and noneducators alike became aware of some of the negative features of tracking students (Oakes, 1992). General concerns included the perception that teachers of lower tracked groups have less effective teaching styles, as well as the overrepresentation of minorities in those groups. Cooperative learning was adopted as the general solution for these problems, and, throughout the United States, its popularity expanded.

Cooperative learning can be an effective teaching tool; however, it is easy for this strategy to result in the academic "exploitation" of gifted students. For example, the bright student in the cooperative learning group often assumes the role of the teacher, explaining concepts to students with less aptitude. This can be especially frustrating for highly able students because their thought processes may be entirely different from the thought process of the student with less aptitude for the topic.

> Although students who explain material to others benefit from this experience if the material is new to them as well, too many repeated explanations may result in constant review. Cooperative learning groups must be structured to eliminate the "free rider" effect that allows some students to carry the instructional burden and others not to contribute to the common goal. (Robinson, 1991, p. 6)

For cooperative learning to be effective for gifted students, Robinson (1991) recommended several points:

1. Gifted students should be grouped together occasionally or allowed to choose their own groups.
2. Gifted students' roles should require higher level thinking.
3. Assigned projects should not allow groups to depend on one person's efforts.
4. Group grades should be avoided.

5. Cooperative learning should not be substituted for specialized programs and services for talented students.
6. Cooperative learning models that encourage access to materials beyond grade level should be employed.
7. Cooperative learning models should permit flexible pacing.
8. Achievement disparities between cooperative learning group members should not be too severe.
9. Academically talented students should have opportunities for autonomy and individual pursuits during the school day.

## Technology

Television, computers, distance learning over the Internet, e-mail, word processors, color laser printers, fiber-optic transmission of televised broadcasts, CD-ROMs, and listservs are all aspects of the seemingly boundless frontier of technology. It is an understatement to suggest that technology will play an increasingly large role in the lives of all people. The reason we mention it in this chapter is that, through technology, students and teachers have greater access to curricula and resources than ever before. If a teacher of gifted students has a question about curricula or assessment, he or she can e-mail that question to a listserv (see "Resources"), and, within minutes, the question will be answered, often prompting other discussion. Parents of students who are ready for an advanced curriculum that is not easily available through the school will often pursue acquisition of the advanced course through electronic correspondence courses (see "Resources").

Technology has eliminated some of the geographic and psychological barriers that impeded the academic development of gifted students, especially those who live in rural or isolated areas or have extraordinary talents. However, technology cannot serve as a substitute for peer interaction and the teacher-student relationship. Therefore, we encourage the use of technology, but strongly recommend that it be considered a component of, not a replacement for, the classroom learning environment.

## Modifying Regular Education Classroom Practices

With the seemingly constant bombardment of "innovations," how does a teacher know which ones are effective for modifying the curriculum along with classroom practices to meet the needs of mathematically talented students? Single professional-development events seldom cause changes in the ways teachers teach. It is particularly difficult to achieve transformational changes, those that require numerous, significant alterations in the classroom (Johnsen, Haensly, Ryser, & Ford, 2002). Johnson et al. suggested the following components for professional development activities:

1.  Involve all of the stakeholders who will be affected by the change, including teachers, counselors, the community, and administrators. Strong leadership is necessary when these changes are being developed and implemented. These factors are helpful in developing a positive attitude, which is essential to effecting change.
2.  The professional development must simulate the desired practices so that the participants will identify with the innovation and be stimulated to make changes.
3.  The practices need to be clearly defined so that teachers will be able to transfer new practices to the classroom. Research also shows that teachers need follow-up support as they are implementing the changes.
4.  The teachers should have a voice in the type and degree of change they will incorporate into their classrooms. This freedom both empowers teachers and builds positive attitudes toward the change.
5.  Teachers need ongoing material and human support to make the changes. These types of support include staff-development days, peer and mentor support, leadership support, materials, and time to implement the desired changes.

---

### Table 8.1
### Factors That Facilitate Change

- Strong leadership and involvement of the stakeholders
- Professional development simulates the desired practices
- Clear definition of new practices and follow-up support
- Teachers should have a voice in the type and degree of change in their classroom
- Material and human support:
  - —Collaboration with peers
  - —Mentoring
  - —Resources
  - —Time to implement

*Note.* From "Changing General Education Classroom Practices to Adapt for Gifted Students," by S. K. Johnsen, P. A. Haensly, G. R. Ryser, & R. F. Ford, 2002, *Gifted Child Quarterly, 46,* 45–63.

---

Croft (2003) has highlighted the critical role of the teacher in the lives of gifted students. Among the many salient points is the fact that the role of a teacher of the gifted must extend far beyond that of the typical classroom teacher (e.g., the gifted education teacher is often the individual who coordinates student involvement in competitions and other academic activities). This seemingly obvious fact has significant implications for those who are currently in the profession, as well as for those who will choose to become teachers. Westberg and Archambault (1997) described teachers who were already successfully implementing curricular differentiation practices for high-ability students. The following factors were evident:

1. Teachers who successfully differentiated for gifted students had advanced training and knowledge. This training included graduate degrees in gifted education or special education, frequent participation in profes-

sional development experiences, and a continued interest in improving their practices.

2. Teachers were willing and ready to embrace change. These teachers experimented with new strategies and were willing to take risks and spend extra time and effort to make changes in their practices.

3. Teachers collaborated with colleagues, including other grade-level teachers, gifted education specialists, and curriculum specialists. These teachers were either provided time within the school schedule or they made the time outside of school to collaborate with others.

4. Teachers viewed their students as individuals who would benefit from differentiated instruction. The teachers were aware of their students' strengths, and they did not expect all of their students to complete all of the same work within the same period of time. They focused on organizing learning opportunities instead of dispensing knowledge.

5. School administrators took on a leadership role in advocating for differentiated programming for gifted students. For example, superintendents spoke publicly about providing programs for gifted students.

6. Teachers were given both autonomy and support in implementing new practices. The culture of the schools was described as "supportive" and "collaborative."

"We maintain that typical teachers tailor instruction to students' similarities; but truly effective teachers tailor instruction to students' differences as well as their similarities" (Westburg & Archambault, 1997, p. 50).

## Changing Attitudes: An Example of a Successful Professional Development Program

Although the personal quality that most strongly influences the education of gifted learners is teacher attitude (Feldhusen, 1985, Maker 1993), it is often omitted from professional development experiences (Feldhusen, 1997). Professional development can successfully increase a teacher's sense of confidence in planning and implementing activities (Croft, 2003); but, to successfully work with mathematically talented students, an effective professional development program must strive to turn a teacher's negative attitude about gifted learners into a positive one.

Heckenberg (1998) reported on the Belin-Blank Fellowship Teacher Training Program (BBFTTP), a successful professional development program at the University of Iowa. The BBFTTP, ongoing since 1980, has changed the attitudes of general education teachers toward gifted learners and gifted education. In her report, Heckenberg described the change in attitude as primarily experiential in nature. This is logical because pre-inservice attitudes tend to have experiential origins, including a teacher's own learning and teaching experiences.

The philosophical foundation for BBFTTP is that increasing a teacher's knowledge about gifted learners will translate into positive attitudes about gifted learners, which will then open the teacher's thinking to the possibility of implementing appropriate curricular differentiation. Teachers spend a week in residence on the university campus. This residency requirement permits the participants to suspend "business as usual" and allows intensive time for reading extensive journal articles, attending lectures and discussions where views of both proponents and opponents of gifted education are presented, and observing student programs that are specifically designed for academically gifted students. Although it has evolved over the past decades, there are several consistent ingredients that have led to this program's success:

1. There have been only four main instructors for the program since its inception, and each adheres to the same philosophy, goals, and curriculum. Thus, there is continuity from one year to the next.
2. Although knowledge and pedagogical skills are addressed, they are not the main focus of discussion. The primary focus is attitude.

3.  Only a limited number of participants are allowed each year so that a small-group environment is guaranteed. Participants must live on the university campus, which promotes the notion of an academic community.
4.  The group of participants includes elementary and secondary teachers from all discipline areas. It is especially important that the participants are not segregated by content area or grade level.
5.  Activities include lectures, readings, small-group discussions, and observations of classes with gifted learners, as well as out-of-class recreational and cultural events. Especially important is the requirement of participants to maintain a daily journal about their personal and professional reactions to the readings.
6.  The importance of program evaluation is demonstrated through the program's self-evaluation, including measures of preworkshop attitude and knowledge.

What kinds of attitude change have been made as a result of this program? Heckenberg (1998) analyzed pre- and post-workshop responses to an attitude scale and found that attitudes about gifted learners shifted from negative to positive upon completion of the workshop. Three of the attitude shifts were statistically significant:

1.  Gifted children tend to display a degrading disrespect for the teacher.
2.  Too many high IQs together create many problems — the interests are too great and too varied for the teacher.
3.  Parents of gifted children interfere with teachers and the teaching of the children.

Heckenberg (1998) also found that participants made more pro-gifted education responses. For example, there was a significant increase in positive responses to the statement "Gifted students can be taught more effectively when grouped with other gifted children than when grouped with nongifted children." These positive changes are attributed to exposure to information in a setting in which attitudes and biases regarding the information can be challenged and explored.

## Conclusion

The field of education and the role of the teacher have evolved dramatically over the past few decades. These changes have impacted the professional development of teachers. Before teachers enter the profession, they have extensive preservice preparation. Once teachers enter the profession, they are often involved in in-service training. Throughout this chapter, we have presented the major educational issues confronting parents and teachers, including the fact that, despite all of their preservice and in-service training, teachers still need more exposure to content and often have attitudes that are not conducive to the academic development of their talented students.

*A teacher affects eternity;*
*he can never tell where his influence stops.*
*—Henry Brooks Adams*

# 9 Case Studies

## Key Points

- Mathematically talented students can be identified at a young age, and their parents are often the first to recognize their talents.

- Objective information is essential in helping parents to be effective advocates for their children.

- The Diagnostic Testing→Prescriptive Instruction model helps ensure that exceptionally mathematically talented students study mathematics at a steady rate.

- Long-term planning is essential so that students are always studying an appropriately challenging level of mathematics.

- Mathematically talented students benefit from finding an intellectual peer group; this may be especially important for mathematically talented girls.

WE HAVE WORKED WITH THOUSANDS OF STUDENTS over the past few decades. From this work, we have identified case studies that highlight the main points of this book. We are grateful to the families who so willingly shared their experiences and insights with us in order to help other families with mathematically gifted students.

We found the case-study approach to be exceptionally helpful in our research and to the families with whom we work. The stories we describe here help to illustrate the points we have made throughout this book. Although case studies are anecdotal in nature, they are valuable to parents and educators who are looking for a general model to apply to individual students. Many parents have told us that they like reading case studies because they realize they are not alone in their situations. Our case studies are somewhat unique because they integrate specific individual information with a robust theoretical approach that has been proven to be effective with hundreds of thousands of students (see Chapter 5).

## Christopher:
### "He wants to learn math as much as he wants air."

Christopher's parents knew from a young age that he was bright. By the age of 1, he memorized books and knew the numbers 1–10, and by the age of 2 he knew the alphabet. At this young age, Christopher became obsessed with numbers. He made his mother sit with him for hours to practice writing numbers and letters. He memorized house numbers, added and subtracted two-digit numbers at the age of 3, and was fascinated with mechanical things.

At the age of 3, he figured out negative numbers by playing with a calculator, and he asked his parents, "Zero is a non-number, isn't it?" It was at this point that his parents first contacted Julian Stanley at Johns Hopkins University, founder of the talent search model. Dr. Stanley kindly forwarded the inquiry to us (see Figure 9.1 with examples of Christopher's handwritten work done at the age of 3).

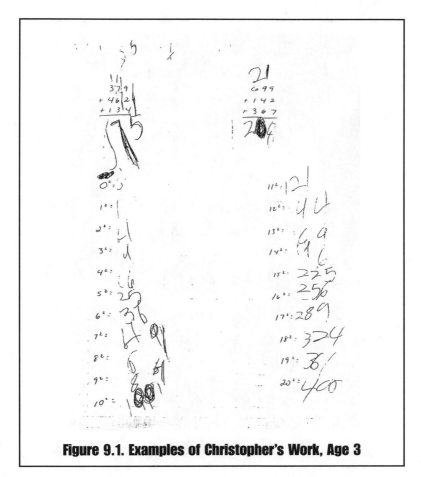

## Figure 9.1. Examples of Christopher's Work, Age 3

Christopher was also talented at writing. He liked writing stories, but they were always about numbers. He dictated his stories to his parents, who typed them out on the computer. His stories always ran along the lines of, "Once there was a 10. And then there was a 15. One day they found a 12." When he was 3, he woke up in the middle of the night crying. On his way to respond to Christopher, his father jokingly said to his mother that Christopher was probably having a nightmare that someone came and took away all of the numbers, since

$\sqrt{289} : 17$

$2^3 = 8$

$(7 \times 3) + 2 = 23$

$(1 + 1)^2 = 4$

$1^0 + 2^0 = 2$

$10 \div 2 = 5$

$\sqrt{144} : 12$

$5^4 : 625$

$4 - 2 = 2$

$2 - 4 = -2$

$10 - 3 = 7$

$14 \div 7 = 2$

If $A = 9$ then $A^2 = 81$

If $B = 3$ then $B + 2 = 5$

If $C = 8$ then $10 - C = +2$

If $\mathbb{D} + 5 = 7$ then $\mathbb{D} = 2$

If $\mathbb{X} - 4 = 1$ then $\mathbb{X} = 5$

**Figure 9.1 continued**

"numbers are his life." It turned out that Christopher had been dreaming that he couldn't find the number 79.

When Christopher was 4, he could read, multiply, and divide (he said he preferred multiplication). He understood squares and square roots, played with numbers on the computer (he liked *Math Blaster*), and figured out powers on his own. About this time, he showed an interest in infinity and negative infinity.

By the time Christopher entered kindergarten at the age of 5, he was reading at the third-grade level. As a programming

DEAR DR. STANLEY,

I HEARD   YOU LIKE   NUMBERS. SO DO I.

WOULD   YOU              PLEASE

LOOK AT MY  WORK..

  THANK U.

SINCERELY,,

CHRISTOPHER

P.S. I AM 3 YEARS OLD.

**Figure 9.1 continued**

option for his advanced reading level, he was pulled out of kindergarten for a special reading program. The reading teacher reported to Christopher's mother that his "attention span was short," but his mother believed that his behavior reflected that he didn't like being separated from his kindergarten class.

When Christopher entered first grade, he demonstrated such superior understanding of mathematics that he clearly did not fit into the regular mathematics classroom. He needed a formal assessment of his mathematical abilities so that a clear educational program could be developed. His parents asked us to do that assessment. Midway through his first-grade year, we gave him the Quantitative section of the Lower Level of the Secondary School Admission Test (SSAT-Q; previously, we had used this test with gifted third through fifth graders; it was normed on private school students in grades 5–7). The administration of the SSAT-Q occurred as the first step of the Diagnostic Testing→Prescriptive Instruction process that we have found to be so helpful in devising appropriate programs for mathematically talented youth (see Chapter 4). On the SSAT-Q, Christopher (a first grader) earned a score that placed him at the 60th percentile when compared to the fifth-grade national norms. When compared to norms that we had gathered on gifted third graders, his score was at the 93rd percentile.

His advanced quantitative reasoning skills were clearly not a fluke, nor were they the result of external "pushing" on the part of his parents. The attitude that a child's performance is primarily attributable to pushy parents or chance behavior is often expressed by educators; however, the fact that, as a first grader, he earned a score that was higher than the scores earned by 60% of the national group of fifth graders for whom the test was normed *and* his score surpassed 93% of the SSAT-Q scores earned by gifted third graders would refute the "chance" or "pushy parent" attribution for Christopher's success.

The next step in determining the appropriate curriculum for him was to administer a test that provided more specific achievement information. This was accomplished by administering the Mathematics sections of the Sequential Tests of Educational Progress (STEP). On the most basic level of the STEP Basic Concepts test, he earned a score at the 82nd percentile when compared to first-semester fourth graders. On the same level of the STEP Computation test, he earned a score at the 80th percentile compared to first-semester fourth graders (he was compared to fourth graders because this was the grade level for whom that level of the test was developed). Clearly, Christopher had a great deal of mathematical aptitude and achievement. Although his exceptional performance did not indicate that he had mastered all of elementary school mathematics or even all of fourth-grade mathematics, it pointed to the fact that, if Christopher was going to be challenged in mathematics, he would need a program that was substantially different from that of the average first grader and even that of a gifted third or fourth grader. No specific accommodations were made for Christopher's mathematics education at that time; however, a plan was formulated for the beginning of second grade. The idea was for the gifted education teacher to teach him math. Although this seemed like a good idea, it was not a good student-teacher match. His mother recalled,

> The teacher had a difficult time accepting [Christopher's] abilities and often insisted that he solve word problems her way. She would scold him for working problems different ways even when his way was logical and resulted in the correct answer. She kept insisting that the third-grade math was beyond him. As proof that he was working on material beyond his abilities, she reported that one time he had slapped her hand. When we questioned [Christopher] about the incident, he told us that, every time he started to work a problem (and before he had a chance to complete it), the teacher would push his hand away and tell him he was doing the problem incorrectly and to start over. He apparently got so frustrated that he finally slapped her hand.

At the beginning of second grade, school personnel suggested having Christopher skip at least one grade, but his parents thought he was not emotionally or physically ready for that. Together, his parents and school district personnel decided to place Christopher with three advanced fourth-grade boys. Together, the four boys studied fifth-grade mathematics with a high school mathematics teacher whose salary was paid by the district. Although this was a highly unusual situation, it seemed to work well for Christopher and the other students. Sometimes, Christopher got a little "teary" when he didn't get the right answer immediately, but his parents recognized that it was good for Christopher to have other children with him.

This arrangement continued for both Christopher's second- and third-grade year. As the end of third grade approached, Christopher's parents began making plans for the next school year. (Planning ahead is an excellent strategy, as it gives all parties involved a lot of time to work out solutions.) Christopher did well with the advanced math material. At the beginning of the next year, though, the fifth-grade boys (his peers) would be moving on to middle school, leaving Christopher with 2 more years in his elementary school without any math peers. The high school teacher continued to be concerned that Christopher wasn't grasping all of the material being taught. She acknowledged that he seemed to understand what was being presented to him, but she admitted that she did not know for sure what he understood because she had never taught so young a student.

By the end of third grade, Christopher had finished all of the sixth-grade math curriculum plus most of the seventh. His father noted that Christopher benefited from being with the other boys because it allowed him to see that he was not always the best. Two of the fifth graders usually did a little better than Christopher, and he usually did better than one of them. When they took their end-of the-year sixth-grade math test, Christopher correctly answered 89% of the material. He took the prealgebra test at the end of the year and did well. The school district administrators usually require a raw score of 60 to select students for advanced programming, and Christopher earned a 59. (Christopher's father noted that it was a timed test, and Christopher didn't finish 8 or 9 of the questions.) Christopher's father said that he sensed that the high school math tutor "could never accept that Christopher could understand this work. She told me that she expected Christopher to do well on the prealgebra test, not because he really understood the math, but simply because he had learned it. I am still trying to figure that one out."

In January of third grade, Christopher took the EXPLORE test and earned a 20 on English (92nd percentile compared to eighth graders), 16 on Math (72nd percentile compared to eighth graders), 15 on Reading (60th percentile), 15 on Science (60th percentile), and 17 Composite (75th percentile). Christopher's excellent scores once again confirmed his extraordinarily high abilities.

During fourth grade, Christopher covered the first half of the Algebra I book. Although the high school teacher wanted Christopher to finish Algebra I by the end of fourth grade, Christopher's parents thought she was requiring too much homework, preventing him from doing other things they thought were important. As a consequence of their request, Christopher did not finish Algebra I until the end of fifth grade. His mother reported that, "He is currently in the sixth grade and taking Algebra II with the advanced eighth graders. He has done very well, earning As both terms thus far. Next year, he will take Geometry with the eighth-grade class. (Algebra II and Geometry are only offered in alternating years at his school.) His teacher tells me that in his eighth-grade year, she will teach him trigonometry and calculus privately since it is not offered in the middle school."

Christopher's family was successful in devising an appropriately challenging program in mathematics for him for a number of reasons. First, they recognized his abilities at a young age. Second, they did a great deal of research on their own to find the needed resources and experts. Third, they worked with their school district and kept the school district informed. Fourth, they constantly looked at Christopher's future mathematics education as they made plans for the current school year. It also helped that Christopher's parents were well educated and lived in an affluent school district that could afford to send a high school teacher to the elementary school for mentoring, not to mention that district personnel recognized Christopher's extraordinary abilities and were willing to devote special resources to meeting his needs.

Even though they were in such a good situation, they still experienced difficulties. For example, the high school math teacher demonstrated the hesitation that so many math teachers show: she could hardly believe that Christopher could do the math, even though he demonstrated his knowledge to her over and over.

## Billy: "If he does third-grade math in second grade, what will he do in third grade?"

According to his mother, Billy had an "unquenchable" thirst for learning and he constantly asked for something harder and more challenging. He was an "extremely intense and driven child." At the age of 2, Billy became utterly fascinated with numbers. He counted everything, everywhere. He enjoyed doing dot-to-dot books because he was able to follow the numerical order of the numbers. For additional challenge, he began creating his own dot-to-dot puzzles.

Billy also showed an interest in letters and reading at a very young age. For example, at 18 months, he recognized all of the letters of the alphabet. He loved playing with his ABC puzzle. After removing all the letters and mixing them up in a pile, he would complete the puzzle in correct order with no hesitation. Throughout the day, he searched for letters, pointing to and announcing letters wherever he happened to be (in the store, in the car, etc.). Because of his enjoyment of letters, he enjoyed watching Wheel of Fortune from his playpen.

Billy taught himself to tell time and to calculate minutes on a traditional clock at the age of 3. One evening at dinner—out of nowhere—he looked up at the clock and told his parents it was 5:22 and, in 38 minutes, it would be 6:00. That was the first time they realized he could tell time and that he was adding and subtracting. After that day, he began to add and subtract minutes on a daily basis. He became obsessed with calculations. He would calculate anything he could. He also became obsessed with television game shows. He would rush home from preschool so that he could watch *The Price is Right*. At church, he would take all the numbers of the songs from the song book and add them together.

One day, Billy's mother found him on his bed surrounded by supermarket ads. He was adding up all the prices with a calculator. One of his favorite activities was going grocery shopping. By the age of 4, he could deduct coupons from the grocery bill total and calculate the change his mother should receive before the cashier did. One incident in particular stood out in his mother's mind. Her total was $207.60. She had $175 in cash, and was planning to write a check for the balance. Before the cashier could calculate the difference on the cash register, Billy said the check needed to be for $32.60. The cashier was amazed.

At age 4, Billy knew the correct locations of all 50 states on a United States puzzle. He also knew all of the capitols. He played Yahtzee daily. It was one of his favorite games because of the numbers. He also liked to calculate all of the players' scores in his head. His parents realized he could read when, one night during his bath, he read the back of a shampoo bottle. From then on, he read everything he could and phonetically sounded out what he could not. He began reading first-grade level books at home.

When Billy was 5, he entered kindergarten at a local parochial school. It quickly became evident that he was well beyond his peers and the course material that was offered. His parents were frustrated by his first report card. It showed "satisfactory" performance. It did not show any advanced knowledge or abilities beyond those of an average kindergarten student. The report card stated that he could recognize numbers 1–12, when, in fact, he could recognize numbers in the thousands. He was adding, subtracting, and doing simple multiplication and division problems at home. His report card also stated that he was reading at Level 1, which was the expectation for the average student. Billy's mother took two mathematics workbooks with her to the first parent-teacher conference to show what Billy was working on at home. She attempted to show those books to the teacher as evidence of his ability, asking if the teacher could provide some first-grade work. The teacher would not even look through the workbooks, and she said she couldn't make any notes of advanced ability or advanced work on his report card other than what was expected or "satisfactory." She said she would not give him any extra work and that maybe they should look into sending him to a public school. When Billy's mother met with the school principal, she received the same responses. Like his teacher, the principal wouldn't even look at the workbooks, and it seemed as though she didn't believe that Billy was exceptional.

Standardized testing that spring showed that Billy was performing in the 99th percentile for his grade (Cognitive Abilities Test: Verbal, 85th percentile; Quantitative 99th percentile, Nonverbal 99th percentile; and Composite, 99th percentile). Billy's parents became aware that the public school district had a gifted program in which Billy could participate.

He was tested using the Stanford-Binet (4th edition) and earned a Composite standard score of 148 (in the Very Superior or Gifted range), a Verbal Reasoning Standard Score of 127, an Abstract/Visual Reasoning score of 143, and a Quantitative Reasoning standard score of 163. On the Wechsler Individual Achievement Test, Billy's Basic Reading standard score was 149, and his Math Reasoning standard score was 160.

Clearly qualified, he started the district's gifted program in the fall of first grade. He continued to attend his parochial school and was pulled out for 30 minutes twice a week to attend the public school gifted program. Billy's regular first-grade class was filled with worksheet after worksheet, and he was happy to participate in the gifted program because he did a lot of above-level reading (third- and fourth-grade level), math work, and projects.

At home, Billy worked on third-grade math workbooks on his own initiative. He enjoyed a subscription to a magazine filled with math puzzles and logical thinking activities. He especially enjoyed board games involving money and geography. He continued to enjoy grocery shopping—still deducting coupons and calculating change—but now also figuring out the best buy for Mom. On one shopping trip, he instructed her to buy a certain brand of raisins because the "price per ounce" made it a better deal.

Second grade was a turning point for Billy and his family. He sat through regular classes at school. He woke up early most mornings in order to work on his fourth- and fifth-grade math workbooks before getting on the bus for school. He still attended the pull-out gifted classes and was very excited by them. For those classes, he had an excellent teacher who realized his potential and need for challenge. Billy enthusiastically worked on several independent study projects, mostly in math. He also developed an intense interest in the solar system. He attended his first C-MITES weekend workshop at Carnegie Mellon, which he thoroughly enjoyed.

At the first parent-teacher conference of the year, his parents were presented with Billy's Iowa Tests of Basic Skills scores, which indicated he performed at the 99th percentile in many areas. Billy's mother asked his teacher about giving him more advanced work. They discussed the possibility of having him sit in on third-grade math classes, but the idea was vetoed by the principal, who said, "If he does third-grade math in second grade, what will he do in third grade?" The only challenge he was given was a sheet of third-grade math homework on a fairly regular basis.

Up to this point, the parochial school had done very little to support Billy's exceptional abilities. Instead of the administration being proud to have a student like Billy in the school, they thought of him as a problem. In turn, his parents were viewed as problems for being his advocates. School personnel didn't know how to handle the situation or what to do with Billy. His parents found this lack of school support and interest quite unexpected. They quickly realized that the role of playing advocate for their son wasn't going to be an easy one.

Several years before, Billy's mother had contacted Dr. Shoplik at Carnegie Mellon University and had received a lot of information about mathematically talented youth, some of which discussed mentoring (see Chapter 4 for details about the information received by Billy's parents). His parents decided that, if Billy could be placed in a mentoring program at his school, it might solve their problems. His mother discussed this idea with the public school gifted teacher, who thought it sounded like a great idea and even volunteered to accompany Billy's mother to the meeting scheduled with the principal and Billy's second-grade teacher.

Although the principal said she previously had not heard of a math-mentor program, she was willing to discuss the idea with the Diocese (the supervisory body for the parochial schools in the area) and gain approval from her supervisors. Second grader Billy then took the STEP Mathematics Basic Concepts test. His score was at the 46th percentile when compared with the sixth-grade norm group. He scored at the 37th percentile on STEP Computation when compared to sixth graders. Billy also took the second- and third-grade end-of-the year math tests. The results of these tests showed his mastery of the second- and third-grade material. Clearly, Billy was performing well above grade level in mathematics.

Testing occurred in February, and Diocesan approval was received in early May (a lag of 2 or 3 months between testing and the administrative decision is not unusual; see Chapter 2). With only about 6 weeks of school left, Billy was finally able to begin working with his mentor, with whom he met twice a week in lieu of his regularly scheduled math classes. On the remaining 3 days of the week, he worked on mentor-assigned homework and e-mailed his mentor with his progress or to ask questions. He loved it. Billy and his mentor worked on permutations, scientific notation, associative and commutative properties, and probability games.

Billy's mother remembers that he had experienced some social difficulties in school during second grade. He got the distinct impression that it wasn't "cool" to be smart. The other students seemed to resent his intelligence and his enthusiasm for learning. In one math class, another student beat him at flashcards, and the whole class cheered. He was crushed and couldn't understand why kids who used to be his friends were treating him this way.

Although the mentor program was wonderful and Billy and his family were very pleased with the results, it targeted only mathematics for Billy. They thought he needed acceleration and challenge in other areas, as well. They decided to look into other schools. Billy was excited about the idea, saying that it would be nice to attend a school that would be challenging and also where there would be more "kids like me." They found a local private school that seemed to be a good fit, and he began attending that school in third grade.

Billy's mother said,

> We are very content with our decision. As parents, we were searching for a school that would provide challenge without being overwhelming and where [Billy] could be the enthusiastic, inquisitive student he needs to be. From the time he was a toddler, he has had an unquenchable thirst for knowledge. We believe his new

school provides him the atmosphere in which he can thrive. Our beliefs were confirmed when, at our first parent-teacher conference at the new school, his teacher said that [Billy] was at the top of his class and was "made" for the school. Because of his personality and his intense desire to learn, the transition to his new school has been a very smooth one, as indicated by all of his teachers. He is finally happy and content. He is with other children like himself where it is acceptable to be smart, and he is able to accelerate within the class. For example, in reading, his teacher is recommending he read fifth-grade-level books for his monthly book reports. In math, he is in a small group that is working on the same subject matter as the rest of the class, but at a higher level and a quicker pace. Billy has his own math folder, as do other students, which is filled with math activities geared toward his ability: critical thinking, logical thinking, algebra, and so forth. There are several centers in the classroom, and students are able to choose a center at which to work. The key here is that he is not being restricted by anyone, and an entire class is not being rushed ahead because of him. The administration and teaching staff are supportive, and they are thrilled to have Billy and students like him attend their school. What made him so difficult at his former school has impressed his new school.

Our parting with the previous school was amicable. They understood our position and said they couldn't structure their curriculum to accommodate students like Billy. They had to target the average student. We believed our son had so much potential and that it would be an injustice to let him remain in a school where it wasn't possible for him to develop to his full potential.

Billy took the EXPLORE test in third grade and earned the following scores: 17 English (73rd percentile compared to eighth graders), 15 Math (62nd percentile compared to eighth graders),

12 Reading (44th percentile compared to eighth graders), 17 Science (76th percentile compared to eighth graders), and 15 Composite (61st percentile compared to eighth graders). His performance on the EXPLORE test was exceptional. Specifically in mathematics, third grader Billy had outperformed the average eighth grader, who had 5 more years of experience in mathematics than he did. Once again, Billy's above-level test scores indicated his tremendous abilities and potential in mathematics and his need for differentiated programming.

Personnel at Billy's new school went to great lengths to create a mathematics curriculum that would satisfy both Billy and his parents. Billy's parents met with the school headmaster, the fourth-grade teachers, the upper-school math teacher, and other parents to discuss ideas for the upcoming years with regard to Billy's mathematics curriculum. For fourth grade, Billy and five other students were separated into an accelerated mathematics group and were taught fifth-grade math. It worked well.

For fifth grade, after careful consideration, school personnel moved this group of six fifth-grade students directly into the sixth-grade accelerated math class. It was also decided that this acceleration plan would follow this group of students through the eighth grade. Again, this plan worked out extremely well. The sixth graders accepted the group of fifth graders immediately, both socially and academically. Billy was at the top of his class. He also participated and placed in several math contests at the sixth-grade level.

Presently, Billy is in the sixth grade, and he attends the seventh-grade accelerated prealgebra classes. He is at the "right" grade level for his age, although he is accelerated in math by one year. In addition to his prealgebra class five times a week, he attends a math computer class weekly. He is at the top of the class and has participated in several math contests at a seventh-grade level (e.g., Continental Math League, American Math Competition). He has earned straight A+s in math since he started attending the private school in third grade.

Next year, when Billy is in seventh grade, he will attend eighth-grade Algebra I and plans to participate in several math contests offered at his school. He will also be eligible to try out for the school MathCounts team. He expects to take Algebra II in eighth grade.

Billy's parents are very pleased with his progress. They believe that their decision to move him to a different school was critical. Billy is now in an environment where his talents are valued and nurtured. His mother commented,

> It is not easy to parent a gifted child. Over the years, we have had to hurdle many educational roadblocks because of the guidelines established by standard curricula. Most of the time, parents are the only advocates a gifted child has. We also learned that standing up for your gifted child is not always the "popular" thing to do. In fact, when we made the decision to move our son from the parochial school to the private school, certain parents [from the parochial school] started to act differently toward us. One comment was, "He can't be that smart. Who do they think they are?" Why should we feel the need to apologize for our son's exceptional abilities? But, that is exactly how many people have made us feel. . . .These thoughts of mine are important, I think, to other parents who are just beginning their journey into the world of educating the gifted child. I know that, when I first read *Jane and Johnny Love Math*, it was comforting to realize that our family was not alone.

We are pleased that Billy and his parents are content with the decisions they have made and with the curricula that have been made available to Billy at the private school. We think it is interesting, however, that the private school made such an issue out of accelerating their mathematically talented students by one year. Clearly, the students were ready for that type of acceleration, and Billy might have benefited from even more radical acceleration in mathematics. In relation to that, we wonder why there was any question about what the students should do after completing fifth-grade math. What other choice should they have except to go on to sixth-grade math? Should they have repeated fifth-grade math? This lack of logical thinking doesn't surprise us because we hear these stories frequently, but we are always disappointed by it.

## Arthur: "Is he being challenged enough?"

Mrs. A. first contacted us when Arthur was a first grader in a suburban school district. She explained that he was in the school's gifted program and had demonstrated that he could do fourth-grade work. Arthur had shown high ability in mathematics since he was quite young. For example, he could tell time at the age of 2. When he was 4, he understood sophisticated concepts such as "There are 18 minutes left until I can go to preschool" or "I got home 23 minutes ago."

Arthur's mother explained that he didn't learn anything academic in kindergarten, except how to make 7s the right way. One day, in kindergarten, the students were talking about numbers, and the problem 10 – 14 came up. The teacher told the students that, "You can't take 14 from 10." Arthur replied, "Yes, you can. It's –4!"

Arthur was identified for the district's gifted program with a gifted individualized educational plan (IEP) in kindergarten. Although Arthur's academic abilities were recognized at this young age, his school did not provide a special program for him in mathematics. He was in the district's gifted program, but it met only once a week for half a day. Arthur enjoyed the projects they did in the class, but the rest of the week, his math program was unaffected.

In the spring of second grade, Arthur was permitted to work on some third-grade mathematics problems in his regular second-grade classroom. His parents began considering whether or not he should move up a grade in mathematics and start taking fourth-grade math when he was in third grade. They did not have to make that decision, however, because they moved to another state in the summer following second grade.

The new district had much lower academic standards than their previous home district. Arthur and his sister found they were repeating information they had previously learned. At this point, Arthur's parents insisted that he be given the opportunity to study fourth-grade mathematics in third grade. So, his teacher tested him and determined where his gaps were in third-grade math. She tutored him a bit on rounding, and he began studying fourth-grade math. Unfortunately, he studied this advanced math in the back of his third-grade classroom on his own while his teacher continued to teach the rest of the third graders in the regular mathematics class. An aide and a special needs student shared the same table with Arthur, and other students in the class often asked him questions and interrupted his work. His teacher reported that he "had trouble focusing" on his work. He earned Bs in math for most of the school year, although he got an A in the final quarter. Arthur felt he was being punished for being smart. He recognized that he could have received As if he had stayed in third-grade math.

Arthur did find that he was challenged by the fourth-grade math he was studying. He learned how to do long division that year, but he found it difficult to learn on his own. He was used to knowing how to do math instinctively, so not knowing how to do something was a new experience for him.

After Arthur completed third grade, he and his family moved back to his former school district. We checked in on him when he was in fourth grade. His new school grouped students for mathematics. Arthur was in the "high" group, and, within that group, he was grouped with a smaller cluster of mathematically talented students. On the same day Arthur attended the half-day gifted program, the gifted teacher went into his math class and offered enrichment. So far that year, the students had been studying "Hands-On Equations" (an algebra program for elementary students), which Arthur enjoyed very much. This weekly math program ended after the fall semester and was replaced by a Great Books class for the second half of the year.

Once every 3 or 4 weeks, Arthur joined a group of mathematically talented students in a districtwide math program. Students qualified for this program through a two-step testing process: First, they had to score at the 98th percentile on the California Achievement Test, then they had to score 90% or above on a seventh- or eighth-grade math test. In this special program, students were bussed to a central location for half a day every 3 weeks to do enrichment in mathematics, such as studying the Fibonacci sequence, which Arthur loved.

In the regular classroom, Arthur repeated the fourth-grade math material he taught himself in the back of his third-grade classroom, partly because his parents were concerned that he might have some gaps in his background from last year's experience. The gifted coordinator in the district also advocated for not advancing Arthur. She said, "What's the rush? He'll end up in 11th grade with nothing to take in mathematics." His parents decided he could be accelerated in math later, if needed.

Arthur loves problem solving, and he loves to tinker with things. During the summer before fourth grade, he participated in Camp Invention (a program designed to promote creativity and problem solving) at a local school. One of his assignments was to take a broken clock radio apart and make an imaginary invention out of it. He thrived in this open atmosphere, saying, "I wish school could be like that."

Arthur's father gives him brain teasers to think about at night before he goes to bed. When Arthur comes in for breakfast the next morning, he has solved the problem. He loves having something to think about.

Arthur sometimes solves math problems in unconventional ways. For example, when doing three-digit addition, he always starts in the hundreds column and works toward the right. He says, "But on paper, I do it the right way, so I don't get in trouble."

Arthur still loves math. Is he challenged right now? "I don't know," replied his mother. "He gets 100s on most of his tests and he doesn't study." Arthur and his family know he didn't like the way he studied math in third grade. He doesn't want to repeat that experience. They are pleased that he has been identified for a special math class in the district. Although they would like the class to meet more often than once every 3 weeks, they feel that being identified for special programming in math is a great benefit of the program. They believe that this current identification will lead to being recognized as mathematically talented in the future, and it will help draw attention to him for math programs as he moves on to high school.

Arthur took the EXPLORE tests in fourth grade and scored 17 in English, 16 in Math, 8 in Reading, 16 in Science Reasoning, and 14 on the Composite. These scores are exceptional, and Arthur clearly has the aptitude for accelerated study of mathematics. Arthur's parents ask, "What are the advantages to accelerating Arthur, given [our] circumstances?" They know that he is not being stretched in math this year, but they think he needs to work on his language arts. He got a B in the subject in the first quarter, and he hates to read and write. They have decided to focus on that this year, in the hopes of making Arthur a little more well-rounded. They also believe he needs to practice math facts such as 7 x 8 and 6 x 7, so they don't think there is any harm in letting him have an extra year of computing.

Maintaining a balance in his life and being well-rounded are very important to the members of this family. Arthur is active in soccer, baseball, church youth group, and piano lessons. They see Arthur's strength in mathematics in contrast to his relative "weakness" in English and reading, and they are interested in helping him to achieve more in that area.

Arthur's parents are taking a conservative approach. They are not interested in "rushing" Arthur through school. They do recognize that he is repeating material he learned last year, and they are disappointed that he isn't being challenged more, although they appreciate the efforts their school district has made to group students and to offer periodic enrichment classes in mathematics.

School personnel have correctly diagnosed Arthur as being talented in mathematics and needing special programming. However, our belief is that Arthur's programming does not progress in a systematic fashion. Although they correctly identified Arthur as mathematically talented, the program offered to him is inadequate. It is simply not enough for him to participate in a challenging math class just once every 3 or 4 weeks.

We checked in on Arthur again, shortly before this book was published, when he was in fifth grade. By this time, his school district had developed a special accelerated mathematics program. Arthur and other gifted students were tested and identified for special programming (using the Diagnostic Testing→ Prescriptive Instruction approach described in Chapter 4). Arthur is grouped with seven other advanced students for a math class that meets first period every day (three of the students are bussed in from another school in the district). This mathematics class covers material that is 2 years above grade level. Next year, Arthur will be eligible for another advanced mathematics class that will result in his being accelerated in mathematics by 3 years. According to his mother, Arthur's performance in language arts has improved. She said it seemed as if he learned how to work harder as a result of the advanced math class, and the study skills he is beginning to learn have helped him in other areas. We are pleased that Arthur is finally being challenged.

## Zach: "There are lots of bright kids. Why should we do anything different for him?"

Zach is the first-born in a family of three boys; his mother is a physician and his father is a professor of education at a large university. In describing Zach as a toddler, his mother recalled that Zach learned the alphabet before his speech was coherent. Both parents described a restaurant scene in which they were amusing their not-quite-2-year-old by writing out words like *Mommy*, *Daddy*, and *Zach*, and just as Zach was identifying the words, their waitress approached their table. Much to their chagrin, the sight of such a young child who apparently knew the alphabet shocked the waitress. Zach's parents felt compelled to explain to this stranger that their son really couldn't read, rather he recognized the initial letters of each word and knew what letter went with what word.

Zach also loved numbers from the time he was a toddler and demonstrated his early affinity for them by counting and arranging things in groups. He spent more time with books that involved counting and numbers than with any other books. When Zach entered kindergarten, his parents were aware that he had a strong interest in math, but they weren't sure just how strong it was. Since Zach was their first child, they were naïve with respect to the role the school system would play in identifying and nurturing his academic strengths.

Fortunately, Zach had an excellent kindergarten teacher, who allowed him to use his creative mind to keep himself occupied. For example, when he would complete the required kindergarten math, which was essentially a set of developmental tasks that consisted of sorting and grouping, his teacher allowed him to then act out elaborate fantasies with the characters used in the developmental tasks. Because Zach remained occupied with the regular kindergarten curriculum, neither his parents nor his kindergarten teacher were aware of how profound his abilities in math were. It is also worth noting that, in Zach's school district, gifted education opportunities typically begin in third grade. However, Zach's kindergarten teacher recommended that Zach be included in the pull-out gifted program as early as kindergarten.

Despite his early ability to recognize letters, Zach did not read independently until he was well into first grade. In describing Zach's behaviors prior to being able to read independently, his parents referred to Zach as an avid story listener who was demanding about being read to. As mentioned, Zach did not read independently until late first grade; but, as his parents perceived it, he didn't want to bother with the types of stories he could easily read because they were not interesting. He much preferred hearing stories that were at his comprehension level. At some point during the second half of his first-grade year (when he had already turned 7), reading books that were of interest to him became worth his effort. Zach credits the reading of *Pippi Longstocking* to him as his motivation to spend more effort learning to read. By the middle of the summer between first and second grade, he was reading chapter books and had read all of the *Pippi Longstocking* books, as well as *Winnie the Pooh*, *Peter Pan*, and *Henry and Ribsy*.

While he was in grades 1 and 2, Zach's parents maintained a relatively neutral attitude concerning the development of their son's academic strengths. When Zach was in third grade, he was eligible for the Elementary Student Talent Search (described in Chapter 5). For Zach's parents, the results of the EXPLORE test were a watershed. Zach's Mathematics score, for example, was 13 out of 25, placing him at the 48th percentile compared to eighth graders. This indicated that he performed about as well in mathematics as students 5 years older than he. From these results, Zach's parents realized that his needs were even more extraordinary than those of the many bright children in their son's class. Zach's parents now realized he needed differentiated programming, and they relied heavily on the above-level testing results to help them in their advocacy for academic programming commensurate with his academic needs.

Despite the fact that Zach's father is a professor of education, he was required to advocate for appropriate programming in the same way all other parents were. In the first parent-teacher conference in which they shared the results of the above-level testing, the response they received from the administration was a question: "There are lots of bright kids in this school. Why should we do something different for Zach?" Zach's parents explained that they agreed there were lots of bright kids in Zach's class; nevertheless, his needs were different from even the very bright students in the school. The talent search group results were instrumental in discussing this point.

In Figure 9.2, the story of Zach's parent's efforts at advocacy unfolds. The first part of the personalized educational plan (PEP), "Standard Curriculum Modifications (Subject Modifications, Monitors/Evaluators)" represents the time period prior to the above-level EXPLORE testing. In the absence of above-level testing results, Zach's programming was primarily enrichment, including mathematics projects. For the projects, Zach worked both independently and with a partner and in small groups. Note, however, that the time allocated for the extended learning program (ELP) was 50 minutes a week. After the results of the EXPLORE were shared with Zach's educators, an additional 30–40 minutes of ELP was allowed to permit independent study in computer programming. As the reader can see from our comments on the PEP, we were quite disappointed by the PEP and the recommendations made for Zach (see Chapter 3 for more information on the types of PEP comments we find most helpful).

In order to obtain more systematic programming for Zach, his parents made a request to the school district for an evaluation that would be specifically focused on the curriculum. Since Zach was in third grade when this plan was under consideration, the math coordinator for the district began the curriculum-based assessment with the end-of-year fourth-grade assessment. As noted on the PEP, this assessment resulted in Zach earning a score of 72% correct on the Concepts and Computation and a score of 75% correct on Problem Solving. The coordinator also identified specific gaps in fractions, decimals, and rounding. As can be seen, even though Zach did not quite make the 80% guideline, school personnel agreed to place him in fifth-grade math. The language that was used in the "Special Considerations" section of the PEP is, from our perspective, disappointing. Rather than focusing on his strengths, it seemed as though undue attention was directed toward his seemingly minor gaps in computation.

When Zach entered fourth grade, he went to fifth grade for math, but his accelerated programming was focused only on that subject. The educators in this district were cautious concerning any acceleration. Zach retook the EXPLORE when he was in fourth grade and earned a score of 16 on Math (see Table 9.1). Although he had already taken EXPLORE two times, he re-took it again as a fifth grader because he loved the challenge provided by above-level testing. He earned a 24 on the EXPLORE Mathematics test and actually came close to the ceiling on all of the EXPLORE tests. He demonstrated the most growth in math, which was most likely due to the fact that math was the one subject in which he received appropriate accelerative programming.

The discussions with his teachers began to focus on having him take the prealgebra curriculum while in fifth grade so that he could take algebra in sixth grade. In his school system, grade 6 is the final year spent in the elementary building.

*Student name:* Zach      *School Year:* 199–      Grade: 3

*Plan Developed by:* ELP teacher, third-grade math teacher, homeroom teacher, district math coordinator, 5/6-math teacher

[Author comment: Zach's parents were not invited to this meeting. There was no parental input into this plan; it was just handed to them.]

*Strength areas:* All academic areas. Especially math.

*Interest areas:* None reported

[Author comment: No interest areas were reported because parents were not involved in this meeting and they were not given the opportunity to provide input.]

*Standard Curriculum modifications (subject modifications, monitors/evaluations):* Zach has had math compacted this year to allow time for enrichment and more challenging projects in math. He has worked independently, with a partner, and sometimes a small group on these projects.

*Additions to standard curriculum (Mentors, groups, enrich/accelerate, and independent study):* ELP (Extended Learning Program) class 50 minutes weekly. As of March 27, an additional 30–40 minutes in ELP is spent on an independent study in computer programming using Logo Plus.)

[Author comment: This additional time was added after the parents provided the results of the above-level EXPLORE testing.]

*Special Considerations:* Zach's math strengths indicated a need for additional assessment in order to provide the appropriate level of challenge in fourth grade. The district fourth-grade end-of-year assessment provided by the math coordinator was given in early April. Results: Concepts and Computation (72%); Problem Solving (75%).

He has some definite gaps in fractions, decimals, and rounding. In addition, he had some curious errors, which could have been carelessness. Typically 80% correct is the guideline for recommending acceleration. However, it was the math coordinator's recommendation that he would probably be okay in fifth grade with help in the weak areas.

[Author comments: It is unfortunate that the language focuses on his relative weakness as opposed to his strengths. Note also, there was no mention of Zach's participation in the above-level talent search. The district did not use information from other sources.]

*April meeting:* Meeting with 3/4 teachers (ELP teacher, 5/6 homeroom teacher, 5/6 math teacher) to discuss the results and possible options for next year. Classroom teacher suggested that she work with Zach this year on the gaps indicated in the assessment. It was the consensus of the group that Zach be accelerated in math only for the next school year. It was also suggested that he possibly be placed in the 4/5-combination group.

Math coordinator will be sending information to the 3/4 teacher so she can plan to address Zach's needs as indicated on the assessment.

[Author note: The comment that "Zach be accelerated in math" is unfortunate. First of all, it sounds like Zach is the problem and needs to be "fixed." Rather than using language that emphasizes his strengths and what curriculum will meet his needs, the action is placed on the person. Also, this PEP shows remarkably limited vision. Parents were given this plan after it was completed, but they did not have input into it.]

## Figure 9.2: Zach's Personalized Educational Plan

Students spend grades 7 and 8 in a junior high building and grades 9–12 in a senior high building. The discussions about full-grade acceleration included a scenario in which Zach would skip grade 7 and go directly to grade 8. Concurrently,

| Table 9.1 Zach's EXPLORE—Mathematics Scores | | | |
|---|---|---|---|
| Grade tested | Standard Score | Talent Search Percentile | 8th Grade Percentile |
| 3rd | 13 | 91 | 48 |
| 4th | 16 | 96 | 72 |
| 5th | 24 | 99 | 99 |

his school system had just implemented a pilot program in which a select number of eighth graders were allowed to take geometry. The creation of the cohort was made possible by the advocacy efforts of the gifted educators who negotiated with administrators to allow them to have prealgebra in grade 6, thus permitting algebra in grade 7 and geometry in grade 8.

As a 13-year-old eighth grader, Zach had a cohort comprised of students at his grade level who also demonstrated talent in mathematics. Along with these students, he took the SAT, again demonstrating how different he was from his bright peers. On the verbal section of the SAT, he earned a score of 720, which is equivalent to the 97th percentile of college-bound juniors and seniors. He earned a mathematics score of 760, which is at the 98th percentile.

Outside of school, Zach was very involved in chess. In eighth grade, he was the state chess champion for junior high, and placed fifth in the state in the 19-and-under tournament even though his parents indicated that, outside of the tournaments, he spent very little time on chess because it cut into his reading time!

When Zach was a youngster, his parents kept him occupied by posing math problems to him. As a teenager, Zach posed problems to his parents on a near-daily basis, many of which he thought up. He got along well with the rest of his family and was described by his parents as a "good citizen," who pitched in when they needed help and didn't ridicule those for whom academics don't come as easily.

Although Zach is very talented in mathematics, he is talented in other areas as well. He fantasizes that, as an adult, he will be a writer or a cartoonist. He plans to vicariously enjoy children with his future nieces and nephews. Time will tell! Meanwhile, he is now on an academically challenging path, which began with above-level testing.

### Elizabeth: A Scientifically/Mathematically Gifted Female Whose Parents Don't Want Her to Be Different

We became aware of Elizabeth because of a phone call from her mother, which occurred after many years of discussions (but little action) with school personnel. In those discussions, the most specific issue concerned whole-grade acceleration and its pros and cons. At that time, Elizabeth was in fourth grade and her mother was concerned about the lack of academic challenge in her daughter's education. Elizabeth's mother was worried that an unchallenging curriculum would have a negative impact on Elizabeth's self-esteem, possibly leading to boredom and eventually to acting-out behaviors. At the same time, Elizabeth's mother expressed concern that any recommended placement options not make her daughter "different from her classmates."

Our first response to her request for our consultation was to highlight the need for specific, objective information prior to making any educational programming decisions, including acceleration. We also suggested that it would be best for the school to conduct any assessments (with our consultation) so that they would feel more ownership of the results, as well as the recommendations. We thought it was important to have collaboration among the school, the parents, and us. Fortunately for Elizabeth, the collaborative process was possible because of the very capable gifted education teacher who worked with her in the school's enrichment-focused pull-out program.

Elizabeth was one of the most able students in her school's pull-out program, which consisted of an hour of enrichment per week. However, her teacher for this enrichment program was the first to recognize that this level of programming was not providing Elizabeth with the systematic, high-level curriculum she needed in mathematics or in science.

The first step in identifying Elizabeth's educational needs was to see how she compared to others in her grade. Elizabeth had consistently scored at the 99th percentile on the Iowa Tests of Basic Skills (ITBS); a careful examination of the item profile for her ITBS results indicated that she never missed an item. It was obvious that she was talented—achieving at a level that was higher than others in her grade—but the grade-level assessment could not reveal the level for which curriculum/instruction was most appropriate for her. The only given was the fact that Elizabeth and her parents were convinced that she needed a challenging mathematics curriculum. We decided to administer the quantitative sections from the Secondary School Admission Test–Lower Level (SSAT) as an out-of-level test. On that test, while in fourth grade, Elizabeth scored at the 79th percentile when compared to sixth graders.

We then used the Sequential Tests of Educational Progress (STEP) tests that were normed for grades 5–8, and compared Elizabeth's scores to spring-semester sixth graders. Elizabeth earned a score at the 87th percentile on the STEP Basic Concepts. On the same level of the STEP Computation test, Elizabeth earned a score at the 25th percentile—a score that was considerably lower than her Basic Concepts score. This did not surprise us since we had already anticipated that her computation skills, like those of many mathematically gifted students, lagged behind her conceptualization of mathematics (Rotigel, 2000). An interesting observation concerned the fact that Elizabeth was able to earn a high Computation score when she was allowed to complete the items in an untimed setting. Nevertheless, it was apparent that she needed to have a firmer foundation for computation. From the results of the diagnostic testing we recommended that Elizabeth begin pre-algebra as soon as possible. A late-spring (of Elizabeth's fourth-grade year) meeting including teachers, parents, principal, and us was set to identify instructional goals for systematically working through the prealgebra curriculum during fifth and sixth grade.

During these discussions, we addressed the parents' concerns about Elizabeth being "different" from her classmates. Interestingly enough, this was not and still is not a concern for Elizabeth. We also discussed the parents' concerns that their daughter might be stressed by doing advanced work. We shared with them our perspective on the differences between stress and stretch. Because the parents felt the need for further discussions regarding their daughter's giftedness and its impact on her and their family, they were referred to a family counselor who had specific training in working with issues unique to families of gifted students.

Our impressions of Elizabeth were that she seemed like many academically able girls: self-effacing with respect to her abilities and simultaneously anxious to please her teachers. Fortunately, she had both a classroom teacher and an enrichment program teacher who very much wanted to see Elizabeth appropriately challenged and were willing to work together to differentiate the curriculum to do so.

These two teachers "stretched" the prealgebra curriculum through fifth and sixth grade. Also, when Elizabeth was in fifth grade, she participated in the Elementary Student Talent Search. Her scores on EXPLORE were superior (see Table 9.2) and demonstrated exceptional scores in both math and science reasoning. Because she seemed to be appropriately "stretched" in science through an enrichment project in which she built a camera, less emphasis was placed on providing specific programming in this subject area.

When Elizabeth was in seventh grade, she was allowed to do algebra, which was a rare occurrence for her district, since mathematically able students were only accelerated into algebra in grade 8. Unfortunately, she didn't have any math as an option in her school when she was in eighth grade, and she did not have the transportation to get to the high school for additional math classes. Because the district was not willing to provide programming for her, she played with a computer in the back of the mathematics classroom during her eighth-grade year. At that time, there was still not much available for summer programs in her area, so she was unable to take

| Table 9.2<br>Elizabeth's EXPLORE Scores in Fifth Grade | | | |
|---|---|---|---|
| EXPLORE<br>tests | Standard<br>Score | Talent Search<br>Percentile | 8th Grade<br>Percentile |
| Math | 13 | 48 | 48 |
| Science<br>Reasoning | 21 | 93 | 93 |

advantage of that sort of opportunity.

However, once she entered high school, she took full advantage of the opportunities. She took as many science classes as were available, often "doubling up." She completed the college-entrance requirements fairly quickly and participated in the postsecondary enrollment option available in many districts. This opportunity permitted her to do research with a physics professor throughout her junior and senior years. More importantly, working with a college professor while still in high school gave her added confidence. She also got back on track in mathematics and completed calculus as a senior. When it came time to consider colleges, she applied and was accepted at prestigious technical institutes on both coasts, but chose the institution that fully covered her tuition (and is located on the warmer of the two coasts). Her declared major was physics.

In the first conversation with Elizabeth's mother, the concern about her daughter being "different" as a result of a program intervention was a major point of discussion. We clearly remember advising the mother that, with respect to a need for a very challenging curriculum, Elizabeth *was* different from her classmates and that our consultation would provide objective information that could be used to develop such a curriculum.

If we knew then what we know today about mathematically (and scientifically) talented students, we would have done things slightly differently in three areas. First, we would have addressed Elizabeth's talent in science, as well as in math. Additionally, we would have strongly insisted on long-term planning in both of her talent areas. This would have avoided the lost year in which Elizabeth sat at the back of the classroom and worked on the computer. Finally, we would have tried to "normalize" Elizabeth's talents. That is, we would have encouraged the mother's efforts at advocacy for her daughter, and emphasized that her daughter is normal with some unique academic needs.

Elizabeth has continued on a unique path by choosing a field that has typically attracted very few females. Realization of her academic talent means that Elizabeth is destined to be different.

## Lessons Learned

As a result of working with Christopher, Billy, Arthur, Zach, Elizabeth, and many other students, we have learned numerous lessons.

1. Parents know their kids. They are essential advocates for their children.

Parents' specific anecdotes about their children's activities at certain ages are very useful in identifying mathematically talented students. This information, combined with objective information about aptitude and achievement, is critical to obtaining appropriate programming. Christopher's parents noted his unusual facility with numbers even when he was 3 years old. As soon as he began articulating his observations about numbers, they began to take note, and their observations proved extremely useful in alerting educators to Christopher's abilities.

2. Mathematical ability can be recognized at a young age.

The cases of Billy and Christopher illustrate this point clearly. Some of the early indicators of mathematical ability include:

- telling time early and showing an early interest in numbers (e.g., counting objects; Waxman, Robinson, & Mukhopadhayay, 1996a);

- an early sustained interest in manipulating numbers (e.g., 3-year-old Matthew spontaneously added the numbers he saw on a truck, 369 + 369, and shouted out, "738!"); and
- ability to construct their own understanding of mathematics without direct instruction. (For example, Peter demonstrated an intuitive understanding of multiplication at the age of 2. He was counting out three raisins for each gingerbread man he and his mother were making. When he was told they would make four more cookies, he said, "Then we need 12 more raisins!")

These early indicators of mathematical ability are first observed by the parents, which again illustrates our earlier point that it is critical to listen to parents' stories about their children. Of course, not all mathematically talented students are recognized early. As we have already mentioned, Zach's parents did not think the things he did at a young age were remarkable because he was their first-born and they didn't have any other young children with whom he could be compared.

3.  Because school personnel often take a "wait and see" attitude or "just say no," parents need to be persistent in their advocacy efforts.

Over and over again, we hear stories about parents being dismissed by school personnel or told to "give it more time." Some of our favorite quotes include: "All kids need enrichment and that enrichment will satisfy his or her need." "We don't do acceleration here." "We accelerate only 1 year." "No student is ready for algebra before age 13 or 14." These statements have been made by real school personnel, and these ideas represent educational myths.

We've also heard interesting stalling tactics, such as "Let's put Anthony in the regular classroom this fall and see how it goes. If he has trouble, we'll test him in November. Then, it'll be Christmas vacation, and we shouldn't start any special programs. Let's plan to start something in January." This is why it is important to plan in the spring for the following school year. Then, the principal and guidance counselor (and whoever else is involved with scheduling) can take into account a child's special needs when doing the scheduling. Christopher's parents did an excellent job using this strategy.

We have found that parents and gifted education teachers are the driving force behind discovering mathematically talented students and generating appropriate programming for them. Both parents and gifted educators need to be persistent at creating an appropriately challenging program, and oftentimes this will need to be done in a less-than-supportive environment. We have sometimes experienced the situation where the teacher is willing to give a student more advanced material, but the principal will not support it. This is a difficult situation that can require the negotiating skills of a professional diplomat. It is always helpful to have an advocate within the system, but it is not appropriate to put that advocate at risk in his or her job situation.

4.  School-based assessments are typically grade-level in nature, and many educators are not aware of the need or procedure involved in above-level testing.

Billy's teachers used the standards for the primary grades as indicators of his achievement ("can recognize numbers 1–12"), but didn't attempt to measure what he could do beyond these minimum expectations or what he was ready to learn next. The information we presented in Chapters 3, 4, and 5 should be helpful in determining what level of test to give to a student and how to interpret the resulting scores. As we have stated repeatedly in this book, the goal is to determine what the student already knows and then move on from there. Rather than using grade-level tests that tell us what we already know (the student is performing very well compared to age-level peers), we offer students the opportunity to take a much more challenging test and demonstrate their exceptional abilities. Although the approach we advocate is common sense, few educators have had specific training in providing this type of testing and programming for gifted students.

5.   Children don't need to be tested until they are ready for systematic programming.

Although it is not essential to have standardized testing at a very young age, it is when students enter the school system. We recommend testing right before kindergarten if the child is showing characteristics of exceptional mathematical ability. That way, parents have objective information to show school personnel so that a special program can be put in place at the beginning of the school year, if needed. It is generally not necessary for a child as young as 2 or 3 to have this specialized testing done. Again, we recommend waiting until about 6 months before entering kindergarten. Chapter 3 offers more information about the type of assessment we recommend.

6.   All assessment (testing) needs to be driven by a question.

In our case, the question is, "What is the extent of the child's mathematical ability and what types of programming modification does he or she need?" In this situation, IQ testing is not necessary. It gives a sense of overall ability, but it does not give the specific information needed to develop a systematic mathematics program. Billy's testing in kindergarten and first grade pointed out that he was an exceptionally bright child, but it didn't yield specific recommendations for his math program. The only obvious benefit from his IQ testing was that it helped to identify him for a gifted program, and this resulted in his working with an understanding teacher who became one of his advocates.

7.   The Diagnostic Testing→Prescriptive Instruction model is useful for helping mathematically talented youth study mathematics at the appropriate level and pace.

The skills and content students have mastered in mathematics must be assessed carefully to ensure that instruction begins at the proper point, and the DT→PI approach provides the systematic means of doing so.

Both Zach and Elizabeth exemplified some of the issues that math talented kids have to deal with in a district that focuses only on enrichment. They were lucky because they had teachers who were willing to go outside of the imposed enrichment curriculum and seek assistance through additional testing (DT→PI) to get the right "dosage" of mathematics. With Elizabeth, it wasn't perfect because there was a gap in eighth grade. For Zach, the gap was taken care of because the system was already in place when he needed it.

8.  Even extremely talented students need time to develop the cognitive structures that characterize mathematical maturity.

We are strong advocates of acceleration because it is often the only way in which a student can be truly challenged in mathematics. At the same time, we recognize that students need time to develop intellectually. We are concerned that students who rush ahead before they are ready might learn advanced mathematics by rote without the benefit of deep understanding.

It is important for students to understand the logic underlying elementary mathematics problems before advancing to abstract concepts. We are also concerned that students not have large gaps in their mathematical backgrounds. Thus, while acceleration is appropriate for many mathematically talented students, at the same time it is being planned, it is critical to look at how the time saved will be used. We also advocate using the DT→PI model to ensure that students do not have gaps in their mathematics background (see Chapter 4).

9.  Mathematically talented students should study mathematics at a steady rate.

It is not necessary for a student to meet individually with a mentor for many hours each week to advance in mathematics. Two 1-hour sessions with a mentor, with homework assigned between sessions, might be all the challenge and stimulation a student needs. Students who do accelerate in mathematics also have the luxury of more time for studying enrichment topics in mathematics. This extra time should be put to good use. We encourage students to study enrichment topics that might not be a part of the regular curriculum (see Chapter 7).

Continuous study of mathematics 12 months of the year is not necessary, and students do not need to race through the standard sequence of mathematics. What happened to

Elizabeth should be avoided: moving ahead in mathematics only to be left without any mathematics for a whole school year. Long-term, continuous planning is essential for these students whose needs are very different from the norm.

10. Choices made when students are in elementary school may affect their high school mathematics program. Educators often fear that "students will run out of math" before they graduate from high school.

If the level and pace of instruction are matched to the abilities of mathematically talented students, by definition they will be accelerated. They may run out of mathematics courses that are offered by their school district before they finish high school, but there is plenty of mathematics to be learned. Students may need to take college courses part-time, work with a mentor, complete distance-learning courses, or enter college early in order to have access to an appropriate level of mathematics (see Chapter 6 and the "Resources" section).

11. Students may need to look outside of their school system for appropriate programs in mathematics.

These opportunities include summer and weekend programs offered at universities, distance-learning programs, mentor-paced programs, and competitions. All of the students included in our case studies took advantage of programs offered by local universities, zoos, museums, and other educational groups, and their parents were constantly on the lookout for new and interesting opportunities for their children ("Resources" provides information about many of these opportunities).

12. Mathematically talented girls may have special needs.

Research and personal experience has shown that it is important that mathematically talented girls be placed in a challenging, supportive atmosphere so that their talents can be fully realized. As we have mentioned elsewhere, we find many more mathematically talented boys than girls. Many more parents of boys than girls call us seeking our advice. This seems especially true with the youngest students. We have also noticed that parents of girls seem to be more concerned about social issues, stress the fact that they don't want their daughters to be different (as in Elizabeth's case), and are more willing to allow school personnel to talk them out of seeking accelerative options or other special educational programming.

We recommend that parents of mathematically talented girls be especially aware of the social pressures that encourage girls *not* to demonstrate their exceptional abilities. These students benefit from opportunities to explore mathematics in a supportive atmosphere, work with female role models, and study mathematics with other similarly talented girls. Experiences provided by programs such as those listed in the Resources section may be especially important for their mathematical development. (A more detailed discussion about issues affecting mathematically talented females is presented in Reis & Gavin, 1999).

13. Students should strive to achieve a balance among studying mathematics at an accelerated pace, studying other academic subjects, and participating in extracurricular activities.

Students need time to study other subjects, to play with friends, and to be alone. It is important to us to help these students achieve a balance in their lives while also making sure that they study mathematics at the appropriate level. We recognize that accelerated students still have the opportunity to be with same-age peers in many other situations, such as scouts, religious youth groups, recess, and lunch, even if they are not grouped with their age peers for any of their academic activities. We encourage students to try out different types of activities, including sports and music, not in an effort to be "well-rounded," but in an effort to be exposed to different situations and different people.

14. Talented students benefit from finding an intellectual peer group.

This is why academic summer programs and weekend programs are so valuable. Talented students can be placed together with others who have similar interests. They enjoy the rewards of being challenged intellectually while also becoming friends with others like themselves. Christopher and Zach both benefited from this type of experience during their regular school day; they were grouped with other mathematically talented students who also happened to be older than they were. The benefits of this type of grouping include the realization that they are not the only ones who like and are good at math. Again, this experience may be especially important for mathematically talented girls.

15.   Most parents of talented students we have met are not "pushing" their children.

Most of the parents with whom we work are simply responding to their child's needs and interests. These parents have not been showing their children flashcards from birth. Billy's case illustrates this point clearly. He spontaneously demonstrated his capability to tell time, calculate, and read; his parents did not teach him these feats directly. Instead of pushing their children, these parents are being pulled by their children, who consistently demand, "More math!"

## Conclusion

The case studies in this chapter illustrate many of the points we have made throughout this book. Mathematically talented students can be identified at a young age, and they benefit from programming that matches the curriculum and pace of instruction to their specific academic abilities and needs. Talent searches, first pioneered by Julian Stanley in 1972 for seventh graders and now offered by several universities for elementary, middle school, and junior high school students, provide a systematic method for identifying precocious youth and providing appropriate programs for them. The Diagnostic Testing→Prescriptive Instruction model, used by the talent searches and by a number of schools, has been effective in helping exceptionally talented students to study the appropriate level of mathematics.

# Resources

THIS SECTION PRESENTS GENERAL INFOR-
mation and resources relevant for mathematically gifted students, their parents, and their
teachers. It begins with a listing of talent
searches and programs for talented youth. Next,
we indicate programs that provide for early
entrance to college and distance-learning opportunities. The section continues with an alpha-
betical listing of major competitions and
contests, as well as a listing of printed materials,
including periodicals and books, and computer
software. This section concludes with a list of
other resources, Web sites and listservs, and a
recommended reading list.

When parents and educators are informed,
they can make general policy decisions, as well as
individual program plans, based upon objective
information, rather than subjective experience.

## Talent Searches

**Academic Talent Search** (talent searches, as well as summer and weekend programs for students in grades 6–9)
School of Education, California State University, 6000 J St., Sacramento, CA 95819-6098; http://edweb.csus.edu/projects/ATS

**ADVANCE Program for Young Scholars** (grades 7–11)
P.O. Box 5671, Natchitoches, LA 71497; http://www.advanceprogram.org

**Belin-Blank International Center for Gifted Education and Talent Development** (talent searches [Belin-Blank Exceptional Student Talent Search–BESTS], grades 2–9; commuter and residential programs, grades 3–12)
Blank Honors Center, The University of Iowa, Iowa City, IA 52242; http://www.uiowa.edu/~belinctr

**Canada/USA Mathcamp** (ages 13–18)
129 Hancock St., Cambridge, MA 0213; http://www.math-camp.org

**Carnegie Mellon Institute for Talented Elementary Students (C-MITES)**
(talent search, grades 3–6; commuter programs throughout Pennsylvania, grades K–7)
4902 Forbes Ave., #6261, Carnegie Mellon University, Pittsburgh, PA 15213; http://www.cmu.edu/cmites

**Center for Talent Development** (talent searches, grades 4–9; summer and weekend programs, commuter and residential, grades K–12)
School of Education and Social Policy, Northwestern University, 617 Dartmouth Place, Evanston, IL 60208-4175; http:// www.ctd.nwu.edu

**Center for Talented Youth (CTY)** (commuter and residential programs, elementary and secondary students; correspondence courses for various ages)

Johns Hopkins University, 3400 N. Charles St., Baltimore, MD 21218; http://www.cty.jhu.edu

**Frances A. Karnes Center for Gifted Studies** (grades 7–10)
The University of Southern Mississippi, Box 8207, Hattiesburg, MS 39406-8207; http://www-dept.usm.edu/~gifted

**Hampshire College Summer Studies in Mathematics** (programs for mathematically talented and motivated high school students)
Hampshire College, Amherst, MA 01002; http://www.hcssim.org

**Math for Young Achievers (MYA)**
Program Coordinator, Arts & Sciences Continuing Education, University of Wisconsin at Eau Claire, Eau Claire, WI 54702-4004; http://www.uwec.edu/ce/Youth/Math/Math.html

**Office of Precollegiate Programs for Talented and Gifted (OPP-TAG)** (residential summer classes in a variety of subjects, grades 7–9; classes in mathematics during the school year are available for local students)
310 Pearson Hall, Iowa State University, Ames, IA 50010-2200; http://www.public.iastate.edu/~opptag_info

**Pennsylvania Governor's Schools of Excellence** (summer residential programs for artistically or academically talented high school students who have completed grades 10 or 11 includes the following areas: the Arts, Agricultural Sciences, Health Care, International Studies, Sciences, and Teaching; a number of other states also offer "Governor's Schools")
http:// www.pde.state.pa.us/excellence

**Program in Mathematics for Young Scientists (PROMYS)** (a challenging program designed to encourage ambitious high school students to explore the creative world of mathematics)
Dept. of Mathematics, Boston University, 111 Cummington St., Boston, MA 02215; http://math.bu.edu/people/promys

**Purdue University Gifted Education Resource Institute (GERI)** (grades 7–12)
Beering Hall, 100 N. University St., Purdue University, West Lafayette, IN 47907-2067; http://www.geri.soe.purdue.edu

**Research Science Institute** (a mentor program in the sciences for rising high school seniors)
140 Park St. SE, Second Floor, Vienna, VA 22180-4627; http://www.cee.org/rsi/index.shtml

**Rocky Mountain Talent Search and Summer Institute (RMTS)** (residential and commuter programs, ages 11–16)
1981 South University Blvd., Denver, CO 80208; http://www.du.edu/education/ces/si.html

**Ross Mathematics Program** (for 14- to 17-year-olds deeply interested in math and science; intense math courses)
Dept. of Mathematics, Ohio State University, 231 W. 18th Ave., Columbus, OH 43210; http://www.math.ohio-state.edu/ross

**Southern Methodist University Gifted Students Institute and Precollege Programs** (grades 7–11)
The Gifted Students Institute, Southern Methodist University, P.O. Box 750383, Dallas, TX 75275-0383; http://www.smu.edu/~gsi

**Summer Program for Verbally and Mathematically Precocious Youth** (grades 7–10)
The Center for Gifted Studies at Western Kentucky University, Bowling Green, KY; http://www.wku.edu/gifted

**Talent Identification Program (TIP)** (residential summer program, grades 7–12; educational information provided to students in grades 4–6)
Duke University, Box 90747, Durham, NC 27708; http://www.tip.duke.edu

**Wisconsin Center for Academically Talented Youth (WCATY)** (grades 4–12)
2909 Landmark Place, Madison, WI 53713; http://www.wcaty.org

**University of Minnesota Talented Youth Mathematics Program (UMTYMP)** (commuter program in accelerated mathematics, grades 5–12)
Institute of Technology Center for Educational Programs, 4 Vincent Hall, 206 Church St. SE, University of Minnesota, Minneapolis, MN 55455; http://www.math.umn.edu/itcep/umtymp

## Early Entrance to College Programs

**Accelerated College Entrance Center, California State University, Sacramento** (grades 9–12)
6000 J St., Sacramento, CA 95819-6098; http://www.educ.csus.edu/projects/ace

**The Advanced Academy of Georgia** (apply in 10th grade and complete 11th and 12th grade and first 2 years of college simultaneously)
Director, The Advanced Academy of Georgia, Honors House, State University of West Georgia, 1600 Maple St. Carrollton, GA, 30118-5130; http://www.westga.edu/~academy

**The Clarkson School** (for students who have completed 11th grade; early admission to college)
Director of Admissions and Financial Aid, The Clarkson School, Box 5650, Potsdam, NY 13699-5650; http://www.clarkson.edu/tcs

**The National Academy of Arts, Sciences, and Engineering at the University of Iowa** (for high school students who have completed the equivalent of 11th grade)
http://www.uiowa.edu/~belinctr/programs/naase/naase.html

**Program for the Exceptionally Gifted** (girls may apply to this program as early as the eighth grade; students generally complete their bachelor's degree within 4 years)
Mary Baldwin College, Staunton, VA 24401; http://www.mbc.edu/peg/index.htm

**Simon's Rock** (early entrance to college for students who have completed 10th grade)
Director of Admission, Simon's Rock of Bard College, 84 Alford Road, Great Barrington, MA 01230-9702; http://www.simons-rock.edu

**Halbert and Nancy Robinson Center for Young Scholars, University of Washington**
P.O. Box 351630, Seattle, WA 98195-1630; (206) 543-4160; http://www.depts.washington.edu/cscy

## Distance Learning

**Advanced Placement Program**
The College Board, P.O. Box 6671, Princeton, NJ 08541-6671; http:// apcentral.collegeboard.com.
Courses offered in many high schools. National examinations given in May each year. High scores earn college credit. Currently, 35 courses in 19 subject areas, including biology, chemistry, English literature, physics, psychology, languages, history, art, and calculus, are available. Students who do not have access to AP courses in their high schools, may enroll in online courses through APEX Learning Corporation (http://www.apexlearning.com). Many states have state-sponsored grants to pay for online AP courses through APEX.

**Education Program for Gifted Youth (EPGY)**
Ventura Hall, Stanford University, Stanford, CA 94305-4115; http://epgy.stanford.edu
Computer-based correspondence courses in mathematics, mathematical sciences, and expository writing for academically talented students in kindergarten through 12th grades.

### The Home Education Network (THEN)
12975 Coral Tree Pl., Los Angles, CA 90066; http://www.onlinelearning.net
Offers distance-learning online education in business management, organizational behavior, risk management, accounting, screenwriting, fiction writing, test preparation, and teacher certification. THEN online courseware is offered in conjunction with the UCLA Extension University. At-home study courses can be completed online or through employers and an affiliated Internet training and distance-education network.

### Intelligent Education
2859 Paces Ferry Rd., Suite 1200, Overlook III, Atlanta, GA 30339; http://www.intelligented.com

### The University of Nebraska Independent Study High School
Clifford Hardin Nebraska Center for Continuing Education, Room 269, Lincoln, NE 68583-9801; http://dcs.unl.edu/ishs

## Contests and Competitions

### American Mathematics Competition (formerly the AHSME)
P.O. Box 839400, University of Nebraska–Lincoln, Lincoln, NE 68583-9400; http://www.unl.edu/amc
Any student who has not graduated from high school is eligible. High-scoring students move on to the American Invitational Mathematics Exam, USA Mathematical Olympiad, and International Mathematical Olympiad.

### American Regions Mathematics League (ARML)
ARML Executive Director, 1315 John's Creek Road, Wilmington, NC 28409; http://www.arml.com
An annual national mathematics competition for high school students. ARML is held simultaneously at three sites: Penn State, University of Iowa, and San Jose State University.

### Future Problem Solving Program
2028 Regency Road, Lexington, KY 40503-2309;

http://www. fpsp.org
Curricular and cocurricular competitive and noncompetitive activities in creative problem solving.

### Intel Science Talent Search (formerly the Westinghouse Science Talent Search)
1719 N St. NW, Washington, DC 20036; http://www.sciserv. org/sts
High school seniors submit independent research projects by November 29th each year. Winners receive college scholarships.

### Junior Engineering Technical Society (JETS)
1420 King St., Ste. 405, Alexandria, VA 22314; http://www. jets.org
A national educational organization offering competitions and programs to high school students to promote interest in engineering, science, mathematics, and technology.

### MATHCOUNTS
1420 King St., Alexandria, VA 22314; http://www.mathcounts.org
A series of competitions designed for seventh and eighth graders. It is a four-stage, year-long program run jointly by the National Society of Professional Engineers, the National Council of Teachers of Mathematics, NASA, and the CNA Foundation.

### Mathematical Olympiads for Elementary and Middle Schools (MOEMS)
2154 Bellmore Ave., Bellmore, NY 11710-5645; http:// www.moems.org
This is an in-school academic year competition for students in eighth grade and younger. There are two divisions: E for grades 4–6, and M for grades 6–8.

### National Merit Scholarships
1560 Sherman Ave., Suite 200, Evanston, IL 60201-4897; http://www.nationalmerit.org
Students scoring high on the PSAT (taken in 11th grade) advance to other levels in the competition. Winners receive college scholarships.

## Science Olympiad

5955 Little Pine Lane, Rochester, MI 48306; http://www. soinc.org

Competitions, classroom activities, and training workshops used to improve the quality of science education, increase student interest in science, and provide recognition for outstanding achievement in science education by both students and teachers. Focuses on the disciplines of biology, Earth science, chemistry, physics, computers, and technology.

## U.S. Chemistry Team (High School)

American Chemical Society, Education Division, 1155 Sixteenth St. NW, Washington, DC 20036; http://www.acs. org/education/student/olympiad.html

## U.S. Physics Team, (High School)

American Association of Physics Teachers, American Center for Physics, Programs and Conferences Department, One Physics Ellipse, College Park, MD 20740.

## Printed Materials

Books

Assouline, S. G., Colangelo, N., Lupkowski-Shoplik, A. E., & Lipscomb, J. (1999). *Iowa acceleration scale.* Scottsdale, AZ: Great Potential Press. This guidance instrument provides a systematic and thorough method of decision making for educators and parents who are considering whole-grade acceleration for students in kindergarten through eighth grade.

Colangelo, N., & Davis, G. A. (Eds.). (2003). *Handbook of gifted education* (3rd ed.). Needham Heights, MA: Allyn and Bacon.

*Directory of Science Training for High Ability Pre–college Students.* Send requests for this free publication to

Science Services, 1719 N Street NW, Washington, DC 20036; http://www.sciserv.org/stp

*Educational Opportunity Guide*, from Duke University's Talent Identification Program (TIP). This guide is published annually. Lists many summer and school-year programs throughout the U.S. Students who score high in TIP's Talent Search get a free copy. Contact TIP, P.O. Box 90747, Durham, NC 27701; http://www.tip.duke.edu.

Johnson, D. T., & Sher, B. T. (1997). *Resource guide to mathematics curriculum materials for high-ability learners in grades K–8*. Williamsburg, VA: Center for Gifted Education, College of William and Mary.

Karnes, F. A., & Riley, T. L. (1996). *Competitions: Maximizing your abilities*. Waco, TX: Prufrock Press. This book lists many different contests and competitions.

Lupkowski, A., & Assouline, S. G. (1992). *Jane and Johnny love math: Recognizing and encouraging mathematical talent in elementary students*. Unionville, NY: Royal Fireworks Press.

*Peterson's Summer Opportunities for Kids and Teenagers.* This publication is a source of information about summer "camps" and is updated annually. Order copies through a local bookstore or call (800) 338-3282.

*Program Opportunities for Talented Students*, from the Institute for the Academic Advancement of Talented Youth (IAAY) Office of Public Information, Johns Hopkins University, 3400 N. Charles St., Baltimore, MD 21218.

Sheffield, L. J. (Ed.). (1999). *Developing mathematically promising students*. Reston, VA: National Council of Teachers of Mathematics.

Waxman, B., Robinson, N. M., & Mukhopadhyay, S. (1996). *Teachers nurturing math-talented young children* (RM96228). Storrs: The National Research Center on the Gifted and Talented, University of Connecticut.

Wickelgren, W. A., & Wickelgren, I. (2001). *Math coach: A parent's guide to helping children succeed in math*. New York: Berkley Books.

Willoughby, S. S. (1991). *Mathematics for a changing world.* Alexandria, VA: Association for Supervision and Curriculum Development.

Periodicals

*Advanced Development Journal*
Institute for the Study of Advanced Development
1452 Marion St., Denver, CO 80228; (303) 837-8378 or (888) 443-8331; http://www.gifteddevelopment.com

*Gifted Child Quarterly*
National Association for Gifted Children (NAGC)
1707 L Street NW, Ste. 550, Washington, DC 20036; (202) 785-4268; http://www.nagc.org
Contains articles of interest to professionals and those with some reading experience in the field of gifted education.

*Gifted Child Today*
Prufrock Press, Inc.
P.O. Box 8813, Waco, TX 76714; (800) 998-2208; http://www.prufrock.com
Directed at teachers and parents, it avoids jargon and provides practical advice on working with gifted, creative, and talented children.

*Imagine*
Center for Talented Youth at Johns Hopkins University
http://www.jhu.edu/~gifted/imagine
A magazine for academically talented students published five times a year.

*Journal for the Education of the Gifted*
The Association for the Gifted (TAG), a division of the Council for Exceptional Children
1110 North Glebe Road, Ste. 300, Arlington, VA 22201; http://www.cec.sped.org
Journal aimed at the experienced reader of the literature.

*Parenting for High Potential*
National Association for Gifted Children (NAGC)
1707 L Street NW, Ste. 550, Washington, DC 20036; (202) 785-4268; http://www.nagc.org
An excellent magazine designed for parents.

*Roeper Review*
The Roeper School
P.O. Box 329, Bloomfield Hills, MI 48303-0329; http://www.roeperreview.org
This publication is designed for professionals. The articles are research-based and often deal with both theoretical and practical issues concerning gifted individuals.

*Understanding Our Gifted*
Open Space Communications, Inc.
P.O. Box 18268, Boulder, CO 80308; (303) 444-7020 or (800) 494-6178; http://www.our-gifted.com

*Vision*
The Connie Belin & Jacqueline N. Blank International Center for Gifted Education and Talent Development
The University of Iowa College of Education, Blank Honors Center, Iowa City, IA 52242-1529; (319) 335-6148 or (800) 336-6463; http://www.uiowa.edu/~belinctr/pubs/vision

## Sources of Math Enrichment Materials

Books and Manipulatives

**AMSCO School Publications**
315 Hudson St., New York, NY 10013-1085; http://www.amscopub.com

**Center for Talented Youth (CTY), Johns Hopkins University**
3400 N. Charles St., Baltimore, MD 21218.
CTY distributes materials explaining the curriculum they use and publishes other resources for teachers.

### ETA/Cuisenaire
500 Greenview Ct., Vernon Hills, IL 60061-1838; http://www.etacuisenaire.com

### Free Spirit Publishers
217 Fifth Ave. North, Ste. 200, Minneapolis, MN 55401-1299; http://www.freespirit.com.

### Mathematical Association of America
1529 Eighteenth St. NW, Washington, DC, 20036-1385; http://www.maa.org.
Sponsors the American Mathematics Competitions leading to the International Mathematical Olympiad.

### The Math Forum, Swarthmore College
3210 Cherry St., Philadelphia, PA 19104; http://mathforum.org.

### National Council of Teachers of Mathematics
1906 Association Dr., Reston, VA 20191-1502; http://www.nctm.org.
Publishes books helpful in teaching mathematics in addition to the journals *Mathematics Teacher* and *Mathematics Teaching in the Middle School*.

### Pearson Learning Group
135 S. Mount Zion Rd., P.O. Box 2500, Lebanon, IN 46052; http://www.pearsonlearning.com.
Previously known as Dale Seymour Publications, which joined with other companies to form Pearson Learning Group.

### Prufrock Press
P.O. Box 8813, Waco, TX 76714-8813; http://www.prufrock.com

### Zephyr Press
P.O. Box 66006, Tucson, AZ 85728-6006; http://www.zephyrpress.com.

Computer Software

The following list includes many computer programs for kindergarten-aged children and older. The programs come with user's guides that offer helpful suggestions.

**Courseware Solutions, Inc.**
99 Hayden St. Suite 205 Toronto, ON, Canada, M4Y3B4; http://www.mathville.com.

**Discovery Channel Shopping Online**
P.O. Box 877, Florence, KY 41022-0877; http://shopping. discovery.com

**Mattel Interactive**
http://www.broderbund. com.
This is the new owner of The Learning Company and Broderbund.

**Sunburst Technology**
1550 Executive Dr., Elgin, IL 60121; http://www.sunburst. com

**Ventura Educational Systems**
P.O. Box 425, Grover Beach, CA 93483; http://www. venturaes.com

## Organizations

Most states have a state organization to promote advocacy for gifted and talented students at the state and local level; provide preservice and in-service training in gifted education; and support parent/community awareness, education, and involvement. See the NAGC Web site (http://www.nagc.org) for specific information by state.

**American Association for Gifted Children**
Duke University, P.O. Box 90270, Durham, NC 27708-0270;

http://www.aagc.org
Established in the late 1940s, the AAGC is the nation's oldest advocacy organization for gifted children, AAGC also has a role in the Presidential Scholars program, which recognizes 141 outstanding high school graduates each year.

### The Association for the Gifted (TAG)
1110 North Glebe Road, Ste. 300, Arlington, VA 22201; http://www.cec.sped.org
A special interest group of the Council for Exceptional Children (CEC).

### Hollingworth Center for Highly Gifted Children
827 Center Ave. #282, Dover, NH 03820-2506; (303) 554-7895; http://www.hollingworth.org

### National Association for Gifted Children
1707 L St. NW, Ste. 550, Washington, DC 20036; http://www.nagc.org
NAGC is a nonprofit organization that has been in existence for more than 50 years. It hosts an annual convention and publishes two periodicals, a magazine for parents (*Parenting for High Potential*) and a journal for professionals (*Gifted Child Quarterly*). As an organization, its purpose is to serve parents, educators, community leaders, and other professionals who work on behalf of gifted children.

### National Foundation for Gifted and Creative Children
395 Diamond Hill Road, Warwick, RI 02886; (401) 738-0937; http://www.nfgcc.org
This is a nonprofit organization focusing on the problems of overprescription of drugs to gifted and creative children. Incorporated in 1969.

### Supporting Emotional Needs of the Gifted (SENG)
P.O. Box 6550, Scottsdale, AZ 85261; (206) 498-6744; http://www.sengifted.org

**TAG Family Network**
A national association for parents started in Oregon in 1990 and continuing nationwide. Information is available by e-mail: rkaltwas@teleport.com. There is also a TAG Hotline: (503) 378-7851.

## Web Sites and Listservs

**Afterschool.gov** (http://www.afterschool.gov)
**Ben's Guide to the U.S. Government for Kids K–12** (http://bensguide.gpo.gov)
**Cultural Project** (http://web.mit.edu/french/culturaNEH)
**Cyberkids** (http://www.cyberkids.com)
**Davidson Institute** (http://www.davidson-institute.org) This site is a comprehensive resource for parents and educators. It includes an interactive, comprehensive database of use for both parents and students.
**Discovery Channel School** (http://www.school.discovery.com)
**Early Entrance Programs** (http://earlyentrance.org) A comprehensive site developed by a student who entered college early. Very informative for both parents and students.
**Exploring the Solar System** (http://www.nytimes.com/library/national/science/solar-index.html)
**Federal Resources for Educational Excellence** (http://www.ed.gov/free)
**The Hoagies Gifted Education Page** (http://www.hoagiesgifted.org) Parents love this Web site because it is a general introductory resource for families.
**Kidlink** (http://www.kidlink.org)
**KidSource** (http://www.kidsource.com/kidsource/pages/ed.gifted.html)
**Kids Web** (http://www.npac.syr.edu/textbook/newkidsweb)
**Learning Network: On This Day** (http://www.nytimes.com/learning/general/onthisday)
**The Learning Page** (http://lcweb2.loc.gov/ammem/ndlpedu/index.html)
**Mathematics Education at Northern Kentucky University** (http://www.nku.edu/~mathed/gifted.html)

**National Gallery of Art** (http://www.nga.gov/education/
education.htm)
**National Park Service Museum Exhibits** (http://www.cr.nps.
gov/museum/exhibits/index.htm)
**Prometric** (http://prime.prometric.com) A worldwide distribution network for computer-based testing services.
**ShowMe Center** (http://www.showmecenter.missouri.edu)

In addition to the Web sites described above, there are many
listservs that are designed to keep people informed of current
events. A listserv is only useful if it is well-managed. Many educators have indicated that they find the listserv hosted by the
professional development administrator at the Belin-Blank
Center to be very informative. To subscribe to this listserv, send
an email message to gifted-teachers-request@list.uiowa.edu.
Please leave the subject line blank and include the following
commands in the message text:
  subscribe
  end

## Articles

Below is a short list of selected articles that may be useful to
parents and educators. This list was compiled by the staff of
the Belin-Blank Professional Development Program (see
Chapter 8).

### Acceleration

Charlton, J. C., & Marolf, D. M. (1994). Follow-up insights on
  rapid educational acceleration. *Roeper Review, 17,*
  123–139.
Sayler, M., & Lupkowski, A. E. (1992, March/April). Early
  entrance to college: Weighing the options. *Gifted Child
  Today, 15*(2), 24–29.
Southern, W. T., & Jones, E. D. (1992, March/April). The real
  problems with academic acceleration. *Gifted Child
  Today, 15*(2), 34–38.

Advocacy

O'Connell Ross, P. (1991). Advocacy for gifted programs in the new educational climate. *Gifted Child Quarterly, 35,* 173–176. [Note: This article is considered to be "In the Public Interest" and may be reproduced without permission of the publisher.]

Career Planning

Achter, J. A., Benbow, C. P., & Lubinski, D. (1991). Rethinking multipotentiality among the intellectually gifted: A critical review and recommendations. *Gifted Child Quarterly, 41,* 5–15.

Case Studies

White, W. L. (1990) Interviews with Child I, Child J, and Child L. *Gifted Child Quarterly,* 12, 222–228.

Curriculum

Reis, S. M., Westberg, K. L., Kulikowich, J. M., & Prucell, J. H. (1998). Curriculum compacting and achievement test scores: What does the research say? *Gifted Child Quarterly, 42,* 123–129.

Effective Teachers

Ford, D. Y., Grantham, T. C., & Harris, J. J., III. (1997). The recruitment and retention of minority teachers in gifted education. *Roeper Review, 19,*213–220.

Gallagher, J. J., Coleman, M. R., & Nelson, S. (1995). Perceptions of educational reform by educators representing middle schools, cooperative learning, and gifted education. *Gifted Child Quarterly, 39,* 66–76.

Reilly, J. (1992, May/June). When does a student really need a professional mentor? *Gifted Child Today, 15*(3) 3–8.

Whitlock, M. S., & DuCette, J. P. (1989). Outstanding and average teachers of the gifted: A comparative study. Gifted *Child Quarterly, 33*, 15–21.

## Identification

Birch, J. W. (1984). Is any identification procedure necessary? *Gifted Child Quarterly, 28*, 157–161.
Runco, M. A. (1997). Is every child gifted? *Roeper Review, 19*, 220–224.

## Family

May, K. (2000). Gifted children and their families. *Family Journal, 8*(1), 58–60.
Weissler, K. & Landau, E. (1993). Characteristics of families with no, one, or more than one gifted child. *Journal of Psychology, 127*, 143–153.

## Underachievement

Emerick, L. J. (1992). Academic underachievement among the gifted: Students' perceptions of factors that reverse the pattern. *Gifted Child Quarterly, 36*, 140–146.

# Glossary

**Above-average:** A "normal distribution" of "normal" (i.e., "typical") students is shaped like a bell curve. If 100 students' scores are plotted on a graph, a bell curve would likely be generated. Most of the scores will fall in the middle of the curve. Average scores are those in the middle two-thirds of the curve. Students who earn scores above the average scores are above-average. Compared to the other 100 scores, their scores are better than 85%; they are at the 85th percentile or above. The top 3–5% of scores earned by a group of 100 "typical" students of a particular age and/or grade—those whose scores were at or above the 97th or 95th percentile—are sometimes considered for gifted programming.

**Above-level test:** A test designed for older students is given to younger, academically talented students. The above-level test is presumably more difficult than grade-level tests. Having more difficult items helps us to measure the students' abilities more accurately and to devise more appropriate programs. The concept of above-level testing is the foundation upon which the talent search model was built.

**Above-level testing:** Giving a test that was developed for students who are several years older. Also called out-of-level testing or beyond-level testing.

**Acceleration**: Moving at a faster pace through the curriculum than is typical. This can be accomplished by entering kindergarten, first grade, or college early (early admission); skipping an entire grade (grade skipping), or advancing in a subject area more rapidly than is typical (subject-matter acceleration).

**Achievement test**: Tests that measure what a student has learned. These are usually given to students after completing a course or topic. Achievement test results are also useful for adapting instruction to individual needs because this information helps instructors determine what topics a student does or does not know.

**Age-equivalent**: Students' scores on tests are sometimes compared to the performance of a typical child at a given age level. A student's score on a test will correspond to the highest year/grade level that he or she can successfully complete. However, caution needs to be used in drawing conclusions regarding most age-equivalent scores, as scores at the extremes are usually extrapolations and not actually based upon performance. For example, a 6-year-old who earns an age-equivalent of 14 years on a reading test has actually earned an age-equivalent score that is based upon an extrapolation of data, not upon an assessment of 14-year-olds.

**Age-in-grade grouping**: Placing a student with other students of the same chronological age and grade level.

**Aptitude tests**: Tests that are used to predict performance in specific areas, such as verbal comprehension, mathematical ability, mechanical aptitude, spatial relations aptitude, or non-verbal reasoning ability. Aptitude tests have more specific content than intelligence tests do (i.e., they measure only one or a few abilities, rather than a wide variety of abilities).

**Ceiling effect**: When a test does not have enough difficult items to measure a student's abilities accurately, the test is said to not have enough "ceiling." Students who correctly answer all or almost all of the items on the test are said to have reached the "ceiling" of the test.

**Chronological age:** An individual's age based upon birth date. Usually represented in years and months.

**Curriculum compacting:** A method developed for eliminating unnecessary repetition of material already learned. By pretesting or some other means, what a student already knows is determined and then he or she is allowed to move on. The time saved can be used for engaging in enrichment activities or for studying more advanced material.

**Curriculum scope and sequence:** The range of topics of subject-matter content and the order in which those topics are covered during an academic year and from grade to grade.

**Diagnostic Testing→Prescriptive Instruction (DT→PI) model:** A model for educating talented youth that is useful for determining specific strengths and weaknesses in a subject. This information is then related to instructional prescriptions. DT→PI model participants are first given aptitude tests. High-scoring students are recommended for further testing using beyond-level achievement tests. Instruction is prescribed based upon those test results. Students work on the topics they do not fully understand, and they spend little time on topics they already know well. After studying a topic, students are retested to assess their level of mastery.

**Differentiated curriculum:** A curriculum that is designed specifically for gifted students and is defensibly different from the curriculum offered to average students. Can refer to a medley of educational programs, including acceleration and enrichment.

**Enrichment:** Students are given opportunities to study subjects or content not covered in the typical school curriculum or an in-depth exploration of topics covered in the regular curriculum. Students participating in enrichment activities study richer, broader, and more varied content.

**Grade-equivalent:** A standard score that is designed to indicate growth from one academic year (i.e., 10 months) to another academic year. For example, a score of 5.0 refers to average performance compared to other students at the beginning of fifth grade. One year later, those same students would be expected to have an average growth reflected in a grade-equivalent score of 6.0. However, for populations of gifted students, because they tend to gain more than 10 months in one year, grade-equivalent scores can be misinterpreted. A specific grade-equivalent score does not necessarily mean that the student is ready to begin instruction at that grade level, nor does it mean that a student will be challenged by material at the grade-equivalent grade.

**Intelligence test:** Designed to sample a wide variety of functions in order to estimate the individual's general intellectual level.

**IQ (Intelligence Quotient):** The score earned on an intelligence test. The average score on an IQ test is 100. A score of 130 is at the 98th percentile, which represents the top 2% of a typical group of individuals within an age range. Because this score is earned by no more than 2% of a population, it is often considered a score earned by a "gifted" individual.

**Mastery:** The point at which the student demonstrates thorough understanding of the subject-matter content.

**Mentor:** Mentors serve as instructors for talented students and are well-trained in the subject matter beyond what they are expected to teach. Typically, mentors work with only one or two students at a time. They present new information, rather than reviewing already-studied material the way a tutor would. Mentors help their students (sometimes called "mentees") to move through material at a challenging pace.

Mentors also clarify and extend the material to be learned. The goal of mentoring is to help students learn self-teaching skills, not to spoon feed them information.

**Norm group:** As a part of the test-development process, a test is administered to a large group of students among whom the scores will be compared; thus, the group is called the "normative" or "comparison" group. Later, when individual students are tested, their scores can be compared to those in the norm group. The student's performance might be average, above average, or below average when compared to that norm group.

**Parallel forms of a test (alternate forms):** Two or more tests containing different items that cover the same material at the same level of difficulty. The measurement specialists who develop the tests have used statistical techniques that make the tests equivalent, but not identical. Parallel forms of a test are useful for pre- and posttesting.

**Percentile rank:** Allows the student's score on a test to be compared to other children his or her age. An average score on a test yields a percentile ranking of 50, meaning that the child scored higher than 50% of the children in the comparison group. Talented children tend to score at the 97th percentile or above when compared to their own age group.

**Precocious:** Showing exceptionally early development and achievement. For example, a precocious mathematics student may multiply and divide at the age of 4.

**Pretest:** Before instruction begins, students are given a test on the material. The purpose of pretesting is to determine what students know, as well as what they are ready to learn. Instruction can then focus on teaching the student new material, rather than reviewing material already mastered.

**Psychological assessment:** Can include intelligence testing, achievement testing, personality profiles, and information about affective development, including social and emotional maturity. This assessment provides information about a student when compared to others of the same age.

**Reliability:** A term used in educational testing to describe how consistent test results are from one administration to another.

**Spiral approach to mathematics curriculum:** Mathematics is presented to students a little bit at a time. Students then return to the topic year after year, each time at a slightly more advanced level. For example, in first grade, students learn one-digit addition; in second grade, they learn two-digit addition; and, in third grade, they learn three-digit addition. We do not advocate this approach for talented youth because it is usually not challenging to bright students.

**Standardized tests:** Ability, aptitude, or achievement tests developed by testing specialists such as Educational Testing Service, the Iowa Testing Program, and ACT, Inc. These tests are developed so that scores earned by students can be compared to each other. Teacher-made tests assess the students' understanding of the material that was studied. Standardized tests assess the students' performance compared to a norm group.

**Study of Mathematically Precocious Youth (SMPY):** Founded in 1971 by Julian C. Stanley at Johns Hopkins University. The purpose of SMPY was to conduct research and offer programs and services for mathematically talented students. Some participants in SMPY participate in a longitudinal study housed at Peabody College, Vanderbilt University (codirected by Camilla Benbow and David Lubinski). SMPY has evolved to include the Study of Exceptional Talent (SET) at Johns University. SET is directed by Linda Brody and housed in the Center for Talented Youth (CTY).

**Validity:** A term used in educational testing to describe how well a test measures what it sets out to measure.

# Appendix: 1998–1999 Mathematical Olympiad Problems (Division E)

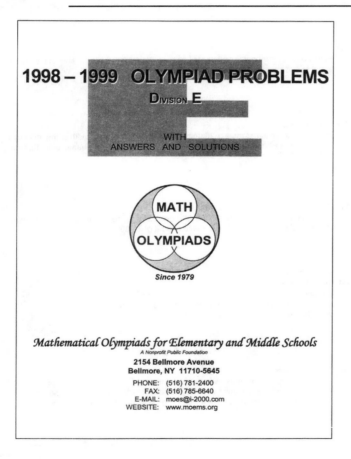

1998 – 1999 OLYMPIAD PROBLEMS

Dᵢᵥᵢₛᵢₒₙ E

WITH
ANSWERS AND SOLUTIONS

MATH OLYMPIADS

Since 1979

*Mathematical Olympiads for Elementary and Middle Schools*
A Nonprofit Public Foundation

2154 Bellmore Avenue
Bellmore, NY 11710-5645

PHONE: (516) 781-2400
FAX: (516) 785-6640
E-MAIL: moes@i-2000.com
WEBSITE: www.moems.org

**Division** **E**     — *Mathematical Olympiads* —
**NOVEMBER 17, 1998**
*for Elementary and Middle Schools*
**Contest 1**

**1A** *Time: 4 minutes*

How many different natural numbers between 10 and 200 have the sum of their digits equal to 6, if zero is not a digit of any of the numbers?

**1B** *Time: 5 minutes*

The perimeter of a rectangle is 26 units. Each of the length and width of the rectangle is measured in natural numbers. What is the largest area in square units that the rectangle could have?

**1C** *Time: 5 minutes*

Bryan can buy candy canes at 4 for 50¢ and can sell them at 3 for 50¢. How many canes must Bryan sell in order to make a profit of $5.00?

**1D** *Time: 5 minutes*

A supermarket clerk makes a solid pyramid out of identical cereal boxes. The top five layers are shown. What is the total number of cereal boxes in the top five layers as shown?

**1E** *Time: 6 minutes*

A normal duck has two legs. A lame duck has one leg. A sitting duck has no legs. Donald has 33 ducks. He has two more normal ducks than lame ducks and two more lame ducks than sitting ducks. How many legs in all do the 33 ducks have?

**2A** *Time: 5 minutes*
Roberta throws five darts at the target shown. Each dart lands in a region of the target, scoring the points shown. Of the following total scores, list all that are *not* possible:

6,  14,  17,  38,  42,  58

**2B** *Time: 4 minutes*
Kelly made two purchases. She gave one cashier $20 for a compact disc and received $6 change. Then she gave another cashier $15 for a bracelet and received $3 change. After these purchases she had $28. How many dollars did she have before buying the compact disc and the bracelet?

**2C** *Time: 5 minutes*
On a 100 cm measuring stick, marks are made at 19, N, and 99 cm, from left to right. The distance between the marks at N and 99 cm is three times the distance between the marks at N and 19 cm. What number is N?

**2D** *Time: 5 minutes*
A cube has 6 faces: top, bottom, and all 4 sides. The object shown is made of six congruent cubes. Not all faces are visible. All outer faces of the object including the bottom are painted blue. How many faces of the cubes are painted blue?

**2E** *Time: 7 minutes*
Assume that a post office issues only 3¢ and 8¢ stamps and all postage is in whole numbers of cents. What is the largest amount of postage in cents which *cannot* be made using only 3¢ and 8¢ stamps?

**Division E**

**Mathematical Olympiads**
**JANUARY 12, 1999**
*for Elementary and Middle Schools*

**Contest 3**

**3A** *Time: 4 minutes*
Suppose Sandy writes every whole number from 1 to 100 properly and without skipping any numbers. How many times will Sandy write the digit "2"?

**3B** *Time: 4 minutes*
Paul has half as many pieces of candy as Jennifer. Jennifer has half as many as Charles. Charles has 12 times as many as Susan. Susan has 4 pieces. How many pieces do Charles and Paul have altogether?

**3C** *Time: 5 minutes*
Consider all pairs of natural numbers whose sum is less than 11. The two members of a pair could be either the same as each other or different. How many different products are possible if the two numbers are multiplied?

**3D** *Time: 6 minutes*
Mary's rectangular garden and Kevin's rectangular garden each have the same area, 36 square meters. Each side is measured in whole meters. Mary's garden is 1 m wider than Kevin's garden, but Kevin's garden is 3 m longer than Mary's garden. How wide is Mary's garden, in meters?

**3E** *Time: 7 minutes*
Each of eight traffic lights on Main Street shows green for 2 minutes, then switches to other colors. The traffic lights turn green 10 seconds apart, from the first light to the eighth light. From the time that the first light turns green until it switches to another color, for how many seconds will all eight lights show green at the same time?

| Division | *Mathematical Olympiads* | Contest |
|---|---|---|
| **E** | **FEBRUARY 9, 1999** *for Elementary and Middle Schools* | **4** |

**4A** *Time: 4 minutes*

Each of PQ and RS represents a 2-digit number. Different letters represent different digits, chosen from 6, 7, 8, and 9. What is the largest product that PQ × RS can have?

**4B** *Time: 4 minutes*

Exactly 10 disks are in a bowl. Each is marked with a different natural number selected from 1 through 10. Gina and Monique each selects 5 disks. Two of Gina's disks are marked 2 and 8. Two of Monique's disks are marked 7 and 9. What is the largest sum that Gina's disks can have?

**4C** *Time: 5 minutes*

A "fast" clock gains time at the same rate every hour. It is set to the correct time at 10 AM. When the fast clock shows 11 AM the same day, the correct time is 10:52 AM. When the fast clock shows 3:30 PM that day, what is the correct time?

**4D** *Time: 6 minutes*

All counting numbers are arranged in the triangular pattern as shown by the first four rows. What is the first number in the 13ᵗʰ row?

```
        1
      2  3  4
    5  6  7  8  9
10 11 12 13 14 15 16
```
*. . . and so on.*

**4E** *Time: 6 minutes*

A 14-digit number **N** is created by writing 8 as both the first and last digits and then placing the 3-digit number 793 between the two 8s four times. What is the remainder when **N** is divided by 7?

**5A** *Time: 4 minutes*
In this addition different letters represents different digits.
What digits do A, B, C, and D represent?

```
   6,B 5 2
     9 C 4
 + A,3 7 D
  1 1,1 1 1
```

**5B** *Time: 4 minutes*
Each of AB and BA represents a two-digit number having the same digits, but in reverse order. If the difference of the two numbers is 54 and A + B = 10, find both numbers, AB and BA.

**5C** *Time: 5 minutes*
The length of each segment in the overlapping rectangles, as shown, is given in cm. Find the sum of the areas of the shaded regions, in sq cm.

**5D** *Time: 6 minutes*
How many different natural numbers less than 200 are exactly divisible by either 6 or 9 or by both?

**5E** *Time: 6 minutes*
In the number 203,500, the last two zeroes are called *terminal zeros*. The zero after the digit 2 is not a terminal zero. How many terminal zeros does the product of the first 30 counting numbers (1×2×3× . . . ×30) have?

**ANSWERS AND SOLUTIONS**

*Note: Number in parentheses indicates percent of all competitors with a correct answer.*

## CONTEST 1                    NOVEMBER 17, 1998

**Answers:**   [A] 9   [B] 42 *(sq. units)*   [C] 120 *(canes)*   [D] 100 *(boxes)*   [E] 37 *(legs)*

**1A.**  *Strategy: List 2- and 3-digit numbers separately.*                    **28% correct**
                2-digit numbers:   15, 24, 33, 42, 51
                3-digit numbers:   114, 123, 132, 141
According to conditions of the problem, 6, 60, 105, 150 must be excluded.
**There are 9 numbers.**

*FOLLOW-UPS:  (1) If we allow 0 as a digit, and also eliminate the lower and upper limits (10 and 200), what patterns occur in the solution?*
      *(2) What patterns occur if the digit-sum is 2, 3, 4, 5, etc.?*

**1B**  *Strategy: Make a table of all possible lengths and widths and compute the areas.*    **17%**
The perimeter is 26, so the sum of the length and width (called the semiperimeter) is 13.

| WIDTH | LENGTH | AREA |
|:---:|:---:|:---:|
| 1 | 13 - 1 = 12 | 1 × 12 = 12 |
| 2 | 13 - 2 = 11 | 2 × 11 = 22 |
| 3 | 13 - 3 = 10 | 3 × 10 = 30 |
| 4 | 13 - 4 = 9 | 4 × 9 = 36 |
| 5 | 13 - 5 = 8 | 5 × 8 = 40 |
| 6 | 13 - 6 = 7 | 6 × 7 = 42 |

No other rectangles are possible.

**The largest area that the rectangle might have is 42 sq units.**

*FOLLOW-UP:  What is the largest whole number area if the perimeter is 18, 22, 30, 24? Find the rule.*
      *[Remind students that a square is a special kind of rectangle.]*

**1C**  *Strategy: Assume he buys and sells 12 canes in order to avoid using fractions.*    **5%**
    12 canes cost Bryan 3×50¢ = $1.50.
    12 canes sell for 4×50¢ = $2.00.
    12 canes bring a profit of $2.00 - $1.50 = $.50.
    Since $5.00 = $.50 × **10**, multiply 12 canes by **10** = 120 canes.
Thus **Bryan must sell 120 candy canes.**

*SUGGESTION: To help your students answer the question that was asked,*
*train them to use the original words of the question in writing their answers.*

58%

**1D** _Strategy:_ Break up the problem by layers, and make a table.

| LAYER | # of ROWS | × | # of BOXES per ROW | = | # of BOXES per LAYER |
|-------|-----------|---|--------------------|---|----------------------|
| Top | 1 | × | 4 | = | 4 |
| 2 | 2 | × | 5 | = | 10 |
| 3 | 3 | × | 6 | = | 18 |
| 4 | 4 | × | 7 | = | 28 |
| 5 | 5 | × | 8 | = | 40 |
| | | | | TOTAL = | 100 |

**In all there are 100 cereal boxes.**

52%

**1E  METHOD 1.** _Strategy: Compare the number of each type of duck to the number of sitting ducks._
Donald has 2 more normal ducks than lame ducks and 2 more lame ducks than sitting ducks, so he has 4 more normal ducks than sitting ducks. Suppose we remove 2 lame ducks and 4 sitting ducks. This gives him the same number of each type of duck. He now has a total of $33 - 2 - 4 = 27$ ducks. Thus he now has $27 + 3 = 9$ of each type of duck.
  Originally, he must have had 9 sitting ducks, $9 + 2 = 11$ lame ducks, and $11 + 2 = 13$ normal ducks. The 9 sitting ducks have 0 legs, the 11 lame ducks have 11 legs and the 13 normal ducks have 26 legs. Hence, **the 33 ducks have a total of $0 + 11 + 26 = 37$ legs.**

**METHOD 1A.** _Strategy: Use algebra.(Increasingly algebra is being introduced into the elementary grades. We will begin to show the use of algebra in solutions as an alternate method.)_
Suppose Donald has S sitting ducks. Then he has S + 2 lame ducks, and S + 4 normal ducks.

1. Then: $\qquad\qquad S + (S + 2) + (S + 4) = 33$
2. Remove parentheses: $\qquad S + S + 2 + S + 4 = 33$
3. Combine like terms: $\qquad\qquad\qquad 3S + 6 = 33$
4. Subtract 6 from each side of the equation: $\qquad 3S = 27$
5. Divide each side of the equation by 3 to isolate S: $\quad S = 9$
6. Add 2 to get the number of lame ducks: $\qquad S + 2 = 11$
7. Add another 2 to get the number of normal ducks: $\quad 11 + 2 = 13$
8. Thus, $9 + 11 + 13 = 33$ ducks have a total of $0 + 11 + 26 = 37$ legs.

**METHOD 2.** _Strategy: Compare the number of legs to the number of ducks._
Pair each sitting duck with a normal duck. In this group there are exactly as many legs as ducks. Remember that four normal ducks are not paired.
  Next add the lame ducks to the group, which then consists of 29 ducks with a total of 29 legs. Now add the unpaired four normal ducks to the group. This results in 33 ducks with $29 + 8 = 37$ legs. Hence, **the 33 ducks have a total of 37 legs.**

**METHOD 3.** _Strategy: Make a table beginning with 1 sitting duck._

| | SITTING | LAME | NORMAL | TOTAL # of DUCKS | |
|--|---------|------|--------|------------------|--|
| | 1 | 3 | 5 | 9 | (This total lacks 24 ducks) |
| (Add 8 ducks to each column) | 9 | 11 | 13 | 33 | |

The 33 ducks have a total of $0 + 11 + 26 = 37$ legs.

## CONTEST 2                    DECEMBER 15, 1998

*Answers:*   [A] 6, 17, 58    [B] 54 ($54)    [C] 39    [D] 26 (faces)    [E] 13(¢)

**2A** *Strategy: Try to duplicate each total separately.*                    `49%`
The minimum score is 5 × 2 = 10. Therefore 6 is not possible.
The maximum score is 5 × 10 = 50. Therefore 58 is not possible.
Since each of the target scores are even, 17 is not possible.
The remaining scores are all possible. One way is shown for each:
  14 = 2+2+2+2+4;  38 = 10+10+10+6+2;  42 = 10+10+10+10+2.
**Thus, 6, 17, and 58 are not possible.**

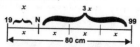

**2B** *Strategy:  Do one thing at a time.*                    `40%`
The CD costs 20 – 6 = $14 and the bracelet costs 15 – 3 = $12, so Kelly spent 14 + 12 = $26.
Then $26 spent plus $28 remaining = $54 to start.
**Kelly had $54 before buying the CD and the bracelet.**

**2C  METHOD 1:** *Strategy: Use the definition of "three times".*                    `22%`

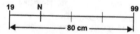

The interval from 19 to 99 is 80 cm. Since the distance from 19 to N is three times the distance
from N to 99, picture the latter distance as consisting of three parts, each equal to the former
distance. Then the entire interval from 19 to 99 consists of 1 + 3 = 4 equal parts. Therefore
each part contains 80 ÷ 4 = 20 cm. Then, **N is 19 + 20 = 39.** Check: 3 × 20 = 60 and 99 – 60
= 39.

   **METHOD 2:** *Strategy: Algebra. (Note: As stated after Olympiad 1, algebraic solutions will be
offered hereafter as an alternative method.)*

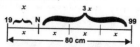

From the diagram: $x + 3x = 80$
               $4x = 80$
               $x = 20$    Then N = 19 + $x$ = 19 + 20 = 39.

**2D  METHOD 1:** *Strategy: Subtract the number of unpainted faces from the total .*                    `24%`
Each cube has 6 faces, so 6 cubes have 36 faces. There are 5 places where 2 cubes touch
face-to-face. Thus a total of 10 faces are *not* painted blue.
Then 36 – 10 = **26 faces of the cubes are painted blue.**

*Method 2 on next page.*

**(2D)**    **METHOD 2:** *Strategy: Separate the faces by category.*
Number of faces that are painted blue:

| | |
|---|---|
| top faces - visible | 4 |
| bottom faces - not visible | 4 |
| vertical faces - visible | 9 |
| vertical faces - not visible | 9    Total = 26 |

26 faces of the cubes are painted blue.

Alternately, look at the faces from each of the six directions: from the top 4 faces are visible, from the bottom 4 faces, from the left 4 vertical faces, from the right 4 faces, from the front 5 faces, and from the back 5 faces. A total of 26 faces of the cubes are painted blue.

**METHOD 2A:** The 4 cubes on the bottom each have 4 painted sides while the two cubes on the top each have 5 exposed sides. Thus, $(4 \times 4) + (2 \times 5) = 16 + 10 = 26$.

4%

**2E**    *Strategy: Check each amount until 3 consecutive values are found.*
Suppose we find three consecutive numbers that can be made. Then the next three consecutive numbers can also be made. All we need to do is add a 3¢ stamp to each. In this way, we can make every amount larger than the first three consecutive amounts.

Small numbers that can be made: 3, 6, 8, 9, 11, 12.
The next numbers that can be made: 14, 15, 16.  ($14 = 2 \times 3 + 8$, $15 = 5 \times 3$ and $16 = 2 \times 8$.)

Since we can make 14, 15, and 16, we can make 17, 18, and 19 by adding 3 to each. Then we can make 20, 21, and 22 by adding 3 again to each. In fact, we can make any amount above 13 by adding some multiple of 3 to 14, 15, or 16.

Thus the largest number which cannot be made by some combination of 3 and 8 is 13. **The largest postage which cannot be made is 13¢.**

*FOLLOW-UPS: (1) Suppose bolts are sold in packages of 4 and 7 each. How many consecutive numbers of bolts are needed in order to guarantee that all numbers above a certain amount can be made? What is the largest number of bolts which cannot be bought by a combination of packages?*
*(2) Suppose the packages contain 5 and 6 bolts, or 4 and 5 bolts. Find the general rule for determining consecutive numbers.*

**CONTEST 3**                                      **JANUARY 12, 1999**
*Answers:*    [A] 20    [B] 60 *(pieces)*    [C] 19    [D] 4 *(cm)*    [E] 50 *(seconds)*

43%

**3A**    *Strategy: Examine each digit separately.*
The digit "2" appears in the ones' place 10 times: 2, 12, 22, . . . , 92.
The digit "2" appears in the tens' place 10 times: 20, 21, 22, . . . , 29.
The digit "2" appears no other times. **Sandy wrote the digit "2" $10 + 10 = 20$ times.**

**3B** _Strategy:_ _Work backwards from Susan's 4 pieces._
Susan has 4 pieces.
Charles has 12 × 4 = 48 pieces.
Jennifer has ½ × 48 = 24 pieces.
Paul has ½ × 24 = 12 pieces.
**Charles and Paul have 48 + 12 = 60 pieces altogether.**

76%

**3C  METHOD 1:** _Strategy:_ _Make a table and cross out duplicates._
Let P and Q represent the two natural numbers.

5%

| P | Q | P × Q | |
|---|---|---|---|
| 1 | 1, 2, 3, . . . .,9 | 1, 2, 3, 4, 5, 6, 7, 8, 9 | 9 products |
| 2 | 1, 2, 3, . . . .,8 | 2, 4, 6, 8, 10, 12, 14, 16 | 4 new products |
| 3 | 1, 2, 3, . . . ,7 | 3, 6, 9, 12, 15, 18, 21 | 3 new products |
| 4 | 1, 2, 3, 4, 5, 6 | 4, 8, 12, 16, 20, 24 | 2 new products |
| 5 | 1, 2, 3, 4, 5 | 5, 10, 15, 20, 25 | 1 new product |

TOTAL = **19 products are possible.**

**METHOD 2:** _Strategy:_ _Eliminate the impossible._
The smallest product possible is 1×1 = 1 and the largest is 5×5 = 25. From the 25 possibilities (1 through 25), eliminate those which are (a) prime numbers greater than 9 and (b) multiples of these primes.
    (a) Eliminate 11, 13, 17, 19 and 23:  (5 products)
    (b) Eliminate 22 = 11×2:  (1 product)
Then 25 − 5 − 1 = 19 products are possible.

_FOLLOW-UP:_ _Two fair dice are tossed. What products are not possible? The answers illustrate both categories listed in method 2, and a third one: 32 is the product of two composites, one of which is larger than 6._

**3D  METHOD 1:** _Strategy:_ _Make a table of all possible dimensions based on an area of 36._
Find a row in which the width increases by 1 and the length decreases by 3. This occurs when we compare Row 4 against Row 3. Therefore **Mary's garden is 4 m wide.**

29%

| Area | = Width × Length | |
|---|---|---|
| 36 | = 1 × 36 | |
| 36 | = 2 × 18 | |
| 36 | = 3 × 12 | [Kevin's garden is 3 m wide.] |
| 36 | = 4 × 9 | [Mary's garden is 4 m wide.] |
| 36 | = 6 × 6 | [A square is a special kind of rectangle] |

**METHOD 2:** _Strategy:_ _Make 2 tables: change the dimensions and then compare areas._
Create Table 2 from Table 1 by increasing the width by 1, decreasing the length by 3, and then computing the area. Then row 3 of the table 2 is the only row in which the area is 36 sq m.

| Kevin's Garden | Mary's Garden | |
|---|---|---|
| W L  Area | W L  Area | |
| 1 × 36 = 36 | 2 × 33 = 66 | |
| 2 × 18 = 36 | 3 × 15 = 45 | |
| 3 × 12 = 36 | 4 × 9 = 36 | [Mary's garden is 4 m wide.] |
| 4 × 9 = 36 | 5 × 6 = 30 | |
| 6 × 6 = 36 | 7 × 3 = 21 | |

23%

**3E** *Strategy:* Track the situation, introducing one traffic light at a time.
**METHOD 1:** Measure the time from when traffic light #1 turns green. Light #2 turns green 10 seconds later, light #3 turns green 10 seconds after light #2 and 20 seconds after light #1, light #4 turns green 30 seconds after light #1, and so on. Then **all eight lights will be green at the same time for the next 120 − 70 = 50 seconds**, until light #1 switches to another color after 120 seconds.

**METHOD 2:** *Strategy:* Make a diagram

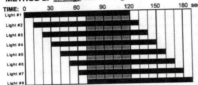

TIME: 0   30   60   90   120   150   180 seconds

Light #1
Light #2
Light #3
Light #4
Light #5
Light #6
Light #7
Light #8

Each bar represents a green light.

All lights show green from the 70th second to the 120th second (see shading).

All eight lights will show green at the same time for 50 seconds.

**METHOD 3:** *Strategy:* Make an organized chart
[Times On and Off = number of seconds measured from the time that Light #1 turns green]

| Light # | Times On and Off |
|---------|------------------|
| 1 | 0 – 120 |
| 2 | 10 – 130 |
| 3 | 20 – 140 |
| 4 | 30 – 150 |
| 5 | 40 – 160 |
| 6 | 50 – 170 |
| 7 | 60 – 180 |
| 8 | 70 – 190 |

Note the 8-way overlap from the 70th second to the 120th second, a total of 50 seconds.

All eight lights will show green at the same time for 50 seconds.

---

## CONTEST 4                    FEBRUARY 9, 1999

*Answers:*    [A] 8352    [B] 31    [C] 2:46 (*PM*)    [D] 145    [E] 4

31%

**4A** *Strategy:* Put the largest digits in the places with the greatest place value.
To form the largest product, the tens' digits must be 9 and 8. That leaves 7 and 6 for the ones' place. Test each arrangement: 97×86 = 8342; 96×87 = 8352. **The largest product is 8352.**

*FOLLOW-UP: Assign different sets of 4 digits. Try to discover a rule for choosing the tens' digits and then a rule for matching up the ones' digits with each tens' digit.*

44%

**4B** *Strategy:* Select the highest available values for Gina's disks.
Gina must draw 10, 6, and 5, and Monique must draw 4, 3, and 1. **The largest sum that Gina's disks can have is 2 + 8 + 10 + 6 + 5 = 31.** The least sum that Monique's disks can have is 7 + 9 + 4 + 3 + 1 = 24.

*Continued on next page.*

---

*Continued from page 11*

**(4B)** FOLLOW-UPS: *(1) If Gina and Monique play a new round, can their totals be equal? Can their totals form a simple ratio?*

*(2) Suppose there are 100 numbered disks, each girl selects half the disks, and Gina draws #2 while Monique draws #98. What is the largest possible sum for Gina's disks? Can the students create a simple general method for this problem?*

---

**4C  METHOD 1:** *Strategy: Compare the elapsed times proportionally.*    **13%**
At 11 AM (fast clock time), the fast clock has gained 8 minutes.
From 10 AM to 3:30 PM (fast clock time), the fast clock shows 5½ hours of elapsed time.
Therefore, at 3:30 PM (fast clock time), the fast clock has gained 5½ hours × 8 minutes per hour = 44 minutes. Then: **The correct time is 3:30 – 0:44 = 2:46 PM.**
[Note: give credit if an answer omits the "PM"]

**METHOD 2:** *Strategy: Construct a table and note the differences in times.*

| Fast Clock | Correct Time | |
|---|---|---|
| 10 AM | 10:00 AM | +52 minutes |
| 11 AM | 10:52 AM | +52 minutes |
| 12 Noon | 11:44 AM | +52 minutes |
| 1 PM | 12:36 PM | +52 minutes |
| 2 PM | 1:28 PM | +52 minutes |
| 3 PM | 2:20 PM | +½ of 52 = 26 minutes |
| 3:30 PM | 2:46 PM | |

From 10:00 to 10:52 is 52 minutes. To 10:00 AM, add 52 minutes for each hour and 26 minutes for the half-hour. The correct time is 2:46 PM.

---

**4D  METHOD 1:** *Strategy: Look for a pattern and then extend it.*    **25%**
Look at the last number in each row. It is a perfect square. That is, the last number in row 1 is 1 = 1×1; the last number in row 2 is 4 = 2×2; the last number in row 3 is 9 = 3×3; the last number in row 4 is 16 = 4×4; and so on. The last number in each row is the square of the row number, so the last number in row 12 is 12×12 = 144. Then **the first number in the 13th row is 145.**

**METHOD 2:** *Strategy: Look for a pattern and then extend it.*
Look at the first number in each row: 1, 2, 5, 10, 17, . . .
Their differences are 1, 3, 5, 7, . . .
To the first number add the sum of the 12 differences:
(1) + (1+3+5+7+9+11+13+15+17+19+21+23) = 1 + 144 = 145.
The first number in the 13th row is 145.

FOLLOW-UP: *Examine the pattern below for a relationship between the middle number on the left side of each line and the value on the right side of that line.*

$$1 = 1^2$$
$$1+3 = 2^2$$
$$1+3+5 = 3^2$$
$$1+3+5+7 = 4^2, \text{ etc.}$$

---

**4E** *Strategy:* *Examine remainders for a pattern after dividing each 793 by 7.* **46%**

$$7\overline{\smash{\big)}\,8\ ^17\ ^39\ ^43\ ^17\ ^39\ ^43\ ^17\ ^39\ ^43\ ^17\ ^39\ ^43\ ^18}$$

The remainders after division are shown. Note that the remainders 1, 3, 4, will repeat because of the repeated division of 7, 9, and 3 by 7. After each "793" is divided by 7, the remainder is 1. Then the last division is 18 ÷ 7, and the last remainder is 4. Hence, **when N is divided by 7, the remainder is 4.**

*FOLLOW-UPS: (1) Divide 4,000,000,000,000,000,000 by 7. What is the remainder if the number is extended by 1, 2, 3, . . . more zeros?*
*(2) What are the remainders if 4,000,000,000,000,000,000 is divided by 9 or 11?*

# CONTEST 5                                        MARCH 9, 1999
*Answers:*   [A] (ABCD =) 3785   [B] 82 and 28   [C] 99 (*sq cm*)   [D] 44   [E] 7(*terminal zeros*)

**5A** *Strategy:* *Add from right to left, replacing the letters in order.*  **67%**
The sum in each column is either 11 or 21.
Ones' column:           2 + 4 + D = 11, so D = 5.
Tens' column:           1 (from the ones' column) + 5 + C + 7 = 21, so C = 8.
Hundreds' column:       2 (from the tens' column) + B + 9 + 3 = 21, so B = 7.
Thousands' column:      2 (from the tens' column) + 6 + A = 11, so A = 3.
Therefore: **A = 3, B = 7, C = 8, D = 5** (written in any order).

```
  6, B 5 2
     9 C 4
+ A, 3 7 D
1 1, 1 1 1
```

*(NOTE: if an answer does not match letter with value, then only the order 3785 is acceptable.)*

**5B** *Strategy:* *Make an organized list based upon A + B = 10.*  **58%**
Let AB be larger than BA.

| AB – BA | = | Difference |
|---------|---|------------|
| 91 – 19 | = | 72 |
| 82 – 28 | = | 54 |
| 73 – 37 | = | 36 |
| 64 – 46 | = | 18 |
| 55 – 55 | = | 0 |

**The two numbers are 82 and 28.**

*FOLLOW-UPS: What is the pattern of differences if A + B = 8 instead of 10?*
*Explore the two patterns of differences for even and odd values for A + B.*

**10%**

**5C** <u>*Strategy:*</u> *Compute the missing lengths first and then compute each area.*

Unshaded rectangle: length = 5 – 3 = 2, and
width = 10 – 6 = 4, so
area = 2 × 4 = 8.

Upper rectangle: area = 5 × 7 = 35.
Shaded area = 35 – 8 = 27.

Lower rectangle: area = 10 × 8 = 80.
Shaded area = 80 – 8 = <u>72.</u>

Adding: 99

**The sum of the areas of the shaded regions is 99 sq cm.**

**11%**

**5D** <u>*Strategy:*</u> *Count the number of multiples of 9, and of 6. Then eliminate duplications.*

**METHOD 1:** 200 ÷ 9 = 22⁺: the interval 1 – 200 contains 22 multiples of 9.
200 ÷ 6 = 33⁺: the interval 1 – 200 contains 33 multiples of 6.

The least common multiple of 9 and 6 is 18. Any multiple of 18 is also a multiple of 6 and of 9 (as well as 2 and 3).
Then 200 ÷ 18 = 11⁺: the interval 1 – 200 contains 11 multiples of 18. That is, 11 of the 22 multiples of 9 are also multiples of 6. They were counted twice. Thus, 22 + 33 – 11 = 44. Thus, **44 numbers in the sequence are exactly divisible by either 6 or 9 or both.**

**METHOD 2:** <u>*Strategy:*</u> *Make a number line.*

Multiples of 6:  6  12  18  24  30  36  42  48  54  60  66  72  90  108  126  144  162  180  198

Multiples of 9:  9  18  27  36  45  54  63  72  90  108  126  144  162  180  198

Every multiple of 18 appears on both lists. Cross out just one of each duplicated number and count all of the remaining numbers. Thus, 44 numbers in the sequence are exactly divisible by either 6 or 9 or by both.

COMMENT: *Method 2 is valid but very inefficient. However, it does help to explain Method 1 more fully.*

**4%**

**5E** <u>*Strategy:*</u> *How can we achieve a product of 10, 100, 1000, etc.?*

For every terminal zero in our product, we need to pair a factor of 5 with a factor of 2. That is, 10 = 5×2, 100 = 5×5×2×2, 1000 = 5×5×5×2×2×2, and so on. In the product of the first 30 counting numbers, 5 appears as a factor 7 times; it is a factor only of 5, 10, 15, 20, 25, and 30, appearing twice as a factor of 25. However, 2 appears as a factor of the product 26 times; it is a factor of 2, 4, 6, 8, 10, ... , 30, appearing as a factor of some numbers (such as 16) several times. Since each factor of 5 must be paired with a factor of 2, there are as many terminal zeros as there are factors of 5.

Thus we can pair the 7 factors of 5 with only 7 of the factors of 2. That is, (5×5×5×5×5×5×5)×(2×2×2×2×2×2×2). Therefore, **the product of the first 30 counting numbers has 7 terminal zeros.**

# References

ACT. (1996). *Evaluating the appropriateness of EXPLORE for BESTS partici-pants.* Iowa City, IA: Author.

ACT. (1997a). *EXPLORE technical manual.* Iowa City, IA: Author.

ACT. (1997b). *Standards for transition: Descriptions of the skills and knowl-edge associated with EXPLORE scores.* Iowa City, IA: Author.

ACT. (1999, Spring). Talent programs use EXPLORE to identify gifted grade schoolers. *ACTIVITY*, p. 4.

Ahmann, J.S. (1985). Review of School and College Ability Tests, Series III. In J. V. Mitchell (Ed.), *The 9th Mental Measurement Yearbook* (pp. 1315–1316). Lincoln: University of Nebraska Press.

*American heritage college dictionary* (3rd ed.). (1993). Boston: Houghton-Mifflin.

Assouline, S., Colangelo, N., Lupkowski-Shoplik, A., & Lipscomb, J. (1998). *Iowa acceleration scale: Manual, form, and summary and planning sheet.* Scottsdale, AZ: Great Potential Press.

Assouline, S. G., Colangelo, N., McNabb T., Lupkowski-Shoplik, A., & Saylor, M. (1993, November). *An investigation to determine guidelines for recommending above-level testing of talented elementary students.* Paper presented at the annual meeting of the National Association for Gifted Children, Atlanta, GA.

Assouline, S. G., & Doellinger, H. L. (2001). Elementary students who can do junior high math: Policy or pedagogy. In N. Colangelo & S. G. Assouline (Eds), *Talent development IV: Proceedings from the 1998 Henry B. and Jocelyn Wallace National Research Symposium on Talent Development* (pp. 123–134) Scottsdale, AZ: Great Potential Press.

Assouline, S. G., & Lupkowski-Shoplik, A. (1997). Talent searches: A model for the discovery and development of academic talent. In N. Colangelo & G. A. Davis (Eds.), *Handbook of gifted education* (2nd ed., pp.170–179). Boston: Allyn and Bacon.

Baldwin, A. L. (1980). *Theories of child development* (2nd ed.). New York: Wiley and Sons.

Barnett, L. B., & Durden, W. G. (1993). Education patterns of academically talented youth. *Gifted Child Quarterly, 37,* 161–168.

Bartkovich, K. G., & George, W. C. (1980). *Teaching the gifted and talented in the mathematics classroom.* Washington, DC: National Education Association.

Bartkovich, K. G., & Mezynski, K. (1981). Fast-paced precalculus mathematics for talented junior-high students: Two recent SMPY [Study of Mathematically Precocious Youth] programs. *Gifted Child Quarterly, 25,* 73–80.

Belcastro, F. P. (1987). *Criteria for evaluation of mathematics programs for mathematically gifted elementary students.* (ERIC Document Reproduction Service No. ED 347 751)

Benbow, C. P. (1986). SMPY's model for teaching mathematically precocious students. In J. S. Renzulli (Ed.), *Systems and models in programming for the gifted and talented* (pp. 1–25). Mansfield Center, CT: Creative Learning Press.

Benbow, C. P. (1988). Sex differences in mathematical reasoning ability in intellectually talented preadolescents: Their nature, effects, and possible causes. *Behavioral and Brain Sciences, 11,* 169–232.

Benbow, C.P. (1992a). Academic achievement in math and science between ages 13 and 23: Are there differences in the top one percent of ability? *Journal of Educational Psycholology, 84,* 51–61.

Benbow, C. P. (1992b). Mathematical talent: Its nature and consequences. In N. Colangelo, S. G. Assouline, & D. L. Ambroson (Eds.), *Talent development: Proceedings from the 1991 Henry B. and Jocelyn Wallace National research Symposium on Talent Development* (pp. 95–123). New York: Trillium Press.

Benbow, C. P., & Arjmand, O. (1990). Predictors of high academic achievement in mathematics and science by mathematically talented students. *Journal of Educational Psychology, 82,* 430–441.

Benbow, C. P., & Lubinski, D. (Eds.). (1996). *Intellectual talent: Psychometric and social issues.* Baltimore: Johns Hopkins Press.

Benbow, C. P., & Lubinski, D. (1997). Intellectually talented children: How can we best meet their needs? In N. Colangelo & G. A. Davis (Eds.), *Handbook of gifted education* (pp. 155–169). Boston: Allyn and Bacon.

Benbow, C. P., Lubinski, D., & Sanjani, H. E. (1999). Our future leaders in science: Who are they? Can we identify them early? In N. Colangelo & S. G. Assouline (Eds.), *Talent development III: Proceedings from the 1995 Henry B. and Jocelyn Wallace National Research Symposium on Talent Development* (pp. 59–70). Scottsdale, AZ: Gifted Psychology Press.

Benbow, C. P., Perkins, S., & Stanley, J. C. (1983). Mathematics taught at a fast pace: A longitudinal evaluation of SMPY's first class. In C. P. Benbow & J. C. Stanley (Eds.), *Academic precocity: Aspects of its development* (pp. 51–78). Baltimore: Johns Hopkins University Press.

Benbow, C. P., & Stanley, J. C. (1980). Sex differences in mathematical ability: Fact or artifact? *Science, 210,* 1262–1264.

Benbow, C. P., & Stanley, J. C. (1982). Consequences in high school and college of sex differences in mathematical reasoning ability: A longitudinal perspective. *American Educational Research Journal, 19,* 598–622.

Benbow, C. P., & Stanley, J. C. (Eds.). (1983). *Academic precocity: Aspects of its development.* Baltimore: Johns Hopkins Press.

Bennett, G. K., Seashore, H. G., & Wesman, A. G. (1947). *The differential aptitudes test.* San Antonio, TX: Psychological Corporation.

Binet, A., & Simon, T. (1905). Méthodes nouvelles pour le diagnostic du niveau intellectuel des anormaux. *L'Année Psychologique, 11,* 191–244.

Bloom, B. S. (1985). *Developing talent in young people.* New York: Ballantine Books.

Borland, J. H. (1997). Evaluating gifted programs. In N. Colangelo & G. A. Davis (Eds.), *Handbook of gifted education* (2nd ed., pp. 253–266). Boston: Allyn and Bacon.

Brody, L. E. (1998). The talent searches: A catalyst for change in higher education. *The Journal of Secondary Gifted Education, 9,* 124–133.

Brody, L. E., & Benbow, C. P. (1987). Accelerative strategies: How effective are they for the gifted? *Gifted Child Quarterly, 31,* 105–109.

Brody, L. E., Lupkowski, A. E., & Stanley, J. C. (1988). Early entrance to college: A study of academic and social adjustment during freshman year. *College and University, 63,* 347–359.

Brown, V. L., Cronin, M., & McEntire E. (1994). *Test of mathematical abilities–Second edition.* Austin, TX: PRO-ED.

Center for Talented Youth (CTY). (1993). *Educational Resources for academically talented adolescents.* Baltimore: Author.

Clasen, D. R., & Hanson, M. (1987). Double mentoring: A process for facilitating mentorships for gifted students. *Roeper Review, 10,* 107–110.

Cohen, J. (1988). *Statistical power for the behavioral sciences* (2nd ed.). Hillsdale, NJ: Erlbaum.

Cohn, S. J. (1991). Talent searches. In N. Colangelo & G. A. Davis (Eds.), *Handbook of gifted education* (pp. 166–177). Boston: Allyn and Bacon.

Colangelo, N. (2003). Counseling gifted student: Issues and practices. In N. Colangelo & G. A. Davis (Eds.), *Handbook of gifted education* (3rd ed., pp. 373–387). Boston: Allyn and Bacon.

Colangelo, N., Assouline, S. G., & Lu, W-H. (1994). Using EXPLORE as an above-level instrument in the search for elementary student talent. In N. Colangelo & S. G. Assouline (Eds.), *Talent development II: Proceedings from the 1993 Henry B. and Jocelyn Wallace National Research Symposium on Talent Development* (pp. 281-298). Dayton: Ohio Psychology Press.

Colangelo, N., & Dettman, D. F. (1982). A conceptual model of four types of parent-school interactions. *Journal for the Education of the Gifted, 5,* 120–126.

Coleman, L. J., & Cross, T. L. (2001). *Being gifted in school: An introduction to development, guidance, and teaching.* Waco, TX: Prufrock Press.

College Entrance Examination Board. (2001). *Facts about the Advanced Placement program.* New York: Author.

Connolly, A. J. (1997). *The Key Math–Revised.* Circle Pines, MN: American Guidance Service.

Council of State Directors of Programs for the Gifted. (1999). *The 1998–1999 state of the states gifted and talented education report.* Longmont, CO: Author.

Croft, L. J. (2003). Teachers of the gifted: Gifted teachers. In N. Colangelo & G. Davis (Eds.), *Handbook of gifted education* (3rd ed., pp.558–571). Needham Heights, MA: Allyn and Bacon.

Csikszentmihalyi, M. (1990). *Flow: The psychology of optimal experience.* New York: Harper & Row.

Csikszentmihalyi, M., Rathunde, K., & Whalen, S. (1993). *Talented teenagers: The roots of success and failure.* Cambridge: Cambridge University Press.

Culpepper, R., Finley, B., Gilreath, S., Powell, S., Cooper, N., & Gentry, M. (2000, November). *Creating a seamless math curriculum.* Paper presented at the annual meeting of the National Association for Gifted Children, Atlanta, GA.

Darling-Hammond, L. (1997). *Doing what matters most: Investing in quality teaching.* New York: National Commission on Teaching & America's Future.

Dauber, S. L. (1988). International Mathematical Olympiad. *Gifted Child Today, 11*(5), 8–11.

Daurio, S. P. (1979). Educational enrichment versus acceleration: A review of the literature. In W. C. George, S. J. Cohn, & J. C. Stanley (Eds.), *Educating the gifted: Acceleration and enrichment* (pp. 13–63). Baltimore: Johns Hopkins University Press.

DeStefano, L. (2001). Review of the Otis-Lennon School Ability Tests–7th Ed. In B. S. Plake & J. C. Impara (Eds.), *The 14th mental measurement yearbook* (pp. 875–879). Lincoln: University of Nebraska Press.

DeVries, A. R. (1996). Another school year: Off to the right start! *Parenting for High Potential, 1*(1), 7.

Ebmeier, H., & Schmulbach, S. (1989). An examination of the selection practices used in the talent search program. *Gifted Child Quarterly, 33,* 134–140.

Educational Records Bureau. (2002). *Comprehensive testing program–IV.* Princeton, NJ: Educational Testing Service.

Educational Testing Service. (1979). *School and college ability test.* Monterey, CA: Publishers Test Service.

Elkind, D. (1988). Acceleration. *Young Children, 43*(4), 2.

Elliot, C. D. (1990). *Differential ability scales.* San Antonio, TX: Psychological Corporation.

Feldhusen, J. (1985). The teacher of gifted students. *Gifted Education International, 3*(2), 87–93.

Feldhusen, J. (1997). Educating teachers for work with talented youth. In N. Colangelo & G. Davis (Eds.), *Handbook of gifted education* (2nd ed., pp. 547–552). Boston: Allyn and Bacon.

Flanagan, D. P., Alfonso, V. C., & Flanagan, R. (1994). A review of the Kaufman Adolescent and Adult Intelligence Test: An advancement in cognitive assessment? *School Psychology Review, 23,* 512–525.

Flanders, J. R. (1987). How much of the content in mathematics textbooks is new? *Arithmetic Teacher, 35*(1), 18–23.

Fleenor, J.W. (1995). Review of the Iowa Algebra Aptitude Test, 4th Ed. In J. C. Conoley & J. C. Impara (Eds.), *The 12th mental measurements yearbook* (pp. 505–506). Lincoln: University of Nebraska Press.

Florian, J. (1999). *Teacher survey of standards-based instruction: Addressing time.* A Mid-continent Research for Education and Learning publication submitted to the U.S. Department of Education, Office of Educational Research and Improvement.

Fullan, M. G., & Stiegelbauer, S. (1991). *The new meaning of educational change.* New York: Teachers College Press.

Gallagher, J. J., Coleman, M. R., & Nelson, S. (1995). Perceptions of educational reform by educators representing middle schools, cooperative learning, and gifted education. *Gifted Child Quarterly, 39,* 66–76.

Gardner, H. (1983). *Frames of mind: The theory of multiple intelligences.* New York: BasicBooks.

Garet, M. S., Birman, B. F., Proter, A. C., Desimone, L. & Herman, R. (1999). *Designing effective professional development: Lessons from the Eisenhower Programs.* Retrieved January 25, 2003, from http://www.ed.gov/inits/teachers/eisenhower

George, W. C., Cohn, S. J., & Stanley, J. C. (Eds.). (1979). *Educating the gifted: Acceleration and enrichment.* Baltimore: Johns Hopkins University Press.

Ginsburg, H. P., & Baroody, A. J. (1990). *Test of early mathematics ability–Second edition.* Austin, TX: PRO-ED.

Goldman, B. A. (2001). Review of the Otis Lennon School Ability Tests–7th Ed. In B. S. Plake & J. C. Impara (Eds.), *The 14th mental measurement yearbook* (pp. 879–881). Lincoln: University of Nebraska Press.

Green, B. F., Jr. (1981). A primer of testing. *American Psychologist, 36,* 1001–1011.

Hanna, G. S. (1998). *Manual for the Orleans-Hanna Algebra Prognosis Test–3rd Edition.* San Antonio, TX: Harcourt Brace.

Heckenberg, L. J. (1998). *Teacher attitudes toward gifted learners and gifted education program: An analysis of the attitudes of participants in the Connie Belin Teacher Training Program from 1981 to 1996.* Unpublished master's thesis, University of Iowa, Iowa City.

Herr, T., & Johnson, K. (1994). *Problem solving strategies: Crossing the river with dogs.* Emeryville, CA: Key Curriculum Press.

Hollingworth, L. (1942). *Children above 180 IQ Stanford-Binet: Origins and development.* Yonkers-on-Hudson, NY: World Books.

Hunt, J. M. (1961). *Intelligence and experience.* New York: Ronald Press.

Institute for the Academic Advancement of Youth (IAAY). (1997). *1997 Young Students Talent Search report.* Baltimore: Johns Hopkins University.

Janos, P. M., & Robinson, N. M. (1985). Psychosocial development in intellectually gifted children. In F. D. Horowitz & M. O'Brien (Eds.), *The gifted and talented: Developmental perspectives* (pp. 149–195). Washington, DC: American Psychological Association.

Johns Hopkins University Institute for the Academic Advancement of Youth. (1999). *Young Students Talent Search report: 1999 Young Students Talent Search: Fifth and sixth grades.* Baltimore: Author.

Johnsen, S. K., Haensly, P. A., Ryser, G. R., & Ford, R. F. (2002). Changing general education classroom practices to adapt for gifted students. *Gifted Child Quarterly, 46,* 45–63.

Johnsen, S. K., & Ryser, G. R. (1998*). Test of mathematical abilities for gifted students.* Austin, TX: PRO-ED.

Johnson, D. T. (1994). Mathematics curriculum for the gifted. In J. VanTassel-Baska, *Comprehensive curriculum for gifted learners* (2nd ed., pp. 231–261). Boston: Allyn and Bacon.

Johnson, D. T., & Sher, B. T. (1997). *Resource guide to mathematics curriculum materials for high ability learners in grades K–8.* Williamsburg, VA: Center for Gifted Education, College of William and Mary

Karnes, F. A., & Marquardt, R. G. (1988). The Pennsylvania Supreme Court decision on gifted education. *Gifted Child Quarterly, 32,* 360–361.

Karnes, F. A., & Marquardt, R. G. (2003). Gifted education and legal issues. In N. Colangelo & G. A. Davis, (Eds.) *Handbook of gifted education* (3rd ed., pp.590–603). Needham Heights, MA : Allyn and Bacon.

Kaufman, A. S., & Kaufman, N. L. (1983). *Kaufman assessment battery for children.* Circle Pines, MN: American Guidance Services.

Kaufman, A. S., & Kaufman, N. L. (1993). *Kaufman adolescent and adult intelligence test.* Circle Pines, MN: American Guidance Service.

Keating, D. P. (1973). *Precocious cognitive development at the level of formal operations.* Unpublished doctoral dissertation, Johns Hopkins University, Baltimore.

Keating, D. P. (1976). *Intellectual talent: Research and development.* Baltimore: Johns Hopkins University Press.

Kuchemann, D. (1985). Review of Orleans-Hanna Algebra Prognosis Test. In J. V. Mitchell (Ed.), *The 9th mental measurement yearbook* (pp. 1105–1106). Lincoln: University of Nebraska Press.

Kulik, S., & Rudnick, J. A. (1992). *Reasoning and problem solving: A handbook for elementary school teachers.* Boston: Allyn and Bacon.

Kulik, J. A., & Kulik, C. C. (1984). Synthesis of research on effects of accelerated instruction. *Educational Leadership, 42,* 84–89.

Kulik, J. A., & Kulik, C. C. (1987). Effects of ability grouping on student achievement. *Equity & Excellence, 23*(1–2), 22–30.

Kulik, J. A., & Kulik, C.-L. C. (1997). Ability grouping. In N. Colangelo and G. A. Davis (Eds.), *Handbook of gifted education* (2nd ed., pp. 230–242). Needham Heights, MA: Allyn and Bacon.

Lenchner, G. (1983). *Creative problem solving in school mathematics.* Boston: Houghton Mifflin.

Lerner, J. W. (1976). *Children with learning disabilities* (2nd ed.). Boston: Houghton Mifflin.

Linn, R. L., & Gronlund, N. E. (1995). *Measurement and assessment in teaching.* Upper Saddle River, NJ: Merrill.

Lohman, D. F., & Hagen. E. (2001a). *The cognitive abilities test* (Form 6). Itasca, IL: Riverside.

Lohman, D. F., & Hagen. E. (2001b). *The cognitive abilities test (Form 6): Interpretive guide for teachers and counselors.* Itasca, IL: Riverside.

Lupkowski, A. E., & Assouline, S. G. (1992). *Jane and Johnny love math: Recognizing and encouraging mathematical talent in elementary students.* Unionville, NY: Trillium Press.

Lupkowski, A. E., & Assouline, S. G. (1993). Identifying mathematically talented elementary students: Using the lower level of the SSAT. *Gifted Child Quarterly, 37,* 118–123.

Lupkowski, A. E., Assouline, S. G., & Stanley, J. C. (1990). Applying a mentor model for young mathematically talented students. *Gifted Child Today, 13*(2), 15–19.

Lupkowski, A. E., Assouline, S. G., & Vestal, J. (1992). Mentors in math. *Gifted Child Today, 15*(3), 26–31.

Lupkowski-Shoplik, A., (1996, Winter). Young math whizzes: Can their needs be met in the regular classroom? *Tempo,* 5–9.

Lupkowski-Shoplik, A. E., & Assouline, S. G. (1994). Evidence of extreme mathematical precocity: Case studies of talented youths. *Roeper Review, 16,* pp. 144–151.

Lupkowski-Shoplik, A. E., & Assouline, S. G. (2001). *Report of ESTS 2001 local item responses.* Unpublished report, Carnegie Mellon University, Pittsburgh, PA.

Lupkowski-Shoplik, A., Benbow, C. P., Assouline, S. G., & Brody, L. E. (2003). Talent searches: Meeting the needs of academically talented youth. In N. Colangelo & G. A. Davis (Eds.), *Handbook of gifted education* (3rd ed., pp. 204–218). Needham Heights, MA: Allyn and Bacon.

Lupkowski-Shoplik, A. E., & Kuhnel, A. (1995). Mathematics enrichment for talented elementary students. *Gifted Child Today, 18*(4), 28–32.

Lupkowski-Shoplik, A. E., Sayler, M. F., & Assouline, S. G. (1994). Mathematics achievement of talented elementary students: Basic concepts vs. computation. In N. Colangelo, S. G. Assouline, & D. L. Ambroson (Eds.), *Talent development: Proceedings from the Henry B. and Jocelyn Wallace National Research Symposium on Talent Development* (pp. 409–414). Dayton, OH: Psychology Press.

Lupkowski-Shoplik, A. E., & Swiatek, M. A. (1999). Elementary student talent searches: Establishing appropriate guidelines for qualifying test scores. *Gifted Child Quarterly, 43,* 265–272.

Maker, C. J. (1993). *Critical issues in gifted education.* Austin, TX: PRO-ED.

Marland, S. P., Jr. (1972). *Education of the gifted and talented: Report to*

*Congress of the United States by the U.S. Commissioner of Education,* 2 vols. Washington, DC: U.S. Government Printing Office. (Government Documents, Y4.L 11/2: G36)

Mathematical Association of America. (1991). *A call for change: Recommendations for the mathematical preparation of teachers of mathematics.* Washington, DC: Author.

McCarthy, C. R. (1998). Assimilating the talent search model into the school day. *Journal of Secondary Gifted Education, 9,* 114–123.

McGrew, K. S., & Flanagan, D. P. (1998). *The intelligence test desk reference.* Needham Heights, MA: Allyn and Bacon.

Mills, C. J. (1992). Academically talented children: The case for early identification and nurturance. *Pediatrics, 89*(1), 156–157.

Mills, C. J., Ablard, K. E., & Gustin, W. C. (1994). Academically talented students' achievement in a flexibly paced mathematics program. *Journal for Research in Mathematics Education, 25,* 495–511.

Mills, C. J., Ablard, K. E., & Lynch, S. J. (1992). Academically talented students' preparation for advanced-level coursework after an individually-paced precalculus class. *Journal for the Education of the Gifted, 16,* 3–17.

Mills, C. J., Ablard, K. E., & Stumpf, H. (1993). Gender differences in academically talented young students' mathematical reasoning: Patterns across ages and subskills. *Journal of Educational Psychology, 85,* 340–346.

Mills, C. J., & Barnett, L. B. (1992). The use of the Secondary School Admission Test (SSAT) to identify academically talented elementary school students. *Gifted Child Quarterly, 36,* 155–159.

Mills, C. J., & Wood, S. (1988). *Fast-paced, individualized arithmetic/prealgebra course, version B: Volume1: Curriculum guide.* Baltimore: Center for Talented Youth, Johns Hopkins University.

Monsaas, J. A. (1995). Review of the Iowa Algebra Aptitude Test, 4th Ed. In J. C. Conoley & J. C. Impara (Eds.), *The 12th mental measurements yearbook* (pp. 506–507). Lincoln: University of Nebraska Press.

Moore, N. D., & Wood, S. S. (1988). Mathematics with a gifted difference. *Roeper Review, 10,* 231–234

Murphy, L. L., Impara, J. C., & Plake, B. S. (1999). *Tests in print V: An index to tests, test reviews, and the literature on specific tests.* Lincoln: Buros Institute of Mental Measurements, University of Nebraska.

National Commission on Teaching and America's Future. (1996). *What matters most: Teaching for America's future* Retrieved April 24, 2002, from http://www.nctaf.org/publications/whatmattersmost.html.

National Council of Teachers of Mathematics (NCTM). (1989). *Curriculum and evaluation standards for school sathematics.* Reston, VA: Author.

National Council of Teachers of Mathematics (NCTM). (1991). *Professional standards for teaching mathematics.* Reston, VA: Author.

National Council of Teachers of Mathematics (NCTM). (1995). *Assessment standards for school mathematics.* Reston, VA: Author.

National Council of Teachers of Mathematics (NCTM). (2000a). *Principles and standards for school mathematics.* Reston, VA: Author.

National Council of Teachers of Mathematics. (2000b). *October News Bulletin, 37*(3).

National Council of Teachers of Mathematics. (2002). *Principles and standards for school mathematics.* Reston, VA: Author.

National Education Commission on Time and Learning. (1994). *Prisoners of time.* Retrieved January 25, 2003, from http://www.ed.gov/pubs/PrisonersOfTime

Nitko, A. J. (1996). *Educational assessment of students* (2nd ed). Englewood Cliffs, NJ: Prentice-Hall.

Oakes, J. (1985). *Keeping track: How schools structure inequality.* New Haven, CT: Yale University Press.

Oakes, J. (1992). Can tracking research inform practice? Technical, normative, and political considerations. *Educational Researcher, 21*(4), 12–21.

Olszewski-Kubilius, P. (1998). Talent search: Purposes, rationale, and role in gifted education. *Journal of Secondary Gifted Education, 9,* 106–113.

Olszewski-Kubilius, P., Kulieke, M. J., Willis, G. B., & Krasney, N. (1989). An analysis of the validity of SAT entrance scores for accelerated classes. *Journal for the Education of the Gifted, 13,* 37–54.

Orleans, J. B., & Orleans, J. S. (1928). *Orleans algebra prognosis test.* San Antonio, TX: Psychological Corporation.

Otis, A. S., & Lennon, R. T. (1996). *Otis-Lennon school ability test–7th ed.* San Antonio, TX: Psychological Corporation.

Parker, J. P. (1989). *Instructional strategies for teaching the gifted.* Boston: Allyn and Bacon.

Passow, H. (1985). Review of School and College Ability Tests, Series III. In J. V. Mitchell (Ed.), *The 9th Mental Measurement Yearbook* (pp. 1317–1318). Lincoln: University of Nebraska Press.

Passow, A. H. (1996). Acceleration over the years. In C. P. Benbow & D. Lubinski (Eds.), *Intellectual talent: Psychometric and social issues* (pp. 93–98). Baltimore: Johns Hopkins University Press.

Piaget, J., & Inhelder, B. (1969). *The psychology of the child.* New York: BasicBooks.

Piskurich, P. J., & Lupkowski-Shoplik, A. (1998). Carnegie Mellon weekend workshops: Weekend fun. *Gifted Child Today, 21,* 14–19.

Plucker, J. A., & McIntire, J. (1996). Academic survivability in high potential, middle school students. *Gifted Child Quarterly, 40,* 7–14.

Popham, W. J. (2002). *Classroom assessment: What teachers need to know* (3rd ed.). Boston: Allyn and Bacon

Poteat, G. M. (1998). Review of the Stanford Diagnostic Mathematics Test, 4th Ed. In J. C. Impara & B. S. Plake (Eds.), *The 13th mental measurements yearbook* (pp. 937–938). Lincoln: University of Nebraska Press.

Pratscher, S., K., Jones, K. L., & Lamb, C. E. (1982). Differentiating instruction in mathematics for talented and gifted youngsters. *School Science and Mathematics, 82,* 365–372.

Raven, J. C., Raven, M. & Styles, I. (1998). *Raven's progressive matrices.* Oxford, England: Oxford Psychologists Press.

Raven, J., Raven, J. C., Court, J. H. (2000). *Raven manual: Section III Standard Progressive Matrices* (2000 Edition). Oxford: Oxford Psychologists Press.

Reis, S. M., & Gavin, M. K. (1999). Why Jane doesn't think she can do math: How teachers can encourage talented girls in mathematics. In L. J. Sheffield (Ed.), *Developing mathematically promising students* (pp. 133–148). Reston, VA: National Council of Teachers of Mathematics.

Reis, S. M., Westberg, K. L., Kulikowich, J., Caillard, F., Hebert, T., Plucker, J., Purcell, J. H., Rogers, J. B., & Smist, J. M. (1993). *Why not let high ability students start school in January? The curriculum compacting study* (RM 93106). Storrs: The National Research Center on the Gifted and Talented, University of Connecticut.

Robinson, A. (1991). *Cooperative learning and the academically talented student.* Storrs: The National Research Center on the Gifted and Talented, University of Connecticut.

Robinson, N. M. (1992). Stanford-Binet IV, of course! Time marches on! *Roeper Review, 15,* 32–34.

Robinson, N. M., & Janos, P. M. (1987). The contribution of intelligence tests to the understanding of special children. In J. D. Day & J. B. Borkowski (Eds), *Intelligence and exceptionality: New directions for theory, assessment, and instructional practices* (pp. 21–56). Greenwich, CT: Ablex.

Robinson, N. S., & Robinson, H. B. (1982). The optimal match: Devising the best compromise for the highly gifted student. In D. Feldman (Ed.), *New directions for child development: Developmental approaches to giftedness and creativity, no. 17* (pp. 79–94). San Francisco: Jossey-Bass.

Rogers, K. B. (2002). *Reforming gifted education: Matching the program to the child.* Scottsdale, AZ: Great Potential Press.

Rotigel, J. V. (2000). *Exceptional mathematical talent: Comparing achievement in concepts and computation.* Unpublished doctoral dissertation, Indiana University of Pennsylvania, Indiana, PA.

Rotigel, J. V., & Lupkowski-Shoplik, A. (1999). Using talent searches to identify and meet the educational needs of mathematically talented youngsters. *School Science and Mathematics, 99,* 330–337.

Ryser, G. R., & Johnsen, S. K. (1998). *Test of Mathematical Abilities for Gifted Students (TOMAGS): Examiner's manual.* Austin, TX: PRO-ED.

Sabers, D. L. (1988). Reviw of the Comprehensive Testing Program III. In J. C. Impara & B. S. Plake (Eds.), *The 13th mental measurements yearbook* (pp. 316–318). Lincoln: University of Nebraska Press.

Sattler, J. M. (2001). *Assessment of children: Cognitive applications* (4th ed.) San Diego, CA.: Jerome M. Sattler.

Schiever, S. W., & Maker, C. J. (1997). Enrichment and acceleration: An overview and new directions. In N. Colangelo & G. A. Davis (Eds.), *Handbook of gifted education* (2nd ed., pp. 113–125). Boston: Allyn and Bacon.

Schmidt, W. H., McKnight, C. C., & Raizen, A. (1996). *Splintered vision: An investigation of U.S. mathematics and science education.* Washington, DC: U.S. National Research Center.

Schoen, H. L., & Ansley, T. M. (1993). *Iowa algebra aptitude test* (4th ed.). Chicago: Riverside.

Schunk, D. H. (1987). Peer models and children's behavioral change. *Review of Educational Research, 57,* 149–174

Secolsky, C. (1985). Review of Orleans-Hanna Algebra Prognosis Test. In J. V. Mitchell (Ed.), *The 9th mental measurement yearbook* (pp. 1105–1106). Lincoln: University of Nebraska Press.

Sheffield, L. J. (1994). *The development of gifted and talented mathematics students and the National Council of Teachers of Mathematics Standards.* Storrs: The National Research Center for the Gifted and Talented, University of Connecticut.

Sheffield, L. J. (Ed.). (1999a). *Developing mathematically promising students.* Reston, VA: National Council of Teachers of Mathematics.

Sheffield, L. J. (1999b). Serving the needs of the mathematically promising. In L. J. Sheffield (Ed.), *Developing mathematically promising students* (pp. 43–55). Reston, VA: National Council of Teachers of Mathematics.

Sicola, P. K. (1990). Where do gifted students fit? An examination of middle school philosophy as it relates to ability grouping and the gifted learner. *Journal for the Education of the Gifted, 14,* 37–49.

Slosson, R. L. (1998). *Slosson Intelligence Test–Revised: Technical manual–Calibrated norms.* Ease Aurora, NY: Slosson Educational Publications.

Slosson, R. L., Nicholson, C. L., & Hibpsham, T. H. (1991). *Slosson intelligence test for children and adults* (Rev. ed. by C. L. Nicholson & T. H. Hibpsham). East Aurora, NY: Slosson Educational Publications.

Sosniak, L. A. (1997). The tortoise, the hare, and the development of talent. In N. Colangelo & G. A. Davis (Eds.), *Handbook of gifted education* (2nd ed., pp. 207–217). Boston: Allyn and Bacon

Southern, W. T., & Jones, E. D. (1991). *The academic acceleration of gifted children.* New York: Teachers College Press.

*Stanford diagnostic mathematics test–4th ed.* (1996). San Antonio, TX: Harcourt Brace Educational Measurement.

Stanley, J. C. (1978, Summer). SMPY's DT-PI model: Diagnostic testing followed by prescriptive instruction. *Intellectually Talented Youth Bulletin, 4*(10), 7–8.

Stanley, J. C. (1979a, February 15). How to use a fast-pacing math mentor. *Intellectually Talented Youth Bulletin, 5*(6), 1–2.

Stanley, J. C. (1979b). Identifying and nurturing the intellectually gifted. In W. C. George, S. J. Cohn, & J. C. Stanley, (Eds.), *Educating the gifted: Acceleration and enrichment* (pp. 172–180). Baltimore: Johns Hopkins University Press.

Stanley, J. C. (1984). Use of general and specific aptitude measures in identification: Some principles and certain cautions. *Roeper Review, 28,* 177–180.

Stanley, J. C. (1990). Leta Hollingworth's contributions to above-level testing of the gifted. *Roeper Review, 12,* 166–171.

Stanley, J. C. (1991). An academic model for educating the mathematically talented. *Gifted Child Quarterly, 24,* 36–42.

Stanley, J. C. (1996). In the beginning: The Study of Mathematically Precocious Youth. In C. P. Benbow & D. Lubinski (Eds.). *Intellectual talent: Psychometric and social issues* (pp. 225–235). Baltimore: Johns Hopkins University Press.

Stanley, J. C. (2001). Helping students learn only what they don't already know. In N. Colangelo & S. G. Assouline (Eds.), *Talent development IV: Proceedings from the 1998 Henry B. and Jocelyn Wallace National Research Symposium on Talent Development* (pp. 293–299). Scottsdale, AZ: Great Potential Press.

Stanley, J. C., & Benbow, C. P. (1986). Youths who reason exceptionally well mathematically. In R. J. Sternberg & J. E. Davidson (Eds), *Conceptions of giftedness* (pp. 361–387). New York: Cambridge University Press.

Stanley, J. C., Keating, D. P., & Fox, L. H. (1974). *Mathematical talent: Discovery, description, and development.* Baltimore: Johns Hopkins University Press.

Stanley, J. C., Lupkowski, A. E., & Assouline, S. G. (1990). Eight considerations for mathematically talented youth. *Gifted Child Today, 13*(2), 2–4.

Sternberg, R. J. (1986). A triarchic theory of intellectual giftedness. In R. J. Sternberg & J. E. Davidson (Eds.), *Conceptions of giftedness* (pp. 223–243). New York: Cambridge University Press.

Swiatek, M. A., & Benbow, C. P. (1991a). A ten-year longitudinal follow-up of ability-matched accelerated and unaccelerated gifted students. *Journal of Educational Psychology, 83*, 528–538.

Swiatek, M. A., & Benbow, C. P. (1991b). A ten-year longitudinal follow-up of participants in a fast-paced mathematics course. *Journal for Research in Mathematics Education, 22*, 138–150.

Swiatek, M. A., & Lupkowski-Shoplik, A. (2000a). Gender differences in academic attitudes among gifted elementary school students. *Journal for the Education of the Gifted, 23*, 360–377.

Swiatek, M. A., & Lupkowski-Shoplik, A. E. (2000b, May). *Predicting performance in a summer enrichment program from above-level EXPLORE scores.* Paper presented at the 5th Biennial Henry B. & Jocelyn Wallace National Research Symposium on Talent Development.

Swiatek, M. A., Lupkowski-Shoplik, A., & O'Donoghue, C. C. (in press). Gender differences in above-level EXPLORE scores of gifted third-through sixth-graders. *Journal of Educational Psychology.*

Terman, L. M, & Merrill, M. A. (1960). *Stanford-Binet intelligence scale.* Boston: Houghton Mifflin.

Thorndike, R. L., Hagen, E. P. & Sattler, J. M. (1986a). *Guide for administering and scoring the Stanford-Binet Intelligence Scale–4th Ed.* Chicago: Riverside.

Thorndike, R. L., Hagen, E. P. & Sattler, J. M. (1986b). *Technical manual, Stanford-Binet Intelligence Scale–4th Ed.* Chicago: Riverside.

Tomlinson, C. A., Coleman, M. R., Allan, S., Udall, A., & Landrum, M. (1996). Interface between gifted education and general education: Toward communication, cooperation, and collaboration. *Gifted Child Quarterly, 40*, 165–171.

U.S. Department of Education. (1991). *America 2000: An education strategy.* Washington, DC: Author.

U.S. Department of Education, Office of Educational Research and Improvement. (1993). *National excellence: A case for developing America's talent.* Washington, DC: U.S. Government Printing Office.

U.S. Department of Education. (1998). Using TIMSS to inform changes in instruction and professional development. In *Policy brief: What the Third International Mathematics and Science Study (TIMSS) means for systematic school improvement.* Retrieved January 25, 2003, from http://www.ed.gov/pubs/TIMSSBrief/newinstruct.html

Usiskin, Z. (1999). The mathematically promising and the mathematically gifted. In L. J. Sheffield (Ed.), *Developing mathematically promising students* (pp. 57–69). Reston, VA: National Council of Teachers of Mathematics.

Usiskin, Z. (2000). The development into the mathematically talented. *Journal of Secondary Gifted Education, 11,* 152–162.

VanTassel-Baska, J. (1996). Contributions to gifted education of the talent search concept. In C. P. Benbow & D. Lubinski (Eds.), *Psychometric and social issues concerning intellect and talent* (pp. 236–245). Baltimore: Johns Hopkins University Press.

VanTassel-Baska, J. (1998). *Excellence in educating gifted and talented learners* (3rd ed.). Denver: Love.

Ward, S. B., & Landrum, M. S. (1994). Resource consultation: An alternative service delivery model for gifted education. *Roeper Review, 16,* 276–279.

Waxman, B., Robinson, N. M., & Mukhopadhayay, S. (1996a). *Parents nurturing math-talented young children.* Seattle: University of Washington.

Waxman, B., Robinson, N. M., & Mukhopadhayay, S. (1996b). *Teachers nurturing math-talented young children* (RM96228). Storrs: The National Research Center on the Gifted and Talented, University of Connecticut.

Wechsler, D. (1949). *Manual for the Wechsler Intelligence Scale for Children.* New York: Psychological Corporation.

Wechsler, D. (1955). *Manual for the Wechsler Adult Intelligence Scale.* New York: Psychological Corporation.

Wechsler, D. (1967). *Manual for the Wechsler Preschool and Primary Scale of Intelligence.* New York: Psychological Corporation.

Wechsler, D. (1974). *Manual for the Wechsler Intelligence Scale for Children–Revised.* New York: Psychological Corporation.

Wechsler, D. (1991). *Wechsler preschool and primary scales of intelligence–Revised.* San Antonio, TX: Psychological Corporation.

Wechsler, D. (1997). *Wechsler adult intelligence scale.* San Antonio, TX: Psychological Corporation.

Wechsler, D. (1991). *Wechsler intelligence scale for children.* San Antonio, TX: Psychological Corporation.

Westberg, K. L., & Archambault, F. X. (1997). A multi-site case study of successful classroom practices for high ability students. *Gifted Child Quarterly, 41,* 42–51.

Wheatley, G. (1983). A mathematics curriculum for the gifted and talented. *Gifted Child Quarterly, 27,* 77–80.

Wheatley, G. H. (1988). Mathematics curriculum for the gifted. In J. VanTassel-Baska (Ed.), *Comprehensive curriculum for gifted learners* (pp. 252–274). Boston: Allyn and Bacon.

Wilson, V., Litle, J., Coleman, M. R., & Gallagher, J. (1998). Distance learning. *Journal of Secondary Gifted Education, 9,* 89–100.

Winebrenner, S. (1992). *Teaching gifted kids in the regular classroom.* Minneapolis: Free Spirit.

Winebrenner, S. (2001). *Teaching gifted kids in the regular classroom: Strategies and techniques every teacher can use to meet the academic needs of the gifted and talented* (2nd ed.). Minneapolis: Free Spirit.

Woodcock, R. W., & Johnson, M. B. (1989). *Woodcock-Johnson psychoeducational battery–Revised.* Itasca, IL: Riverside.

Woodcock, R. W., McGrew, K. S., & Mather N. (2001). *The Woodcock-Johnson III.* Itasca, IL: Riverside.

# Index

# About
# the Authors

**Susan G. Assouline** is the University of Iowa Belin-Blank Center's associate director and clinical supervisor. She has an appoinment as a clinical associate professor in school psychology. She received her B. S. in general science with a teaching endorsement, her Ed.S. in school psychology, and her Ph.D. in psychological and quantitative foundations, all from the University of Iowa. She was awarded a 2-year postdoctoral fellowship at the Study of Mathematically Precocious Youth (SMPY) at Johns Hopkins University and, upon completion, joined the Belin-Blank Center in 1990. She is especially interested in the discovery and development of academic talent in elementary students. This was first articulated in *Jane and Johnny Love Math* (coauthored with Ann Shoplik). She is coeditor with Nicholas Colangelo of the series *Talent Development: Proceedings from the Wallace Research Symposia on Giftedness and Talent Development* and codeveloper, with Nicholas Colangelo, Ann Lupkowski-Shoplik, Jonathan Lipscomb, and Leslie Forstadt of the Iowa Acceleration Scale. She has served as the Center's primary consultant regarding acceleration and mathematically talented students. As a consultant, she has worked with over 100 schools. She has presented to dozens of audiences in the United States, as well as in Australia, Austria, Canada, Chile, Israel, Hong Kong, the Netherlands, New Zealand, and the Philippines.

**Ann Lupkowski-Shoplik** is the director of the Carnegie Mellon Institute for Talented Elementary Students (C-MITES). She earned a Ph.D. in educational psychology from Texas A&M University and then completed a 3-year postdoctoral fellowship at the Study of Mathematically Precocious Youth at Johns Hopkins University in 1989. She was an assistant professor and director of the Study of Mathematically Precocious Youth at the University of North Texas from 1989 to 1991. In 1992, she founded the Carnegie Mellon Institute for Talented Elementary Students (C-MITES) at Carnegie Mellon University, where she continues to conduct research and develop programs on behalf of academically talented youth. She conducts the annual Elementary Student Talent Search throughout Pennsylvania and oversees the C-MITES summer programs and Weekend Workshops for academically talented students in seventh grade and younger. Her research interests include identifying mathematically talented students younger than age 12 and studying their characteristics and academic needs. She has published many articles on gifted education in scholarly journals. Together with Susan Assouline, she wrote *Jane and Johnny Love Math: Recognizing and Encouraging Mathematical Talent in Elementary Students*. She is also a coauthor of the Iowa Acceleration Scale with Susan Assouline, Nicholas Colangelo, Jonathan Lipscomb, and Leslie Forstadt.